Ólöf the Eskimo Lady

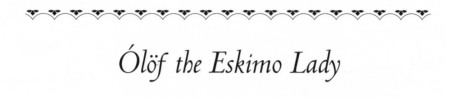

Ólöf the Eskimo Lady

A BIOGRAPHY OF AN
ICELANDIC DWARF IN AMERICA

Inga Dóra Björnsdóttir

English Translator
María Helga Guðmundsdóttir

THE UNIVERSITY OF MICHIGAN PRESS · ANN ARBOR

2013   2012   2011   2010   4   3   2   1

Library of Congress Cataloging-in-Publication Data

Inga Dóra Björnsdóttir, 1952–
      [Ólöf Eskimói . English]
      Ólöf the Eskimo lady : a biography of an Icelandic dwarf in America /
Inga Dóra Björnsdóttir ; English translator, María Helga Guðmundsdóttir.
         p.   cm.
      Includes bibliographical references and index.
      ISBN 978-0-472-11726-0 (cloth : alk. paper)
      1. Krarer, Olof, 1858–1935.   2. Dwarfs—United States—Biography.   3. Lecturers—
United States—Biography.   4. Icelanders—United States—Biography.
5. Impostors and imposture—United States—History.   I. Title.
CT9992.I5413   2010
973.931092—dc22
      [B]   2010004477

Title of original Icelandic edition: *Ólöf eskimói: Ævisaga íslensks dvergs í Vesturheimi.*
Published by agreement with Edda Publishing, www.edda.is.

Lying is the weapon of the powerless against the powerful.
Evelin Sullivan, *The Concise Book of Lying*

Krarer, Olof (Miss), lecturer; b. east coast of Greenland, 1858; ed. Iceland; came to U.S. as child. *Lecture-subjects:* Greenland: What I Have Seen in America; Missionaries; Life in the Frozen North. Began lecturing in Ill., 1888, under Sl.; since listed with Sl. and Bry. Has lectured 80 times in Phila., 14 in Chicago, and 9 in New York. Has filled 1,500 engagements. *Address:* 25 Waverly Pl., Chicago, Ill.
Augustus Wright, ed., *Who's Who in the Lyceum*

Inuk—Greenlander—Eskimo

Scholars disagree about the origin of the word *Eskimo*. It has long been held to mean "meat-eater" and originate from the Algonquin language, spoken by Native Americans living along the St. Lawrence River in Canada. It was later adopted by Christian missionaries and became a general term in the Western world for the indigenous peoples of the far North.[1] However, new research suggests that the word originally comes from the language of the Montagna people and means "those who make snow-shoes."[2]

Irrespective of its origin, the moniker *Eskimo* has a pejorative meaning to the indigenous peoples of the Arctic, and they have never used it to describe themselves. Instead, they use the word *Inuk* (pl. *Inuit*), which means "man" or "person." Although *Inuit* is now the commonly used term, Vilhjálmur Stefánsson was one of the first to suggest that Westerners adopt the word to describe the inhabitants of the Arctic.[3]

In the following text, the word *Eskimo* is used whenever reference is made to the disguised Ólöf, in discussions of Ólöf in disguise, and in her speeches about her imagined tribe in Greenland. The term is also used in direct quotes from speeches and documents from the time when it was still used to describe those indigenous peoples. The term *Greenlander* is used when referring to natives of Greenland, and the term *Inuit* refers to Arctic natives in general.

Translator's Note

During Ólöf's lifetime, two different spellings of the word *Eskimo* were in use: the one that has prevailed as our modern form, and the French spelling *Esquimau.* Of the latter, the plural form *Esquimaux* was commonly used for both singular and plural; this was the case for perhaps the most important document published about Ólöf: her (fictional) biography entitled *The Esquimaux Lady.* The translator of the present work has chosen to use the more commonly accepted *Eskimo* everywhere except in direct quotations and where Ólöf is referred to explicitly as her stage persona, the "Esquimaux Lady."

Wherever Ólöf is discussed or described as her fabricated second self, Olof Krarer the Eskimo, the anglicized spelling of her name, Olof, has been used. Elsewhere she bears her Icelandic name, Ólöf.

Contents

Olof Krarer in her heyday

Prologue

Newnan, Georgia, 1906

William Jennings Bryan, former member of the House of Representatives and Democratic presidential candidate in 1896, did a double-take as he exited the city theater in Newnan, Georgia. The sun was shining brightly and the warm breeze caressed his cheek, while he had expected a blizzard. Bryan laughed quietly to himself. He had been listening to the Eskimo lady Olof Krarer once again, and her speech about life in the Arctic always had this effect on him. Bryan looked at his watch. His train was to depart in just over an hour, and he decided to walk to the train station.

Olof Krarer was a clever lecturer despite her small stature. She had a flair for acting and a unique sense of humor, coupled with a joy of storytelling. When she began to tell her tale of life in Greenland, her audience lost all sense of place and time and sat as if transfixed, until Olof descended from the stage to collect donations to support her siblings, who remained in Iceland. The audience was most generous, for they wished that Olof's siblings could be reunited and might enjoy the bounty of America like their sister.

Olof's biography seemed to border on the impossible, and Bryan never tired of recalling it from memory. Olof was born in a small town on the northeastern coast of Greenland, far, far north of the Arctic Circle, where darkness and cold reigned throughout most of the year. The Eskimos were born in darkness and spent their whole life in spiritual darkness. They did not learn how to walk or talk until the age of three, and as adults they attained the emotional maturity of a ten-year-old child. It wasn't strange, therefore, that they could not count beyond ten. They lived in snow houses insulated with skins, ate raw meat, and drank cod liver oil with their food. Eskimo women had no household tasks to perform, and their life was extremely monotonous. They sat indoors all year round and hushed their children, who weren't allowed to play outdoors in the cold. The children wanted to play indoors, of course, but that wasn't permitted either, and so they were ordered to sit still with their arms crossed. It came as no surprise that Eskimo girls like Olof should have short and knotted arms. Eskimo boys had normal arms because they got to go hunting with their fathers from time to time. Men seemed to be the only ones who enjoyed themselves at all in Greenland.[1] Eskimos punished their children harshly: if they did not obey immediately, they were branded. Bryan shuddered. He couldn't imagine what consequences it could have for an Eskimo who made the mistake of telling a lie.

If Olof had lived her entire life in her village in Greenland, her fate would have been to marry young, bear a few children, die before her time, and, upon her death, be buried without ceremony in the nearest mound of snow. Fortunately, an Icelandic ship stranded off the beach, not far from Olof's hometown, when she was a teenager. The Icelandic sailors made it to land with great difficulty and sought aid from the villagers, who were more than a little shocked at the sight of these blond, blue-eyed ogres. Yet they soon became good friends, and the Icelandic seafarers dwelled in the village in great comfort for over a year.

The sailors' ship had been completely destroyed, so the only way to get back to Iceland was to borrow dogs and sleds from the Eskimos and walk home across the ice. The sled owners wanted to get their sleds and dogs back, and so they decided to join the sailors on their journey home to Iceland. Olof's family was among them. The journey was long, strenuous, and fraught with danger. It took two months.[2]

At this point in the story, the audience never failed to applaud Olof. They were entranced by the endurance and courage of these folk, who took such risks and made it safe and sound across the ice all the way from Greenland to Iceland.

In Iceland the arrival of the sailors and the Eskimos was met with much celebration, and the Eskimos aroused great amusement, as the Icelanders had never seen these small and strange neighbors before.[3]

Bryan was deep in thought over Olof's story when he looked up and saw her as she passed him in her carriage, together with her assistant, on her way to the train station. He picked up his pace.

Iceland was a small and poor country, but inhabited by a nation of people with a Christian cultural heritage. Bryan knew this well. When the Eskimos came to Iceland they were placed in a missionary center immediately. There they were converted to Christianity and taught how to read and write. Olof had attended school for five years in Iceland. It was incredible to think that if she had spent her entire life in Greenland she would have died illiterate and unable to count past the number ten. But now she was a well-educated and sought-after lecturer in the United States. Fortune could move in strange ways.

At that time, many Icelanders were moving to America. Olof came across a book describing the marvels of America and managed to convince her father to go there with her. Her father was a poor man and could only afford to pay the fare for two passengers, Olof and himself. The other seven children remained behind, and now Olof wished to remedy that and was making excellent progress. Within a year, the family would be reunited, all except the mother, who had died of consumption in Iceland.

When Bryan walked into the railway station in Newnan, Olof was standing on the platform and struggling to board the train—the step was too high for her. Her assistant was nowhere to be seen, so Bryan marched rapidly toward her and lifted her up onto the train as if she were a child.[4]

Shortly after the train departed, Bryan glanced over at Olof where she lay comfortably across the train seat and slept. It came as no surprise that this little woman should be tired after a hard day's work.

William Jennings Bryan

William Jennings Bryan was one of the greatest American orators of all time. He was born in 1860 in Salem, Illinois, making him two years younger than Ólöf. He studied law but became active in politics early on and was elected to the House of Representatives for the Democratic Party in Nebraska in 1890, at the age of only thirty.[5]

William Jennings Bryan, congressman and lecturer

At the Democratic National Convention in 1896, Bryan delivered his famous "Cross of Gold" speech for the first time.[6] In the speech he argued that the United States government's financial policies, which were bound to a gold standard, limited the release of currency and caused deflation, which kept farmers mired in debt and workers in a state of poverty.[7]

The speech was so admired that Bryan was named the party's presidential candidate that same year. He ran against the Republican McKinley and lost, perhaps because of his rigorous opposition to the Republicans' expansionist policies.[8] After that Bryan turned to journalism and lecturing, and Americans flocked by the tens of thousands to his lectures to hear him give the "Cross of Gold" speech.[9] In 1953, 227 American professors of history and political science were asked to name the most important documents in the history of the United States, and the "Cross of Gold" speech was listed among the top fifty.[10]

Bryan and Olof Krarer the Eskimo worked for the same agency for a while, traveled together and gave lectures in the same places, and thus knew each other quite well. Bryan passed away in 1925 at the age of sixty-five, ten years before Olof died; therefore, he didn't live long enough to learn that the Eskimo lady he had traveled with had never set foot in Greenland and never seen a real Greenlander. She was just an Icelandic dwarf whose real name was Ólöf Sölvadóttir, and who came from Outer Langamýri in the county of Húnavatnssýsla in northern Iceland.

Iceland—Youth

Ólöf's Birth

In early July 1857, Solveig Stefánsdóttir (1831–70), housewife at Outer Langamýri in Blöndudalur valley, East Húnavatnssýsla county, received confirmation of her suspicions. She was pregnant with her third child. She came from a fertile family, and it appeared that her own brood with Sölvi Sölvason (1829–1903), farmer at Outer Langamýri, would be a large one. They had only been married for two years and already had two daughters, Helga and Gróa.

The third child was due in mid-February, and there was no predicting the weather. But luck was on their side, and after a freeze-thaw followed by a cold spell from Twelfth Night until February 9, the weather stayed mild until mid-Góa.[1]* At this time there was a handful of certified midwives in Iceland, but none of them were stationed in the Húnavatnssýsla county medical district.[2] Solveig therefore had to rely on an uneducated midwife, but the first two births had gone well and there was no reason to expect anything else from the third.

---

*Translator's note: Góa is the fifth month of winter in the old Icelandic calendar, February 12 to March 13.

Solveig went into labor on the eve of February 15, 1858, and the household was abuzz with anticipation over the arrival of the new child. But the joy over the third daughter's birth was quickly replaced with fear and horror when it became apparent that the little girl had serious birth defects. Her head was unusually large, her arms and legs short and knotted, and only her torso seemed to be of normal proportions. There was no need to mince words; the parish priest must be fetched immediately. Such a malformed child could hardly live very long.

Sölvi Sölvason, Ólöf's father

Father Jón Thórdarson of Audkúla in Svínadalur valley could tell immediately from Sölvi Sölvason's facial expression and the manner of his riding that something serious was afoot. Sölvi's wife, Solveig, was expecting a child any day now, and perhaps the birth had gone badly, the mother passed away or the child been stillborn. Father Jón was greatly relieved to hear that nobody had left this world and that the mother was as well as could be expected, but the newborn girl was malformed and there was reason to fear for her life. Father Jón promised to come to Outer Langamýri as soon as possible, and two days later, on February 17, 1858, the girl was baptized in the *badstofa** there and given the name Ólöf. It was the name of her maternal grandmother, who had died sixteen years earlier, on March 28, 1842, only thirty-nine years old.[3] Witnesses to the baptism were Helga Halldórsdóttir, Ólöf's paternal grandmother, who lived on the next farm, South Langamýri, and Jón Halldórsson, a farmhand at South Langamýri.[4]

Sölvi's and Solveig's reaction to Ólöf's birth was exactly the right one. The odds of survival for dwarves like Ólöf are far lower than those for healthy children. Dwarf children are more sensitive to all sorts of infec-

---

*Translator's note: The *badstofa* (pl. *badstofur*) was the main eating, sleeping, and working quarters in an Icelandic farmhouse.

tions and diseases, and the incidence of accidents is far higher than among children of ordinary proportions.[5] Dangerous diseases were making the rounds in Húnavatnssýsla county that winter, and the infant mortality rate was high.[6] Yet none of these sicknesses seemed to affect the strange newborn. Little Ólöf was healthy and had a strong will to live, and no plans to leave this world. On the other hand, her paternal grandmother and baptismal witness, Helga Halldórsdóttir, was soon to meet her maker. She passed away at South Langamýri about five months after Ólöf's birth, on July 13, 1858, at age fifty-six.[7]

As became clear later on, Ólöf's life was to defy all laws of credibility. Nobody who witnessed the birth in the *badstofa* of Outer Langamýri in February of 1858 would have dreamed that this crippled little child was to live long and become rich and famous in America.

First Cousins on Both Sides

Ólöf Sölvadóttir's parents, Solveig Stefánsdóttir and Sölvi Sölvason, were very closely related: they were first cousins on both sides of their families. Solveig's mother, Ólöf, and Sölvi's mother, Helga, were sisters, the daughters of Halldór Jónsson (born about 1764) and Solveig Jónsdóttir (born about 1761), who lived at Outer Langamýri.[8] Stefán, Solveig's father, and Sölvi, Sölvi Sölvason's father, were brothers, the sons of Sigurlaug Sigurdardóttir (born about 1765) and Sveinn Sveinsson (year of birth unknown, died 1827).[9] Sigurlaug and Sveinn purchased South Langamýri in 1806, so the brothers, Stefán and Sölvi, and the sisters, Helga and Ólöf, grew up side by side, and in the fullness of time, Helga Halldórsdóttir married her cousin Sölvi Sveinsson from South Langamýri. Helga and Sölvi took over the farm at South Langamýri, and Sölvi Sölvason, Ólöf's father, grew up there. Ólöf Halldórsdóttir, Helga's sister, married Stefán Sveinsson, Sölvi's brother, and they lived at Outer Langamýri.

Helga and Sölvi, who took over Helga's parents' farm at South Langamýri, were successful farmers. Their homestead was described thus:

> Sölvi was a great farmer, well spoken and keen of mind. He had a good farm and many sheep. He built up the farmhouse at South

Langamýri to a substantial size. Most of the material was driftwood, fetched from Strandir. There were three *badstofur* and a large room with a loft at the front of the southernmost wing of the house, all clad with hardwood and the loft as well.[10]

Stefán and Ólöf, the parents of young Ólöf's mother, Solveig, settled at Outer Langamýri. Stefán was not as successful a farmer as his elder brother Sölvi at South Langamýri.

Stefán and Ólöf soon had many mouths to feed, for in the space of only a few years they had eight children, among them Solveig, young Ólöf's mother.[11]

Soon grief came to call at Outer Langamýri. Ólöf, the lady of the house, died in 1842 at age thirty-nine, leaving eight children behind. Three years later, Stefán married his second wife, a woman named Gudrún Gudmundsdóttir. He continued to be blessed with many heirs: Soon enough Gudrún had borne him six children, so that in twenty-three years Stefán had fathered fourteen children. It was quite a large family, and the farm at Outer Langamýri couldn't support such a large brood, so Stefán accepted a stipend from the county to support his family.[12] Stefán and Gudrún left their farm in 1851 and worked as farmhands from then on. Their longest period of employment was at Kolugil in Vídidalur valley. Some of the children went with them, but the elder ones were sent to foster homes.[13]

Solveig, little Ólöf's mother, was placed in the care of a widow named Ingibjörg Gudmundsdóttir and her son, Thorleifur Thorleifsson, at Stóridalur in Svínavatn, a flourishing farm.[14] Solveig was confirmed in the spring of 1845, and according to parish records, her reading, writing, and knowledge of the Scripture were average and her behavior acceptable. In addition, she had been vaccinated for smallpox.[15]

Unlike Solveig, his cousin and future wife, Sölvi Sölvason grew up in agreeable circumstances with his parents at South Langamýri and lived there the year he was confirmed. According to parish records, his education was average and his behavior acceptable, and like Solveig he had been vaccinated for smallpox, a fact that was to stand him in good stead later in life.[16]

Sölvi Sölvason was intelligent, assertive, and liberal in his opinions.[17]

He was an imposing man with sharp features—a large, straight nose and dark, almond-shaped eyes. He sported a massive untrimmed beard that contrasted with his well-combed hair and gave him a mischievous look. Sölvi was described as "such an entertainer that he was the center of attention wherever he went. He had inherited a gift for poetry from his father, Sölvi Sveinsson, but was considered to be quite a merciless tease in his verse-making."[18]

Sölvi relished in poking fun at people's weaknesses and vanity, and one of his victims was a young man in the district, Ólafur Gíslason from Eyvindarstadir in Blöndudalur valley. Ólafur was a good horseman with a somewhat foppish style of dress, and was the first man in the region to go riding in an overcoat. Sölvi couldn't leave this untouched and wrote numerous verses making fun of Ólafur the dandy, including this one:

> Though the barbs may sting the boy
> And bring the girls a-staring,
> Long-Coat's outfit must enjoy
> Satire unsparing.[19]

Ólafur can't have been too deeply offended at Sölvi's poetic jests, for he ended up becoming the latter's son-in-law.[20]

Solveig was by all accounts an exceptionally beautiful woman, and her close kinship with Sölvi did not prevent them from being drawn to each other.[21] During their courtship, the cousins lived far apart. Sölvi was still at his father's home at South Langamýri, but Solveig lived with her father and stepmother at Kolugil in Vídidalur valley. The distance between South Langamýri and Kolugil did little, though, to prevent Sölvi's frequent visits to Solveig. He was often in a hurry to reach his lover, sometimes grew impatient on the way, and heaped encouragements on his horse in order to reach his destination faster. On one such ride, he rendered the following verses:

> Onward! Faster, faithful steed
> Farther from the homestead,
> That I rest tonight, I plead,
> In my one true love's bed.

On her bosom, blissfully,
I bid farewell to choler;
Langamýri thankfully
Gives way to Víðidalur.[22]

Sölvi did not need to ride great distances to meet his fiancée for long, for Solveig was hired to work at his home at South Langamýri in 1853.[23] Two years later, on June 3, 1855, they were married at Svínavatn Church. Witnesses to their matrimony were Jón Pálmason from Sólheimar and Erlendur Pálmason from Tungunes. The young couple started their own farm at Solveig's childhood home, Outer Langamýri.[24]

The Shock

When Sölvi and Solveig were married, Solveig was five months pregnant. Their eldest daughter, named for her paternal grandmother, Helga, was born four months after the wedding, on October 4, 1855.[25] Their daughter Gróa was born a year later, and Solveig became pregnant again in the summer of 1857. In late winter 1858, Sölvi and Solveig's third daughter, Ólöf, was born.

Ólöf's birth was clearly a great shock to her parents. One may imagine that instead of joy and celebration because of the newborn's arrival, Solveig and Sölvi were filled with grief and even shame. They probably found themselves asking, as the parents of children with birth defects often do, what they had done to deserve such a fate.

They were also probably concerned about Ólöf's future and the heavy burden she would have to shoulder in a society where dwarves were looked down upon and subjected to discrimination and mockery. But as time progressed, Solveig and Sölvi came to accept Ólöf and realized that she was as gifted, talented, and lovely as her two elder sisters, Helga and Gróa.[26]

At the time of Ólöf's birth, Iceland's farming community was deeply rooted in tradition. Farming methods had remained nearly unchanged since Norwegians settled the country in the ninth and tenth centuries.[27] As in other Protestant countries, work was considered a virtue, and every able individual had to do his duty, irrespective of age, sex, and social class. The children of prosperous farmers as well as poor ones worked hard from an early age. Work helped them develop discipline and a sense of responsibility and made them good citizens. Idle children became irresponsible, and as adults they were a burden to their family and society.[28]

It is clear that Ólöf began working at an early age, as the family at Outer Langamýri was large and there were many tasks to be done. Ólöf's work ethic was keen; she was industrious for her entire life and was never a burden to anyone.

In her fabricated biography, recorded by Albert S. Post and published in the United States in 1887, Ólöf paints an accurate picture of life on an Icelandic farm in the nineteenth century. For example, she describes the difficulty of gathering fuel for the winter:

> Picking up fuel was hard work, and took a great deal of time. They had but little wood [in Iceland], and no coal, so that it was necessary to gather the droppings of animals, and make great piles of this kind of stuff in the summer, so that it would be dry enough to burn in the winter.[29]

She also describes Icelandic sheep farming and states that she prefers sheep's milk to cow's milk:

> The Icelanders used sheep's milk a great deal, and I liked it. Sheep's milk is richer and sweeter than cow's milk. They used to put up a lot of milk in barrels, and put in some rennet, which would make it curdle into something like cottage cheese. This they would set aside for winter use, and were very fond of it. The family would be considered very poor who could not put up from eight to ten barrels of this food.[30]

"None Can I Find Fault with You"

Although the parents and siblings of dwarves like Ólöf show them love and affection and usually treat them like healthy individuals, the same is not true of society as a whole. In almost every society there is shame at-

A nineteenth-century turf house, Hólshús, in Eyjafjördur about 1900

tached to being a dwarf, and people with dwarfism are continually reminded of their small stature and unusual body shape. The general public allows itself to either stare at dwarves and make negative comments,
or deliberately ignore them and act as if they are invisible.[31] As a result,
dwarves therefore rarely enjoy the privilege of healthy people, which is to
be seen without being paid any particular attention.[32]

Icelandic society was no exception. Ólöf was often teased, made fun
of, and laughed at.[33] In her biography, Ólöf describes how children at her
"school" in Iceland teased her. Of course she implies that she was teased
because she was an Eskimo rather than because she was a dwarf. According to her, the children were jealous of her because of all the attention
the priest paid to the little girl from Greenland. Ólöf said that in Iceland,
she and her siblings were

> placed in the Lutheran school, and there I studied for five years. My
> teacher was a good and kind man. His name was Ion Thorderson. He

was patient with me and helped me to learn; but some of the scholars were jealous of "the little thing" and made fun of me. For this they had to carry notes home to their parents, and this secured them a good whipping a-piece, so that they were heard to wish "that little thing" had never come into the school.[34]

Because of all this, dwarves often develop an inferiority complex, have low self-esteem, and are emotionally and socially isolated.[35] Ólöf's parents seem to have realized what difficulties accompanied being a dwarf, and did their best to bolster her self-confidence, as can be seen in the following verse of encouragement written by Sölvi to his daughter:

None can I find fault with you,
Rosy-cheekèd Ólöf,
Fairest of my children, too,
Blessing made of God's love.[36]

Ólöf's Future Prospects in Iceland

School attendance was made compulsory in Iceland in 1907, thirty-one years after Ólöf left the country. During Ólöf's youth there were six children's schools in operation in Iceland, all of them located by the sea, and all run at the behest of parents and counties. Apart from that, the households managed education under the guidance of priests. The only requirement was that children learn reading and Scripture. Three years after Ólöf left Iceland, Parliament passed a law mandating the teaching of writing and arithmetic in addition to the previous compulsory curriculum.[37]

On May 19, 1872, Ólöf was confirmed in Audkúla Church by Jón Thórdarson, the priest who had baptized her when she was only two days old. In parish records, Father Jón makes no mention of Ólöf's knowledge of reading and Scripture, only mentioning that she is "quite well behaved."[38] However, according to parish visitation records from 1871, Ólöf knew the entire contents of Luther's *Small Catechism*.[39]

At this time there was only one public secondary school in the country, the Learned School in Reykjavík. The Priests' School was founded in 1847, and in 1876, the year Ólöf sailed west, the Medical School opened its doors.[40] The Learned School was open to men only, and its students were largely the sons of officials. The school played an important role in sustaining the power of the Icelandic upper class.[41]

In 1874, two years before Ólöf left Iceland, the country's first school for women was opened in Reykjavík. The Women's School in Reykjavík was a private school, primarily intended for the daughters of upper-class farmers. These young women were often sent to live with good families in Reykjavík to learn domestic skills in a city household. The housewives in these families were often too busy to attend to the country girls as they should, but the founders of the Women's School thought the school could improve upon this system.[42]

Tuition at the Women's School was high, and only wealthy parents could afford to send their daughters there. If by some strange circumstance a poor farmer like Sölvi Sölvason had had an opportunity to send one of his daughters to the Women's School, it is almost certain that Ólöf would not have been selected. A girl who attended the school could expect to marry a successful farmer and thus join the ranks of important women in Icelandic society. The odds of Ólöf's capturing the attention of one of these men, just over three feet tall as she was, were slim. Indeed, it was rare for dwarves to marry at all.[43]

Yet neither Ólöf's small stature nor her lack of education were to hold her back in America.

Marriage and Labor Bondage

It was not merely Ólöf's stature that governed her chances of marriage in Iceland. Marriage was a privilege there, just as education was. By law, only those people who had a large and fertile enough plot of land to support a large family were permitted to marry. There was a great shortage of land in Iceland at the time. As a consequence, fewer married than would have liked to. Many men never married, and an even larger number of women remained single, for women outnumbered men in Iceland. Marriage rates were extremely low; for example, in 1880 only 23.7 percent of Icelandic women over fifteen years of age were married.[44]

Until the year 1894, eighteen years after Ólöf left the country, farm laborers were bound to their positions by Icelandic law. By law, all single

Women carding wool in a badstofa. *The* badstofa *was the principal workplace of Icelandic women for centuries.*

men or women who did not reside with their parents had to be registered as laborers on a farm.[45] Thus Ólöf's fate in Iceland was already cut out for her: like all other unmarried women, born healthy or not, she would have to work her way through the world as a farmhand. Her one opportunity to improve her circumstances in life would have been to move to a different farm in the hope of receiving better pay and treatment. Ólöf realized early on what her future in Iceland held, and probably entertained dreams of a better life. Those dreams were to come true.

Sölvi and Solveig's Separation

Solveig and Sölvi were very fertile and their family grew rapidly. Ólöf was her parents' third child, and the fact that the third daughter had birth defects did not prevent the family from continuing to expand. When Ólöf was two years old, her parents had their first son, Sölvi. A year later, in 1861, their second son, Sigurdur, was born, and the third, Jón, came along three years later, in 1864. The fourth son, Ásgeir, was born a year later, in 1865, and Sölvi and Solveig's youngest child, their daughter Ingibjörg, was born in 1866. Thus Sölvi and Solveig had eight children in all, four daughters and four sons.[46]

Before long the young couple's life became a never-ending struggle to make ends meet. Outer Langamýri was a farm of average quality at best. As Solveig's parents had learned years before, it could by no means support a large family. In the hope of improving their circumstances, Sölvi and Solveig moved from Outer Langamýri after ten years there, settling at Rútsstadir in Svínadalur valley, but to no avail.[47]

Unlike his father, Sölvi Sveinsson from South Langamýri, Sölvi Sölvason was not much of a farmer and soon became lazy and idle.[48] To make matters worse, he had a tendency to abandon the farm in difficult times and go riding across the surrounding countryside to visit friends, whom he would entertain with clever and often cutting verse. The relationship between husband and wife grew stilted, and Sölvi began having an affair with the household maid, Soffía Eyjólfsdóttir. Soffía was a single mother, and her son, Magnús Björnsson, worked with his mother at Rútsstadir.[49]

Sölvi and Soffía's affair caused emotional turmoil in the household, and Solveig's humiliation was complete when she and Soffía both bore Sölvi a child in the same year, 1866. Sölvi and Solveig's youngest child, Ingibjörg, was born January 25, 1866, and Sölvi and Soffía's daughter was born on December 28 of that same year. According to parish records, this was the first time Sölvi had committed adultery, but it was Soffía's second child born out of wedlock.[50] This situation was far from being unique in Iceland, and since wives usually received very little money after a divorce and lost custody of their children as well, they often accepted their plight and stayed with their husbands.[51]

Sölvi and Soffía's daughter was baptized Solveig, possibly in a bid for forgiveness from the lady of the house. If so, it failed to achieve the intended effect. A year later, in 1867, Solveig left her children and her home and moved to her father and stepmother's home at Kolugil in Vídidalur.

By this point in time, Sölvi had traded Rútsstadir for Mosfell, another farm in the same county.[52] The separation made a deep and permanent impact on the family's life, because the family was dissolved upon

Solveig's departure. Sölvi took a job as a farmhand with his sister Gróa at South Langamýri and her husband, Arnljótur Gudmundsson, taking with him two of his children, Sölvi Jr. and Gróa.[53] The other children were placed in foster care on nearby farms. Ólöf was initially at Outer Langamýri, the farm closest by. Soffía, the mother of Sölvi's child, was a maid at Svínavatn in Svínavatn District.[54]

Sölvi and Soffía were reunited in 1869, when Soffía was hired to work as a maid at South Langamýri. They lived there for two years with their daughter, Solveig, and Sölvi's children, Sölvi Jr. and Gróa, and were then hired to work at Brandsstadir in Blöndudalur valley in 1871.[55]

Ólöf Moves Back Home

Reuniting the family and reclaiming his children was clearly a matter of great importance to Sölvi, and Ólöf moved back in with her father and stepmother in 1872. She had then been in foster care at Mosfell in Svínadalur for three years.[56] In 1874, five of Sölvi and Solveig's eight children lived at Brandsstadir: Sölvi Jr., Jón, Ásgeir, Ólöf, and Ingibjörg. Also living there were Sölvi and Soffía's two children: Solveig and their son Arnljótur, born at Brandsstadir in 1873.[57] Soffía's son, Magnús Björnsson, lived with them as well, but he had previously been a farmhand at the farm Kúlusel in Svínavatn District.[58]

Another maid who was temporarily employed at Brandsstadir, Rósa Jóhannesdóttir, had her eye on Sölvi, and "felt that she was just as well suited for Sölvi's affections as Soffía."[59] Sölvi had no interest in Rósa but was amused by her attentions and wrote the following quatrain about her:

With her eyes off wandering
Where be handsome fellows,
Valley-rose's sense of self
Significantly mellows.

Although Sölvi had no particular interest in Rósa, it is likely that he continued to cast appreciative glances at other women. But he never betrayed Soffía's trust, and they continued to live together without benefit of clergy for some thirty years.[60]

Solveig's Death

Solveig was a competent seamstress, and after she moved to Kolugil she earned her keep sewing clothing for men and women alike. Three years after she and Sölvi separated and Solveig moved to Kolugil, Ólöf and her siblings suffered a still greater shock when their mother died in an accident on March 3, 1870. Her funeral was held in Audkúla Church on March 11.[61]

There are two accounts of the events leading up to Solveig's death. According to one version of events, she was walking on ice across Svínavatn Lake in bad weather when the wind threw her over. She fell badly and broke a few ribs. She barely managed to crawl to the next farm, where she lay down in bed and died shortly thereafter. The other account claims that she was crossing Midfjardarheidi heath with a young man for company when they were caught in a blizzard. The young man is said to have frozen to death on the way, but Solveig made it to the next farm exhausted and chilled to the bone. There she was placed in bed and died soon thereafter. Solveig was thirty-nine years old when she died, and thus reached almost exactly the same age as her mother, Ólöf Halldórsdóttir. Mother and daughter each left eight children behind them.

Ólöf Sölvadóttir was eleven years old when her mother died, and if she had harbored the dream of living close to Solveig again, that dream died with her. Solveig's death marked the passing of the last woman who was close to Ólöf and could provide her with unconditional love, warmth, and shelter. Ólöf, her grandmother and namesake, died sixteen years before she was born, and Helga, her paternal grandmother and godmother, died when Ólöf was only five months old, so she never got to know either of her grandmothers. Thus Ólöf learned at an early age to stand on her own two feet and rely on her own wits, and she soon grew to appreciate the wisdom of the saying that God helps those who help themselves.

Hard Times and Emigration

It is clear that Sölvi was to blame for most of his family's difficulties because of his poor farming skills.[62] He also caused his wife, Solveig, and their children immeasurable pain and grief. Nonetheless, it would be unjust to blame him for the entirety of the family's misfortune. Circumstances in Iceland were by no means favorable for private farmers such as Sölvi, even if they managed their farms well. It was a time of great economic change in Iceland, and these changes were initially to the detriment of the average farmer.[63]

For centuries, Iceland's economy had been firmly entrenched. Farming was conducted in the same way it had been at the time of the country's settlement, and the production capacity was the same. For centuries the population size remained virtually unchanged, and it never exceeded 50,000. Peaks in population growth were followed almost automatically by famine or disease that kept population growth under control.[64]

Things began to change in the nineteenth century, and advances in medicine eradicated smallpox from Iceland as well as other parts of Europe. Transportation between Europe and Iceland improved greatly, ensuring that the population had access to enough food during times of famine.[65] In the wake of these changes, the nation faced an overpopulation crisis, for the farms' productivity did not increase correspondingly. Between 1850 and 1870, there was no balance between population and food production in the country, and during this period the ranks of the poor swelled considerably in number. In 1850, 1.9 percent of the nation was considered poor. Ten years later, in 1860, 2.7 percent of the nation lived in a state of poverty, and by 1870 the proportion of poor people in the country had more than doubled to 5.6 percent.[66]

Rapid population growth called for more land, and large farms were split into smaller patches. The mild climate of the first decades of the nineteenth century enabled people to farm on heaths and in remote valleys where no one had farmed before, nor has since.[67] In good years, small farmers such as Sölvi could live a decent life if their families weren't too large. After 1850, long cold spells made life very difficult on small farms. Sölvi and his family may not have been counted officially among the poor, but they were nonetheless no strangers to poverty and struggled eternally to make ends meet.

At Brandsstadir, Sölvi had three cows and pregnant heifers, one yearling bull, twenty-seven sheep with lambs, and ten infertile sheep, but no wethers or rams above a year old. He also had fourteen yearling lambs, three stallions, and three geldings. Sölvi did not grow vegetables.[68]

It soon became apparent that this livestock could by no means support a large family. Sölvi soon had to send three of his sons, Sölvi Jr., Jón, and Ásgeir, away to foster homes or farm labor positions. Sölvi Jr. went to Hvammur in Svartárdalur valley, Jón's foster home was Sólheimar in Svínavatn District, and Ásgeir went to work at Stóridalur in Svínavatn District, where his mother, Solveig Stefánsdóttir, had worked as a young woman.[69]

As Sölvi's attempt to improve his family's living conditions and reunite his children failed, it is unsurprising that he should have been susceptible to the propositions of the so-called America agents. These agents began to visit the country regularly after 1870 and promised a better life beyond the sea in America.

The Great Emigration of 1876

In the fall of 1875, the Canadian government sent two agents to Iceland, the Canadian W. C. Krieger and the Icelander Sigtryggur Jónsson, who had been one of the first Icelanders to settle in Canada. The purpose of their journey was to convince a group of people to move west and stake claims in the newly founded Icelandic colony, New Iceland, by Lake Winnipeg in Manitoba. With this purpose in mind they distributed leaflets in Icelandic, published by the Canadian consul in London, to the local farms.[70]

At the same time, two representatives of the government of Nova Scotia came to Iceland on a similar errand. Both were Icelanders: Jóhannes Arngrímsson, who had taken the name John Anderson, and Jóhann Straumfjörd. Two years earlier, in 1873, a group of Icelanders had settled in Kinmount, Ontario. They fared very poorly, and the government of Nova Scotia had succeeded, with Jóhannes' assistance, in convincing them to resettle in Mooseland Heights, fifty miles from Halifax. Mooseland Heights proved to be a far better choice than Kinmount, and the Icelanders were quick to give it a new name. They called it Markland and were quite content there.

Now the government of Nova Scotia wanted more Icelandic settlers to come to Markland.[71] The government's offer was very enticing: every man aged fifteen or over was to receive one hundred acres of land free of charge, including one acre that had already been cleared. The land was to include a house, a stove, and other necessary housekeeping implements, enough food to last a year, and a settler's stipend of eleven dollars. Some of the equipment was free, and the rest could be purchased with loans on highly favorable terms.[72]

The America agents fared well that year. By the spring of 1876, 1,200 Icelanders had accepted their offer and decided to leave Iceland permanently. Most were bound for New Iceland, but a few families, including that of Sölvi Sölvason, had accepted the government of Nova Scotia's princely offer and planned to settle in the new Markland.[73]

Across the Ocean

In her fabricated biography, Ólöf Sölvadóttir says it was at her initiative that her family moved to America. She claims that her Eskimo family came to Iceland from Greenland and lived there for a few years in good circumstances. At that point Ólöf chanced to come across a book that described the wonders and riches of America, and managed to convince her father to move there with her. Her father agreed, but the poor man could only afford to pay for two people to travel. He chose Ólöf as his companion, she says, because she was most interested in leaving the country, in addition to being the youngest child and his favorite.[74]

This story is not true. Ólöf did not take the initiative in her family's emigration to America, though she supported the suggestion whole-heartedly from the beginning. But the story clearly illustrates her desire to improve her standing in society and her wish for the undivided attention of her father.

It was Sölvi himself who suggested the move west. He was constantly in financial difficulties, his children had been shunted between farms, and he clearly wanted to make up for this neglect by starting a new and better life in a distant country, far away from the clutches of poverty and old grief. All of Sölvi's children save two sailed west with him in the summer of 1876. Helga, the eldest daughter, flatly refused to go. She was engaged to the very same Ólafur Gíslason whom her father had ridiculed in a poem for riding through the county wearing an overcoat. Helga and Ólafur were married six years after her family left the country, on October

14, 1882, and they lived at Eiríksstadir in Svartárdalur valley all their lives.[75] Sigurdur, Solveig and Sölvi's fifth child, also remained in Iceland but came west seven years later, in 1883. He came with Sigurdur Sölvason, Sölvi's brother, and his wife, Rut Magnúsdóttir. Sigurdur Jr. had been in their foster care for over ten years, first at Steiná in Svartárdalur valley, then at Hvammur in the same district.[76]

Joining Sölvi and Soffía on their westward journey were Gróa, Sölvi's second eldest, age twenty; Ólöf, age eighteen; Sölvi Jr., age sixteen; Jón, age twelve; Ásgeir, age eleven; and Ingibjörg, Solveig and Sölvi's youngest child, who was nine years old. Also with them were Sölvi and Soffía's children, Solveig, nine years old, and Arnljótur, three years old, as well as Soffía's son Magnús Björnsson, who was the same age as Ólöf. Sölvi himself was forty-six years old when he left Iceland, and Soffía was forty-two.[77]

The steamship *Verona*, which was supposed to transport the voyagers on the first leg of the journey from Iceland to Scotland, was expected to arrive in Saudárkrókur in early June. It was essential to arrive on time, and at the beginning of June the passengers began streaming to Saudárkrókur in such droves that the tiny town may never have been as populated. It must have been quite a sight to behold Sölvi's company riding with their pack horses from Húnavatnssýsla county to Skagafjördur, for in addition to his family of eleven there were Gudrún Kristjánsdóttir, housemaid at Brandsstadir, age twenty-three, and her two-year-old daughter, Sigurbjörg Soffía Ólafsdóttir.[78] The wait for the ship was long, though. The winter and spring of 1876 were unusually cold, and even in June there were still ice sheets floating off the northern coast. The ice prevented the *Verona* from arriving on schedule, and the ship did not dock in Saudárkrókur until June 29. Sölvi's family was surely becoming impatient, and they must have rejoiced upon finally boarding the ship and commencing the journey to the promised land.[79]

Like Sölvi himself, most of the emigrants were impoverished people who had sold all their possessions and even taken loans to cover the cost of the trip. America was far across the ocean and the journey was long and taxing, and nobody expected the travelers to return. Sölvi's neighbors and friends knew that he was leaving the country for good. He was no farmer and it was obvious that the country's economy would not suffer

Saudárkrókur in the late nineteenth century. This is the first photograph ever taken in Saudárkrókur, and it dates to 1887–88.

much from his departure, but among revelers he would be sorely missed. Gatherings and festivities in the county would be much duller without Sölvi's cheerfulness, sense of humor, and poetic gifts.[80]

When news of the *Verona*'s arrival finally reached them, a few of Sölvi's friends rode out to Saudárkrókur to bid him and his family farewell one last time. As usual, Sölvi did not disappoint—when he stepped aboard ship he turned around and recited the following verse in farewell:

Steady winds do westward blow,
We fall silent, praying.
Iceland's sons, may God bestow
Blessings on your staying.[81]

Early on the morning of June 30, 1876, the *Verona* finally departed from Saudárkrókur for Akureyri, where more emigrants boarded. Two days later, July 2, the ship was on its way, and the day after that, July 3, most of the passengers saw Iceland for the last time.[82]

The Promised Land

The Transatlantic Voyage

Sölvi and his family attracted immediate attention on board the *Verona,* and Sölvi probably wasted no time in charming his fellow travelers with his poems and stories. Ólöf also attracted attention, but of a different kind. Most of the passengers had never seen a dwarf before and stared and laughed at her. The mocking did not diminish when Ólöf, clearly tired of being teased, said she was going to gain fame and respect in the new land.[1] Like the other emigrants, she hoped for a better life beyond the sea, but it is doubtful that she had anything specific in mind when she answered in this manner. Her statement was to prove prophetic, however. Although some of her fellow voyagers and their descendants were successful in America, few of them made it as far as she did.

As an example of the fate of Ólöf and her family's shipmates in America, one might take Fridrik Fridriksson (Stefánsson), an eight-year-old boy who was traveling with his mother, Gudrídur Gísladóttir. Fridrik was conceived out of wedlock, son of Fridrik Stefánsson, member of parliament from Skálá in Skagafjördur.[2] Fridrik became a printer and worked for *Lögberg,* one of the most important Icelandic newspapers in Canada. He married an Icelandic woman, Anna Olson, who was born in

1877 in New Iceland. Their daughter, Signý, married John David Eaton, grandson of the founder and owner of Eaton's department store in Canada, who took over the business after the death of his father, Sir John Craig Eaton. Signý was always concerned about the well-being of Icelanders in Canada, and supported the establishment of a professorship in Icelandic language and literature at the University of Manitoba.[3]

Writer Torfhildur Hólm was also aboard the same ship as Ólöf. For thirteen years Torfhildur lived in Winnipeg, where she started her writing career and published her first articles and short stories. When she returned to Iceland, she was determined to make her living entirely from her writing. She wrote historical novels based on the *Sagas of the Icelanders*, which became very popular in Iceland and mainland Europe alike. But she received little public support for her work and had to finance her publishing largely out of her own pocket.[4]

Also among Ólöf's fellow travelers were the married couple Jóhann Stefánsson and Ingibjörg Jóhannesdóttir from Kroppur in Hrafnagil District in Eyjafjördur and their four children: Inga, age twelve; Jóhannes, age nine; Stefanía Rósa, age four; and Lárus, barely a year old. In 1879, three years after they arrived in Canada, they had another son, Vilhjálmur Stefánsson, who later became a world-famous Arctic explorer.[5]

Yet another traveler, a young Skagafjördur native named Jóhann Schram, kept a diary of the journey from Iceland to New Iceland. According to Schram, the crossing to Scotland was uneventful. Southwesterly storms made many of the passengers seasick before Iceland vanished from sight. On the third day of the journey, a child was born on board to Margrét, wife of Davíd from Húsabakkar. The birth went well, and mother and child were well taken care of on board. When the *Verona* docked in Granton, Scotland, news of the child that was "born on the sea" was quick to spread through the town, and many women from Granton came down to the ship and gave the newborn money, "approximately eighteen *krónur*, and two beautiful sets of clothing."[6]

That evening they took a train from Granton to Glasgow. The Icelanders had never seen a train before, and the train ride was unforgettable for many of them. Ólöf later said that she had been half-frightened by the noise and violent shaking of the train.[7] She soon grew accustomed to trains, however, and was later a loyal customer of American railway com-

Emigrants on board the Camoens *on their way to Granton, Scotland, in 1883 or 1884*

panies, for her fame and success as a lecturer were highly dependent on efficient rail transport.

In Glasgow, the group enjoyed the hospitality of the Allan Shipping Line's reception house for four days. People used the time to explore the city and saw many a new sight: grand buildings, paved streets and bridges, and "spectacular stores with enticing products, and indeed some of those who had money bought quite a bit." But there were also poor people and rabble on the streets "who behaved in quite an unseemly fashion."[8] After four days in Glasgow, they set out across the ocean in the *Austria*, a grand vessel. Aboard were 743 Icelanders, forty Scots, and a crew of eighty. The weather was good throughout the voyage, as were living conditions, but among the women there was some tendency to seasickness, and one child died on board. It was the child of Pétur from Jónskot on Reykjaströnd and his wife. A funeral was held the same day, and the body cast overboard.[9] On July 21, 1876, the *Austria* sailed through the mouth of the Gulf of Saint Lawrence to Quebec, docking there at 6:00 a.m. on the morning of July 22.[10] Precisely twenty-two days had passed since Sölvi Sölvason and his family had set out from Saudárkrókur.

Disappointment

Sölvi and his family were undoubtedly tired after a long journey but glad to have their feet on solid ground again. They were also bursting with excitement over arriving in Nova Scotia, for they had seen the territory from a distance during the voyage, and the hilly coastline was densely forested and peppered with green pastures and white houses.[11] But the joy of reaching the promised land and the excitement over their arrival in Nova Scotia didn't last long. On the docks stood three Icelanders from Nova Scotia who had with them a letter from other Icelandic Nova Scotians. According to the letter, the government of Nova Scotia had rescinded its offer, and only those Icelanders who could afford to stake their claim were now welcome.[12] This was shocking news, but fourteen Icelanders had signed the letter, so "we could cast no doubt on this message."[13]

The disappointment felt by Sölvi and his family must have been acute. The dream of a new and better life in the west was turning into a nightmare. There they stood empty-handed, having sold their entire property in Iceland to pay for the voyage, and they had no one to turn to. But the Canadian government soon interceded and agreed to grant the stranded travelers a loan to cover the journey to New Iceland and the expense of getting settled there.[14] Sölvi and his family had no other choice than to accept this offer. So it was that they joined their fellow voyagers from the ship and settled in New Iceland rather than Nova Scotia.

Journey on Land

The following day, July 23, 1876, marked the beginning of the Icelanders' journey across Canada. Their first stop was Toronto, a large city with many beautiful buildings, where they stayed for three days and were "all installed into a large and grand warehouse."[15] While in Toronto, Ólöf had an experience that clearly made a deep impression on her. The group of Icelanders went to a museum where rare and unusual objects and phenomena were being exhibited, among them a newlywed dwarf couple. Each guest paid five cents or twenty *aurar* to see the little couple.[16] A few years later, Ólöf herself took a job in a circus where she was exhibited, for a price, as the wife of a dwarf.

On July 28, the group took a train to the city of Sarnia, where they boarded a steamship on Lake Huron and sailed to Duluth, Minnesota. Accommodations on board were dreadful. The ship was hopelessly overbooked with passengers, who shared beds with pigs and other farm animals. The drinking water on board was so foul that several people were taken ill. After three days on Lake Huron, Sölvi and family reached land in Duluth. From there they took a train to Fisherman's Landing on the Red River, which runs through the city of Winnipeg.[17] The prams that transported the travelers on the last leg down the Red River to Winnipeg were also overflowing with people, and the immigrants' center in Winnipeg proved to be far too small for such a large group of Icelanders.

The weather was hot, and the Icelanders were unaccustomed to it. Many of them couldn't bear it and became gravely ill, and before long between thirty and forty Icelanders—mostly infants—had died from the heat.[18] These deaths were only a portent of what was to come.

New Iceland

Immigration by Icelanders to North America began in earnest in 1872. Between 1872 and 1874, Icelanders settled in Wisconsin, Ontario, and Nova Scotia, the original destination of Ólöf's family. The idea of creating a special colony of Icelanders in America soon surfaced and gained in popularity. One of the first topics of discussion of the Icelanders' Society in Milwaukee, Wisconsin, which was founded in 1874, was to find a suitable location for such a colony.[19]

Two conditions were set for the colony: it had to border a lake or the ocean, so the Icelanders could supplement farming with fishing, and it had to be large enough to support all of the Icelanders already in America, as well as all future arrivals. A few Icelanders went on scouting expeditions. They looked at land in Nebraska, Wisconsin, and Alaska, but none of these places was considered good enough—Nebraska and Alaska were too far from the civilized world, and Wisconsin was too densely populated. Finally the Icelanders decided to settle in Manitoba, in the Red River Valley on the west coast of Lake Winnipeg.[20]

The men who explored the land saw many points in its favor. The soil was fertile, and large forests provided plenty of wood for construction of houses. Wild game was abundant, in particular elk and birds of all kinds, and berries and fish were plentiful. The weather was also exceptionally good: summers were sunny but the breeze from Lake Winnipeg kept temperatures down, and evenings were cool. Crickets did not pose a significant threat, and the Native Americans who lived there had been converted to Christianity and were peaceful people. Access to the site was also good, as the Canadian Pacific Railway Company was laying tracks twenty-eight miles to the south.

There were some drawbacks to the land, however. Mosquitoes were common, but fortunately none of them were of the blood-sucking kind. The land was very flat and thus vulnerable to flooding, but these were considered minor inconveniences compared to the many good qualities the area had to offer.[21]

New Iceland: An Independent State

The virtues of the land selected for the colony were considered substantial, but no less remarkable were the terms offered by the Canadian government: the Icelandic settlers were offered the chance to found an independent state where they would have complete autonomy, name their own government, make laws, and found schools. Such a generous offer could hardly be refused, and there was never any question as to the new state's name: it would be called New Iceland.[22]

Just why the leaders of the young Republic of Canada offered such remarkable terms to the inhabitants of a small island in the North Atlantic remains a mystery. Granted, the Canadian government was eager to persuade people to settle the region west of Ontario. The Hudson's Bay Company and the North West Company sent hunters to these areas. The hunters often had love affairs with Native American women, and their descendants, the so-called Métis people, could be tough customers.[23]

In 1812, the Earl of Selkirk had sponsored a small group of Scottish immigrants who settled at the confluence of the Assiniboine and Red

Rivers, where Winnipeg would later rise. That settlement was not long-lived. The Scots came into conflict with the Métis in some of the first fighting between ethnic groups in Canada. The Canadian government therefore realized that neither Scottish nor British immigrants would be prepared to settle there. The government was adamant that a Francophone population must not settle the region; thus the Icelanders were probably an ideal choice. They posed no threat to anyone, and in all likelihood their proposed republic would soon come to an end. But if the promise of an independent state was the way to entice Icelanders to Manitoba, then the promise would be made.[24]

The First Year in New Iceland

The first settlers of New Iceland arrived there in October 1875, about a year before Ólöf's family came. They soon discovered that New Iceland had little in common with the descriptions they had heard of it. The weather was completely different from what they were accustomed to, the flora and fauna were unfamiliar, and farming and fishing methods were not the same as they had been in Iceland. Just after their arrival in New Iceland, the weather was far too hot, but this was followed by a hard winter, one of the coldest in many years. The Icelanders were poorly prepared for it. They lacked warm clothing, especially good shoes and mittens.[25]

The land around Lake Winnipeg was forested. The Icelanders, who had never seen a forest before, were suddenly expected to start felling trees and building log cabins, all in time for the upcoming winter. They had little experience with such work, as most houses in Iceland were built from turf and rock. Their lack of expertise in building log cabins soon became apparent, as the houses were poorly built and insulated. They leaked like sieves and were drafty. In these makeshift shelters the Icelanders weathered the first winter, usually with two or three families in each hut.[26]

Grain cultivation had been discontinued long since in Iceland, and the settlers knew very little about it. Some of them tried: they cleared the land, plowed the earth, and sowed, but the yield was negligible at first. On the other hand, the Icelanders were experienced fishermen, but the

Landing at Willow Point in Winnipeg, 1875. Painting by Árni Sigurdsson.

nets they had brought with them from Iceland were useless for fishing on Lake Winnipeg. The mesh of the net was either too large or too small, so the first fishing attempts yielded nothing worth eating. As a consequence, the people lived on discounted food supplies from the Canadian government for the first years. Merchants in Winnipeg used the opportunity to rid themselves of old stocks, so the flour and other food the settlers received was both old and spoiled.[27] The Icelanders were no strangers to these business practices.

The first winter in New Iceland was very difficult. People suffered from hunger, cold, and damp, and many fell ill and died that winter. Most of them survived the misery, however, and were able to share their experience and give advice to the large group that arrived in August 1876. But the difficulties in the new colony were just beginning.

Steinnes

Sölvi and his family reached New Iceland safe and sound. When they arrived they immediately began clearing the plot of land they had been allotted in Willow Creek, a few miles from the shore of Lake Winnipeg.

There they built a log cabin and a few outhouses, sowed corn, and tried to grow vegetables. They called their new farm Steinnes. Sölvi had never been much of a farmer, and here he was at even more of a disadvantage. He didn't know any farming methods in this strange land and had to learn everything from scratch. He and his family worked hard to build the new farm at Steinnes and to cultivate the land, but their crops were small.[28]

Sölvi and his family did not have a prominent role in the public life of the community. They are only mentioned twice in local documents: the building of Steinnes is mentioned, as is the fact that Sölvi had a child baptized immediately after its birth in the colony's church.[29]

Smallpox and Quarantine

Two months after the family settled in New Iceland, smallpox broke out in the community. There are conflicting accounts of how the disease was brought to New Iceland, but one story says that an Icelandic woman was infected on the steamship that brought the Icelanders up Lake Huron to Duluth. According to this account, the woman barely made it to New Iceland and died there.[30] The smallpox epidemic was mild at first, but grew worse due to the hard winter and poor housing conditions. By the New Year, the disease had taken hold everywhere in the colony, and before it ended in March 1877 over a hundred settlers had died. The Native Americans in the vicinity were also infected, and many of them died as well. The authorities in Winnipeg, fearing the disease would spread across the entirety of Manitoba, imposed a quarantine on New Iceland at the end of November 1876.[31]

Sölvi and family had been in the promised land less than four months when they were effectively placed under a travel injunction. The quarantine was extremely inconvenient for the Icelandic settlers. Their farms were still too small, and they themselves too inexperienced, to make their living completely off the land. During the first year they had looked for work outside the colony, but now even that recourse was unavailable. Once again they were forced to live on food gifts from the government, but the food was bad and of limited quantity.

The settlers considered the quarantine a source of shame, and they

Log cabin of Icelandic settlers at Spanish Fork, Utah, erected in 1875. Ólöf's family lived in a similar house in New Iceland.

were isolated and starving to death. One of them described this winter in the following way:

> The suffering of the sick and their constant care, the strangeness of the people in this queer, isolated place, the poverty and the deaths of loved ones combined to make the lives of the settlers unbearable.[32]

Because of protests and pressure from the residents of New Iceland, the quarantine was finally lifted in July 1877.[33]

Sölvi and his family had not intended to settle in New Iceland, and life there was an immediate disappointment. Every possible obstacle seemed to arise: bad houses, poor crops, a hard winter, smallpox, and quarantine. Ólöf was soon faced with the fact that she had no future in New Iceland. Her life there would be much the same as it had been in Iceland: eternal work and toil. She had learned at a young age to stand on her own two feet, and at the first available opportunity she took a position in the household of an English-speaking family, although she didn't speak a word of English. This was in 1877, and Ólöf was nineteen years old.

Ólöf's move to Winnipeg marks the beginning of her adventures, but first comes the story of her family's fate in America.

Westward to the Sea

In Shanty Town

A year after Ólöf moved to Winnipeg, her father and family also gave up
on life in New Iceland, left Steinnes, and moved to the city. There Sölvi
and his sons worked as day laborers.

Sölvi and his family settled in Shanty Town, one of the first Icelandic
settlements in Winnipeg.[1] Shanty Town was situated on Hudson's Bay
Company land on the banks of the Red River, and the Icelanders who
lived there were too poor to buy or rent homes in the town. Instead, they
bought inexpensive timber or collected old scraps of lumber from Brown
and Rutherford's sawmill. From these and other materials, the Icelanders
constructed huts that they called "sheds" or "scrap shanties."[2]

Shanty Town grew fast, and when Sölvi and his family moved there in
1878 there were already two orderly rows of sheds, seven huts in one row
and four in the other, as well as a few more scattered here and there. The
neighborhood's inhabitants were legal residents of the town by then and
paid rent for the land, about two dollars a month.[3] The huts of Shanty
Town were shoddily constructed, but the winter of 1877–78 was mild
and caused no harm. On the other hand, the first winter Sölvi and his
family spent there, 1878–79, was a very cold one. The family huddled in

Shanty Town in Winnipeg. Ólöf's family lived there for about two years.

its shanty and tried to keep warm by burning driftwood from the Red River, the only fuel available.

Soon the rumor began spreading that the Icelanders in Shanty Town were substance abusers and instigators of violence. The residents refused to tolerate this reputation and sent a letter to *Framfari* (*The Progressive*), the first Icelandic newsletter in Winnipeg, to correct the misconception. The letter appeared on March 7, 1879, and was signed by ten Icelandic residents of Shanty Town, among them Sölvi Sölvason.[4]

While the Icelanders of Shanty Town denied being violent drunkards, many of them were revelers like Sölvi and enjoyed making merry. Every Saturday evening, the largest of the Icelanders' shanties was emptied, a ball was thrown, and people danced late into the night to accordion music. Sometimes a talented Icelandic fiddler by the name of Gudmundur Björnsson accompanied the dance.[5]

Exodus from New Iceland to North Dakota

After being harried by smallpox and quarantine for the better part of a year, the settlers of New Iceland were gripped by general unhappiness and despair over the future of the colony. To add insult to injury, no sooner was the smallpox epidemic over than the area flooded, and insects harassed the livestock so thoroughly that it yielded little of value. The settlers had also fallen into passionate disputes about various local matters, including religion.[6]

In 1878, a three-man group was sent out to scout for new land, and they came to the conclusion that Pembina County in North Dakota, just south of the Manitoba border west of the Red River, was a much better choice than New Iceland. The Icelanders headed there in large numbers, and by 1881 the population of New Iceland had dwindled from 1,000 to 250.[7]

Sölvi's family never felt at home in Shanty Town, and in 1880 they joined the Icelanders who streamed from New Iceland to Pembina County. Jóhann Stefánsson and Ingibjörg Jóhannesdóttir were among those who moved from New Iceland "south of the line" at the same time. A year before they moved, their son, Vilhjálmur Stefánsson, was born. Ólöf was not with her family at that time, so she never saw Vilhjálmur as a young boy. Their paths would cross later in life, however.

Thirteen Years in Hallson, North Dakota

Sölvi and his family moved from Winnipeg, settled in Hallson in Pembina County, and built a house that was far more sound than their New Iceland log cabin or their scrap shanty in Winnipeg. There they got a solid grasp of agriculture and cultivated grains, and Sölvi supplemented their income with homeopathy.[8] The family fared quite well in Hallson, but after thirteen years' residence there, in 1893, Sölvi and Soffía packed up yet again and moved all the way west to the Pacific Coast. Ingibjörg, the youngest daughter of Sölvi and the late Solveig, had married an Icelander named Brynjólfur Jónsson, who had moved to North Dakota at the age of fourteen in 1886. Six years later Brynjólfur married Ingibjörg, who was six years his senior.[9] The young couple wanted to try their luck on the west coast of the state of Washington, and Sölvi and Soffía decided to join them along with their son Arnljótur, who was twenty at the time.

Washington State, a New Paradise

Washington remained one of the most isolated of the United States for a long time. Surrounded by high mountains on three sides, it was the last of the forty-eight contiguous states to be settled by Europeans. For many years its only inhabitants were Native Americans and a few hunters and fur traders of the Hudson's Bay Company, who competed with native tribes for wild game. When the Oregon Trail was opened in 1848, the number of Europeans in Washington began to rise, but the horse-and-wagon journey across the mountain passes took about six months.[10]

Washington's population didn't start growing to any significant degree until railroad tracks were laid all the way to the coast of the Pacific Ocean in 1883. This made it possible to travel on comfortable trains from states like Minnesota all the way to Washington in five days, a journey that would previously have taken half a year.[11] The railway companies advertised aggressively, encouraging people to move westward to the sea, and the response was immediate. Many Norwegian and Swedish immigrants in the Midwest were tired of American-style farming and the low price of grain. They imagined Washington as a home away from home, for there were woods and an ocean there, just like in Scandinavia.[12] The railway companies were so successful that, between 1880 and 1890, the population of Washington grew by 380 percent. Never before had the population of an American state grown so rapidly in such a short time.[13]

Ballard, a Nordic-Style Harbor Town

Many Icelanders were losing patience with farming in the Great Plains, much like the Norwegians and Swedes. Sölvi and his family weren't the only Icelanders who moved "west to the sea" at this time. A large group was enticed by the offers of the railway companies, and many of them settled in Blaine, a fishing village on the Washington coast, just south of the Canadian border. There they soon earned a reputation as skilled fishermen.[14]

Another group of Icelanders, Sölvi's family among them, settled in Ballard, a rapidly expanding sawmill and fishing town just north of Seattle. Most of the inhabitants of Ballard were immigrants, the majority of

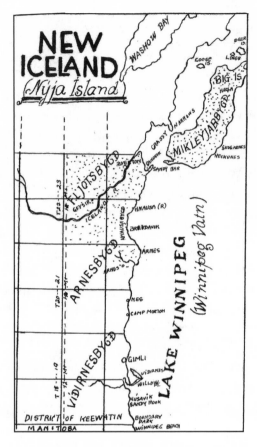

A map of New Iceland

them from Norway. The Norwegians became very successful in the town's fishing industry and lent the community a Nordic flavor.[15]

By 1900, around a hundred Icelanders lived in Ballard, some of them specializing in cod fishing.[16] Others worked in fish processing, at sawmills, in road construction, digging ditches, or building houses. Still others grew trees and fruit. Sumarlidi Sumarlidason, a goldsmith from the island of Æedey, ran a jewelry store on Second Avenue in Ballard, having moved there from North Dakota with his family in 1900.[17]

209 Wilbert Street

In Ballard, Sölvi's family was allotted a plot of land at 209 Wilbert Street. There they built a so-called pioneer farmhouse one-and-a-half stories

Icelandic women in Ballard at a party in honor of midwife Ormsson's birthday in 1921

high, with a single gable, long, high front windows, and a veranda in front. As years went by, people commonly expanded their houses, added a second veranda, and constructed outbuildings.[18]

Each family usually had one cow, a few chickens, a vegetable garden, and fruit trees, the last of which were a great wonder to Icelanders, who cultivated them with the utmost care.[19]

Sölvi, his son-in-law Brynjólfur, and his son Arnljótur, who went by the name Alex, were fishermen. Wilbert Street was within walking distance of the Ballard harbor, and consequently it was easy to go fishing in the morning and bring home the catch in the evening. They rowed an open boat and fished mostly for cod using a hand line. The fishing on Puget Sound was exceptionally good in those years.[20]

The family was very comfortable in Wilbert Street and grew rapidly. In the five years between 1895 and 1900, Ingibjörg and Brynjólfur had three children. The eldest was Sölvi, born in 1895, next was Soffía, born in 1898, and finally Lillian, who was born in 1900.[21] Although there were no hospitals in Ballard and all children were born at home, there were two Icelandic midwives in Ballard, Mrs. Ormsson and Mrs. Solveig Arnbjornsson. The two midwives were revered and respected among Icelandic women in Ballard, who were glad to be able to speak their native tongue while they gave birth and nursed their newborns.[22]

Ingibjörg had been nine years old when she left Iceland and was fluent in English. Her husband, Brynjólfur, also learned English, but Sölvi and Soffía never mastered the language.[23] This caused them no more trouble in Ballard than it had elsewhere, however, for the community of Icelanders in town had a fairly active social life. They had their own church congregation, the Hallgrímur Congregation, as well as a book club called Vestri, which was founded in Sumarlidi Sumarlidason's home. As years went by, the book club amassed a sizable collection of books.[24]

The American Dream Come True—More or Less

In spring of 1903, Sölvi was taken ill with pneumonia. He died on May 17 at his home on 209 Wilbert Street in Ballard, at the age of seventy-four.[25] He is buried in Mt. Pleasant Cemetery in Queen Anne, a Seattle neighborhood near Ballard. A little over a year after Sölvi passed away, Ingibjörg and Brynjólfur sold the house at 209 Wilbert Street and moved north to Blaine with their children and Soffía, Sölvi's widow. By this time Arnljótur was living on Bainbridge Island in Puget Sound.

The years in Ballard were among the best Sölvi and Soffía had after they left Iceland. Their first years in America were characterized by toil, poverty, and disappointment. They ended up in New Iceland against their own wishes, and during their first year there they were quarantined because of the smallpox epidemic. Their new farm at Steinnes did poorly, and after two years they left New Iceland and moved to Winnipeg. This did nothing to improve their circumstances, and they were forced to live in a shanty on the banks of the Red River in the poorest neighborhood of Winnipeg, working as day laborers. Their first break came when they moved to Hallson, North Dakota, but their existence there was a far cry from the life they were to have in Ballard. In Ballard, Sölvi and his family came as close as they ever did to living the American Dream. The environment was spectacularly beautiful, forested from the mountaintops down to the sea, and compared to the climate in Manitoba and Dakota the weather was very good—mild and humid winters and comfortably warm summers. And they no longer had to slave away as

American farmers, but could fish instead. The ocean off the coast near Ballard was full of fish, and the fishing methods were the same as those in Iceland. Their house—bright and spacious and equipped with various modern conveniences—was surrounded by a beautiful yard with apple trees, like the Garden of Eden.

Although Sölvi and Soffía's living conditions were much improved, their social standing remained unchanged. They were always uneducated laborers, but their children were to go far.

The following is known about the lives of Sölvi's children in America, other than Ólöf:

> Gróa, born in 1856, married Gunnar J. Hallson, son of Jóhann Hallson, and lived most of her life in Dakota. Before she married, she had a son, Sölvi Thompson, by an Englishman; Sölvi went by his last name of Thompson for his entire life. Gróa later moved in with her mother's family in Blaine, Washington.
>
> Jón, born in 1864, settled in Bellingham, Washington.
>
> Ásgeir, born in 1865, became a photographer and lived and worked in Seattle. He married an Icelandic woman of the Steinkirkja family, one of the daughters of Gudlaugur from Steinkirkja in Fnjóskadalur valley. They had no descendants.
>
> Sigurdur, born in 1861, who came west seven years after his family left Iceland, settled in Manitoba. He moved back to Iceland for a time, ran a shop there, and sold horse harnesses. He was never content in Iceland and returned to Manitoba, later becoming postmaster in Westborne, Manitoba. He married a woman of Icelandic descent, and their son Rútur later moved back to Iceland.[26]

Helga "Mama" Sölvason

Sölvi and Solveig's youngest child, Ingibjörg (born in 1866), married Brynjólfur Jónsson. When Ingibjörg and Brynjólfur moved from Ballard to Blaine, they had three children. Sölvi and Soffía's son Arnljótur, born in 1873, married a woman of Icelandic descent by the name of Helga. Helga was born in Winnipeg but moved to North Dakota at an early age, and thence to Ballard in 1900. She married Arnljótur not long afterward, and shortly after their marriage they became pioneers on Bainbridge Island in Puget Sound, where Arnljótur made a name for himself in the fishing industry.

Helga and Arnljótur's marriage was very happy but short-lived. Arnljótur died in 1922, only forty-nine years old, leaving his widow with ten children, the eldest nineteen years old and the youngest still in the cradle. With unparalleled courage and determination, Helga managed to hold the family together. She soon passed into local legend on the island and was known as "Mama Sölvason." The children who were old enough lent a hand. A few of them worked for the phone company that was laying phone lines on the island, and two of her daughters became nurses in Seattle. Helga herself cooked for local workers, mostly phone company employees. When food was ready, a big bell on her veranda was rung and the workers streamed to Helga's house for a meal. Helga left the island during the Great Depression. She died at a very advanced age in Seattle in 1963, survived by her ten children and fifteen grandchildren.[27]

Shortly after Helga passed away, her obituary appeared on the front page of the principal newspaper of Bainbridge Island, the *Bainbridge Review*. The obituary was written by journalist Rhea Hannon, who as a child had adored Helga and her children and been a frequent guest in their home. The editor was initially hesitant to publish an obituary about a woman who had left the island almost thirty years previously, but after reading the article he published it on the newspaper's front page.

To all appearances Arnljótur Sölvason, Sölvi Sölvason's youngest son, had made a fine living for himself. He built a large house for his family, with grand living rooms with crystal chandeliers on the ground floor. On the second floor were several large, bright, and spacious bedrooms, each with its own fireplace. The house was always full of life and excitement, and the big family dog, Happy, was especially popular with the journalist Rhea.[28]

Sölvi Sölvason, Buried but Not Forgotten

It is worth mentioning that although Sölvi, Ólöf's father, rests in an unmarked grave on the Pacific coast, he was not entirely forgotten. A year after he died, his passing was mentioned in a Winnipeg publication, the *Almanak* of Ólafur S. Thorgeirsson.[29] And his memory lived among his descendants in both Iceland and North America.

Helga, Sölvi and Solveig's eldest daughter, who remained in Iceland, and her husband, Ólafur Gíslason, the rider in the long overcoat, had three children: Gísli, Hannes, and Vilborg. Vilborg's daughter, Thórhildur Sveinsdóttir (1909–90), was a gifted poet like her great-grandfather Sölvi, and published two books of poetry: *Yesterday and Today* (1968) and *Sunset in the Hills* (1982). In the latter book Thórhildur published the poem "My Great-Grandfathers," two verses of which are dedicated to her great-grandfather Sölvi Sölvason, who left for America. They are as follows:

Limber-worded laysmith
Langamýri's Sölvi
Often did he utter
Erudite poetics.
In his heart he fostered
Faith in God Almighty,
Save but for his Savior,
Submitted to no-one.

Hardship came, and sorrow—
So the tales remember.
Some left land behind them,
Looking never backward.
Sölvi brought the children
Broke new ground to freedom.
Just one daughter tarried,
Though but nine years agèd.[30]

After this brief sketch of Ólöf Sölvadóttir's family, it is time to return to Ólöf herself and to Winnipeg, where she worked as a maid.

Off Adventuring

Ólöf in Winnipeg

Winnipeg was a boom town when Ólöf moved there in 1877. Seven years before, it had been a village of 217 people with a single church and neither a post office nor a bank. When the railroad reached the town in the early 1870s, however, the face of Winnipeg was changed forever. Immigrants poured in at a rate as high as two to five hundred a day, many Icelanders among them. When Ólöf came to Winnipeg, the city boasted about a thousand buildings and a population ten thousand strong. There were forty-five hotels and about three hundred guesthouses, but that was not enough. When the boom was at its peak, immigrants could be seen sleeping in restaurants' dining rooms, in stairwells, on billiard tables, and in wooden crates on the streets.[1]

Town life was vibrant, and in the evenings many people would sit outside drinking at the town's numerous taverns. Manitoba's brewery, Point Douglas, couldn't keep up with the demand for beer, and the company's profits had never been more robust. There was a group of Icelandic young people who participated actively in the nightlife and spent their spare change on fashionable clothing sold in local stores.[2]

However, most Icelanders in Winnipeg kept to themselves and remained aloof from Winnipeg nightlife. Their social life was quite lively, however, and in 1877, the year of Ólöf's arrival, the Winnipeg Icelanders' Society was founded. Its purpose was to uphold the honor of the Icelandic nation abroad and to protect and nourish the nation's love of freedom and progress, which was considered to have been a defining characteristic of Icelanders throughout history. The Icelanders' Society ran a Sunday school for children, assisted poor Icelanders and recent immigrants, and contributed funds to the Icelandic newsletter *Framfari*.[3]

For the first few years the Society had no headquarters. A few of the wealthier Icelanders in town lent their homes for gatherings, where people would play whist, sing, and put on plays. The Icelanders were pious and had the habit of attending church regularly, but at first there was neither an Icelandic church nor an Icelandic pastor in Winnipeg. To compensate for this lack, laymen would preach in Icelandic homes in Winnipeg.[4]

Icelandic Maids in Winnipeg

Maids were in great demand in Winnipeg, and the Icelandic girls in the town often took such positions. This was a logical move—Icelandic girls knew little of tasks other than domestic ones. A young and enterprising Icelander named Fridjón Frederickson seized the opportunity and opened an employment agency for domestic workers.[5]

In their capacity as maids, the Icelandic girls had to learn to cook in Canadian fashion. This proved to be quite challenging at first, as most of them didn't speak English. But soon enough they gained command of the language and of Canadian household management, and before long they became sought after by the finer households in Winnipeg. Lord Dufferin, governor general of Canada, who was known for being sympathetic to Icelanders, praised the diligence of the Icelandic maids in a speech he gave in Winnipeg in 1877.[6]

The salary of a maid like Ólöf, who did not speak English, was four to six dollars (then sixteen to twenty-four Icelandic *krónur*) per month, but rose to eight dollars (thirty-two *krónur*) when she had mastered the language.[7] The Icelandic girls were quite content with their circumstances and often sent glowing descriptions of their employment back home to Iceland. They said that all tools, working hours, and pay were far superior to what was offered in Iceland.[8] The young women were correct in many respects. Homes in Winnipeg were finer and more modern than most Icelandic country households, and working hours were significantly shorter than at home. In Iceland the workday was up to twelve hours long, especially during the busy summer season, and a year's salary was thirty-five *krónur.*[9]

However, employment in an urban Canadian home was often much lonelier than an equivalent position on an Icelandic farm. In Iceland, workers took full part in family life, ate and worked with other members of the household in the *baðstofa,* and often shared a bed with someone. Maids in Canada never ate with the family they served; they dined alone in the kitchen and slept in rooms behind the kitchen or up in the rafters. They were only allowed to leave the household on their day off, which was Sunday afternoon, and although working hours were from eight in the morning to six in the evening, in reality they were on call day and night.

Ólöf and the Circus

The glow of Winnipeg and the maid's position faded fast in Ólöf's eyes. She found domestic chores boring and had little time to enjoy the splendors of the city.[10] The few hours she had off she probably used to visit her family in Shanty Town or attend Icelanders' gatherings.

Ólöf also stood out among maids in Winnipeg more than she had in Iceland. Back home she shared a certain condition with women of normal stature—namely, that of being unable to marry for economic reasons. In America, however, there were no such restrictions. Young couples who were so inclined, even those who could only afford to live in Shanty Town, could get married. Young immigrant women often married early to escape the bondage of the maid's position.[11]

In this respect, the dwarf Ólöf did not enjoy the same prospects as other young women. The odds of her finding a husband were not much better in America than they had been in Iceland. Still, America did offer more to a dwarf woman like Ólöf than simply standing on a stool and washing other people's dishes. That she had discovered years ago when she saw the dwarf couple in the museum in Toronto. When a traveling circus from the United States came to Winnipeg one summer, Ólöf

Advertisement for a human curiosity show in the United States

wasted no time in making an appointment with the director of the circus and asking for a job. Young and fit dwarf women like Ólöf didn't grow on trees, and the director hired her immediately as a part of the circus' human curiosity exhibition. Shortly thereafter, the circus pulled up its tent stakes, and Ólöf left and never looked back.

Ólöf and Her Supposed Husband

The name of the circus that came to Winnipeg and that Ólöf joined, probably in the summer of 1880, is not known. Still surviving, however, is a photograph from Ólöf's circus days, in which she appears as the wife of a dwarf. She and her husband both wear wedding bands on their left hands, and Ólöf looks highly respectable. She is wearing a long, form-fitting black dress in Victorian style. Her hair is well groomed, long and tightly curled. Her serious face is broad, with high cheekbones and re-markably sharp eyes that stare eagerly into the camera.

*Ólöf and her supposed
husband*

Ólöf's supposed husband is also dressed to the nines in a suit, a plaid overcoat, and patent leather shoes. It is clear from his expression that the role of a respectable Victorian husband is outside his usual milieu. His gaze is flighty and his hair long and poorly groomed, suggesting that he was more at home in the role of a wild savage than a respectable husband and citizen.

Ólöf and her husband performed as a respectable married couple, which was supposed to demonstrate that despite their small stature and physical deformity, dwarves had the same feelings and desires as normal people: In the fullness of time, dwarves too would marry and have children.

But despite their respectable appearance, couples like Ólöf and her husband played quite a different and darker role in the human curiosity show. The spectators, usually models of Victorian dignity, gave rather free rein to their sexual fantasies during such shows. They speculated unabashedly on the intimate life of dwarves and allowed themselves to make vulgar and inappropriate remarks and ask intrusive questions about dwarves' sex life.[12] This sexual harassment probably bothered Ólöf, for after she donned her disguise as an Eskimo she downplayed her sexuality as much as possible and cast herself as a cross between an innocent girl and a respected and respectable woman.

Circus as National Unifier?

Ólöf began her work in a circus in the golden age of such establishments in America.[13] The popularity and success of circuses at this time may be attributable to the drastic social and economic changes that followed the Civil War of 1861–65. The end of the war marked the beginning of one of the greatest surges of immigrants to the United States in its entire history, and American society was transformed overnight from a homogeneous farming society to a multinational industrial society. African Americans had been granted freedom and steadily became more visible. Most of the Europeans who came at this time were from eastern and southern Europe and, as such, were much darker than the northern European Protestants who had previously constituted the American majority.

It soon became necessary to mix this disparate group together and at the same time redefine what it meant to be American. Circuses played an important role in carrying out this task.[14] They appealed to everyone and were well attended and popular. Their unifying force lay in the fact that attending the circus became an annual event in the life of many generations of Americans. There they watched men and animals perform their tricks as they mingled with their fellow citizens.

An important prerequisite for the unifying power of the circuses was the fact that with improved rail travel, the same circus could entertain people in New York; in Monterey, California; in Duluth, Minnesota; and in Tallahassee, Florida within a brief time span. As a result, people in all these states kept in their hearts the exact same picture of the wonders of America.[15]

The artists of the circus were from many countries and of different races, but they all performed their tricks with the utmost skill and pushed human abilities to their limits, thereby proving that neither nationality nor race determined a human being's skills, but that all people could achieve as much success as they liked if they only tried: This was

Human curiosity shows consisted of people of exotic races and ethnicities as well as physically disabled white people.

the real core of the American Dream. Circuses were thus an ideal venue to reinforce people's faith that all men were created equal and neither nationality nor race determined an individual's chance of success.[16]

But although the circuses championed the idea that people of all races had the same potential, they undermined this very principle with their human curiosity shows, where healthy representatives of exotic races were displayed alongside disabled delegates of the white race. The conclusion to be drawn was clearly that healthy individuals of foreign races were at the same level of maturity and development as disabled white individuals, for example, dwarves like Ólöf. Thus the circuses actually reinforced the reigning ideas about the inequality of the races.[17]

Within the circuses, participants in the human curiosity shows ranked lower than the circus artists. No particular skills were required of them; they simply performed as they were made by nature, and as a consequence they received lower pay and poorer upkeep than the artists. Despite this, curiosity shows were a popular career choice for people like Ólöf. The disabled people sympathized with each other; they gave one another support and shelter, lived together, and enjoyed life without being harassed.[18]

In the shows, people's birth defects were accentuated and made even more visible than they ordinarily were. Although there was a humiliating aspect to this display, there was also for the performers a certain element of recognition and empowerment in people's willingness to pay to see them. There was an adventurous glow to life in the circus, and a great deal of excitement accompanied the frequent travel. Ólöf seems to have been quite satisfied with life in the circus, and one thing is certain: working as a maid couldn't hold a candle to her new job.[19]

Fleeing the Past

A few years after Ólöf left Winnipeg, her stepbrother Magnús Björnsson, Soffía's son, saw her at the circus. When he came up to greet her, she pretended neither to know him nor to speak Icelandic. Magnús realized that Ólöf's position in the circus was important to her, so he decided to leave her alone and left without making further attempts to contact her. Magnús later interpreted Ólöf's reaction as a sign that she had been completely changed as a person, that the proper, intelligent, and honest young Icelandic woman, Ólöf Sölvadóttir, had fallen into the clutches of a bad "English" woman who had brainwashed her and convinced her to disguise herself first as a circus freak and then later as an Eskimo. This opinion predominated within Ólöf's family.[20]

However, there is no evidence to suggest that Ólöf was forced to join a human curiosity show, much less to become the "Esquimaux Lady," Olof Krarer. She did both at her own behest and of her own free will. Ólöf was very ambitious and self-reliant, and she was determined to improve her station in life. She didn't hesitate to use trickery if necessary, and she seems to have been fully aware of what she was doing from the start.

That being the case, there must have been other reasons for Ólöf's refusal to acknowledge her stepbrother Magnús. She may have feared that he was sent by the family to make her return home, something she was adamantly against doing. She may also have been ashamed to have Magnús see her exhibiting her body for money. Ólöf had received a strict Lutheran upbringing in which girls were taught to conceal their bodies and bodily urges. Showing one's body for money in the way Ólöf was do-

ing bordered on prostitution in the eyes of many Icelanders. Most probably, however, she avoided Magnús because she had begun a new life and
was reluctant to open old wounds.

Magnús was closely connected to the most painful period in Ólöf's
life. They were the same age, and when he was a little boy he moved into
Ólöf's home with his mother, Soffía. Their arrival in the household had
marked the start of a great tragedy. Ólöf's father initiated a relationship
with Soffía, and Solveig, Ólöf's mother, fled her home and eight children
only to die in an accident a few short years later.

The Deception Begins

From the Circus to the Lecture Hall

As a member of the circus, Ólöf traveled between cities and towns, participated in human curiosity shows, and performed in all sorts of guises. After about four years in the circus, she changed course, disguised herself as the Esquimaux Lady, Olof Krarer, and began lecturing on the life and culture of Greenland's Eskimos.[1] But how did it transpire that Ólöf Sölvadóttir from Outer Langamýri in Húnavatnssýsla county masqueraded as an Eskimo and became a popular lecturer for respected institutions in the United States—institutions where a circus performer would seldom be seen in the audience, let alone on the podium?

According to Ólöf's fabricated biography, recorded by Albert S. Post, she told her audience the following story about the advent of her lecturing career:

> When I came to Manitoba, I was sick for nearly two years. The Iceland ministers were very kind to me, and took care of me while I was sick. When I got well, I started out to work for my living. I could not speak one word of English, and I was afraid to try.
>
> The first person I worked for was a half-breed woman, who had a

rough, quarrelsome lot of children that I had to wait upon. Once in a while I was called into the front room, and would find some strangers there. One day the mistress was called away, when I was sent into the room, and the gentleman and lady who were there gave me a quarter each. She had been making money out of me in this way all the while, but all the money I received for some months of hard labor was what these people gave me.

Then I was taken sick with the measles. The woman turned me out of doors. I did not know where to go. I just ran round and round the house. A young lady, from one of the best families in Winnipeg, found me in this plight, took me by the hand and led me home. She nursed me till I was well, and then gave me good clothes and found me a place to work. She told me to come back to her if I was in trouble again.

After working for some time in this place, I came to work for Mrs. C., the lady who is with me now. When she first saw me she thought I was a little child, and did not see how I could be of any use to her. But she pitied me because she thought I was cold, and gave me something to do. I lived with her three months. When I first came to her I could not speak enough English to tell her I liked coffee better than tea. My work was washing dishes. They would help me into a chair so that I could reach the table. When at last I was able to explain, with the help of an Iceland girl who lived next door, that I desired to travel as a curiosity, hoping in this way to make money enough to bring my brothers and sisters from Iceland, Mr. and Mrs. C. consented to come with me.

My father agreed to let me go, if I would go with respectable people and remain with them. I had worn my seal skin suit about in Manitoba until it was worn out, but my father had taken care of my polar bear suit, so I had that to bring with me. He let me bring his new flint and walrus tusk, also.

But a few months afterwards he sent for his spear, because he thought he could not get along without it, so I returned it to him. He is still living in Manitoba, and is 65 years old. This is several years older than people live in Greenland. Oldest people we ever knew were 60 years old. This I know from the Icelanders, who went round to all the snow houses and counted the bones in the different sacks.

Ólöf in Eskimo garb, innocent as an angel

When I reached Minneapolis I was taken sick, and the doctors did not know what to do for me. They kept me in a warm room, and I grew worse every day. At last Mr. C. heard of a doctor who had been in Greenland, and sent for him. Under his advice I was taken to Minnetonka and kept in a cold room, and I got well.

At first I traveled as a curiosity and charged ten cents. All I could do was to let people see me, show my costume, flint and tusk, sing a few songs, etc. But by degrees I learned to answer questions, and at last came to talk pretty well. While we were at a place in Indiana, called Cloverdale, some professors and a minister urged me to give a lecture. They secured a large hall, and when I peeked through a hole in the curtain I saw about 300 people, and was nearly scared out of my wits. But Mrs. C. got me mad over something about my dress, and the curtain went up while I was standing there, and I spoke to them right along. That was Dec. 30th, 1884. Since then I have been lecturing right along, except in some short times of sickness, and the hottest weather. I have been in Minnesota, Wisconsin, Iowa, Ilinois [sic], Michigan, Ohio, Indiana, Missouri, Kansas, and Nebraska, and I hope by next year, to have all my brothers and sisters with me, so that we can travel together and help the missionary teachers in Iceland, where we got our education in the first place.[2]

"I Have Never Seen an Eskimo Before"

Ólöf's account of the start of her career as an Eskimo lecturer is certainly colorful and charming, but of course it is untrue. Vilhjálmur Stefánsson's version is perhaps closer to the truth:

Our North Dakota version of the story ran that Olof had been waitress in a hotel. Seeing how small she was, the guests asked about her and were told, sometimes by herself and sometimes by the hotel people, that she was an Icelander. The comeback was usually: "How interesting! We never saw an Eskimo before." Olof would then explain that Icelanders were not Eskimos and that their blood was chiefly Norwegian with a little mixture of Irish. The interest waned. There were plenty of Norwegians around; the Irish were no rarity. That sort of dwarf was hardly a seven days' wonder.

But there were new guests in the hotel daily, new questions about Olof, and new accents for the tiresome: "How interesting! We never saw an Eskimo before." She became bored, annoyed, outraged. Finally she stopped explaining that Icelanders were not Eskimos and simply flounced off. The interpretation of that was, poor thing, she was ashamed of being an Eskimo. Her silence now gave consent.[3]

But Ólöf cheered up one day when a priest from a local congregation offered her five dollars to give a talk to local Sunday school children about her life and that of her Eskimo family in Greenland. This was a generous offer. Ólöf, who was well acquainted with trickery and deception from her time in the circus, decided to seize the opportunity. It couldn't hurt to tell a lie just this once. She would vanish from town soon enough, never to be heard from again. But the result was very different than she expected. Ólöf's lecture attracted a great deal of attention, and invitations from churches and schools began streaming in. In this she saw a golden opportunity to continue on the same path to fame and glory. She hired a woman, whose name is not known, to manage her appointments and organize lecture tours. She kept her first name, Olof, but took up the last name Krarer.[4] And thus was born the persona that Ólöf would embody in the public eye.[5]

Two Kinds of Disguise

There are two basic ways of misrepresenting one's identity: impersonation and swindling. In the former instance, the deceiver assumes the identity of an existing person, living or deceased, and pretends to be that person. Such impersonators are thus not only frauds but thieves as well. The latter, the swindlers, have more imagination and creativity. They fabricate a new individual and impersonate him or her. The Esquimaux Lady, Olof Krarer, is a good example of the latter. She was the sole creation of Ólöf Sölvadóttir from Outer Langamýri.[6] There was no woman, dead or alive, who had lived her life. Ólöf was at once the creator and the masterpiece itself, and she certainly enjoyed the freedom and power that this dual role gave her.

The Golden Age of Disguises

Ólöf was not alone in this activity. This was the golden age of such deceptions and disguises in America. The idea of the self-made man was at center stage in North America at the time. The will and ambition of each individual were to determine his future, not his ancestry and origins. The inventor and thinker Benjamin Franklin (1706–90) was one of the first advocates of these ideas.[7] The idea of the self-determination of the individual was intended for honest, devout, and reliable white males. But others heard the message as well, and these notions created an ideal environment for unusual people such as Ólöf to change their image drastically and begin a new and better life in disguise.

One of the most popular options was the guise of a Native American. This may be linked to changing sentiments toward American Indians at the time. Initially, European immigrants regarded them as savages who threatened the spread of Western culture in America, and who must consequently be exterminated. As time went by and the Native Americans suffered complete defeat, they ceased to be a threat, and white settlers' views began to change. The European Americans saw Indians as "noble savages," and believed that they could learn much from the latter's wisdom and life experience.[8] White Americans thirsted after insight into Native life and philosophy, but very few of them were suited to such education. Thus a niche developed for Westerners to disguise themselves as Natives for educational and entertainment purposes.

Most famous among those who passed as Indians in America were the Englishman Archie Belaney (1888–1938), who took the name Grey Owl, and the African American Sylvester Long (1890–1932) from North Carolina, who became known under the name Buffalo Child Long Lance.[9]

These men had in common with Ólöf a troubled family background and emotional insecurity. Archie Belaney was born into an upper-class English family, but his father was an alcoholic and drank away the family fortune. His mother was young and inexperienced and incapable of taking care of her son, who was placed in the care of two elderly aunts. Archie Belaney had a very lonely childhood, but as a young boy he was mesmerized by stories of the Wild West and dreamed of being an American Indian. That dream was to come true when he moved to Canada in

Grey Owl

1906 and settled with Native Americans in the wilderness. He took up
the name Grey Owl and claimed to be the son of a Scottish immigrant
who had settled on the American plains and married his mother, an
Apache. He let his hair grow out, dyed it black, and darkened his skin.[10]
Grey Owl was a great lover of nature and soon became an enthusiastic
spokesman in support of wildlife and wilderness conservation.

Like Ólöf, Grey Owl became a popular lecturer. He wrote numerous
articles and a few books about conservation and about his life in the
Canadian wilderness. He also made several wildlife films that attracted
attention. The pinnacle of his career came in 1937, when he went back to
his homeland, England, to give a series of lectures. The king and queen,
who were great fans of Grey Owl, were in attendance.[11]

Long Lance's parents were born into slavery, and he grew up in abject
poverty. Like Ólöf, he began his career in the circus, but he soon discov-

Long Lance

ered that he could rid himself of the burden of being African American by passing as a Native American, as the latter were afforded far more respect than the former. Like Grey Owl, he initially claimed to be of mixed heritage, half white and half Cherokee. He later described himself as pure Blackfoot.[12]

His biography, *Long Lance,* was published in 1928 and became a bestseller. He was also a talented athlete and distance runner, and shoes bearing his name were popular among American athletes.[13] Long Lance's star rose rapidly, and he played the lead role in the film *The Silent Enemy* in 1930. He became an American cultural icon and socialized with the rich and famous. He lived for a time in the headquarters of the famous Explorers Club in New York, whose members included Fridtjof Nansen, Theodore Roosevelt, Robert E. Peary, and Vilhjálmur Stefánsson. Vilhjálmur and Long Lance were good friends.[14]

Long Lance and Ólöf worked for a time for the same agency, the Slayton Lyceum Bureau in Chicago.[15]

A Convincing and Consistent Lie

When Ólöf decided to become the Esquimaux Lady, Olof Krarer, she composed a long and detailed story of her life and the living conditions of Eskimos in Greenland. In order to be convincing and believable, a good lie must resemble the truth in its vivacity and richness of expression, but it must also be consistent and full of details and precise descriptions. The story must be convincing and gripping as well. Ólöf's fiction met all these criteria.[16] Her story was told from the perspective of a native Eskimo and contained a precise and detailed description of Eskimo culture, traditions, and habits. Ólöf's tale was also suitably dramatic, and she often had her listeners holding their breath in suspense.

Little was known about Greenlanders and other Inuit at this time, and Ólöf's story opened up an entirely new world to her audience. Her account was filled with one astonishing description after another, and everything seemed to conflict with Western ideas about human behavior and morality. Although Ólöf's descriptions were crude and exaggerated, they remained internally consistent. On the whole, her message accorded with the American public's preconceptions about the Inuit, the savages of the Arctic. After hearing Ólöf speak, listeners felt that they had learned a great deal, and could scarcely do otherwise than believe she had experienced, body and soul, all that she described.

Where Did Ólöf Come by Her Knowledge of Greenlanders?

It is worth asking where Ólöf found the information about the people of Greenland on which she based her story. Vilhjálmur Stefánsson guessed that when Ólöf agreed to give her first lecture, she ran to the nearest library and read everything she could about life in the Arctic. This would have been neither an impressive nor a long reading list.[17] Sigurdur Nordal gave Ólöf the benefit of the doubt in a 1945 radio broadcast for the Icelandic National Broadcasting Service, suggesting that Ólöf had turned to the works of her countryman, the poet Sigurdur Breidfjörd (1798–

1846). Sigurdur Breidfjörd was a cooper by trade. He lived for a time in Greenland, taught the locals how to build barrels, and wrote his poem *Númarímur* there. He later published the book *From Greenland*, in which he describes his interactions with the Greenlanders and their daily life.

When Ólöf's text is compared with Sigurdur Breidfjörd's narrative from Greenland, it becomes clear that there is no correlation between his descriptions and her story. If Ólöf read Sigurdur's stories from Greenland as a young woman in Iceland, she did not rely on them to create her own biography. Vilhjálmur was probably correct in surmising that Ólöf familiarized herself with some of the public libraries' lighter fare on the subject of Greenland. She was clearly well acquainted with most misconceptions about the Greenlanders, and wove them into her narrative. Ólöf's descriptions of life in Iceland are partly true, but she clearly had no desire to give an accurate picture of life in Greenland. The story was first and foremost Ólöf's own creation, and its purpose was to entertain and shock the audience. She gave her imagination free rein and utilized the rich storytelling tradition she had grown up with in Iceland. Her biography exhibits influences from adventure and fantasy tales and *öfugmælavísur*.*

Ólöf, Innocent as an Angel

Ólöf's lectures were conceived as monologues where she was simultaneously playwright and performer. It was very important to her to win the trust and confidence of her audience, and she usually succeeded in this before she began her tale. In the lecture hall, Ólöf wore white skin clothing, and the podium was decorated with white skins. The choice of the color white evoked Ólöf's snow-covered homeland, Greenland, but there was more to it than that. White symbolizes purity and innocence, and the blank page is also white—nothing has been written on it, and it contains

---

*Translator's note: *Öfugmælavísur* are a form of Icelandic folk poetry in which things are described as opposite to what they really are, with inversions and gross exaggerations used for comic effect. A literal translation of one verse by Bjarni Jónsson reads, "It is best to heap snow on a fire / for this increases its glow, / It is good to have shards of glass in your shoes / when going rock-climbing."

no lies. In her white pelts Ólöf was innocence made flesh, so soft and warm that audiences probably wanted to stroke and embrace her.

Ólöf also had other ways of validating her own story. If somebody in the audience doubted her word, she was quick to respond that she had left her homeland at an early age. It was possible that some details might be incorrect, but on the whole her story was true. She also mentioned in her lectures that if an Eskimo were to lie, an evil spirit would invade his soul and kill him. The fact that she was still alive was an assurance that she never spoke anything but the truth. One of the most important components of her speech was to mention her shock upon discovering that Christians often used lies to their own advantage. She said:

> My people, in spite of their ignorance and misery, are an honest, happy, and contented race . . . They are good to one another; they never steal, and they never lie. I find that when one becomes civilized and educated it is not so uncommon a thing to tell lies—what you call "little white lies," but yet it seems wrong to me—a heathen born.[18]

Unsurprisingly, it occurred to nobody that the person in question was a liar of epic proportions.

Ólöf's Fabricated Biography

Post's Edition of Ólöf's Story

Ólöf's career as Eskimo and lecturer began in 1884, eight years after she first set foot on American soil. Three years after her lecturing career began, the writer Albert S. Post heard her speak. He was so enthralled by the adventures she described that he decided her story should be documented and published. His biography, entitled *Olof Krarer. The Esquimaux Lady. Story of Her Native Home,* was published in Ottawa, Illinois, in 1887. The purpose of the publication was allegedly to collect travel funds for Ólöf's siblings who were still in Iceland.[1]

Post treated Ólöf's tale as the coming-of-age story of a girl who would never have surpassed the maturity of a ten-year-old child had she remained in Greenland her whole life. A series of strange coincidences enabled her to escape to Iceland and later to America. She went through difficult times at first, but at present she had attained great fame and lived a good life telling Americans about her home in northernmost Greenland. In the book's introduction, Ólöf's biographer says the following:

> In writing this little book, it has been our constant aim to make it, as nearly as possible, an autobiography, giving Miss Krarer's own

thoughts and words, avoiding some of the little errors, caused by her imperfect knowledge of English, which are thought by some to add a certain charm to her conversation. If, near the conclusion, I may seem to have departed from this plan, it is only because she desired me to attempt the expression of her thought in more elaborate language than she can herself, at present, make use of.

She is the authority for the facts, from beginning to end.

[I hope] that the story of her eventful life may be as interesting to those who read, as it has already been to thousands who have heard it from her own lips.[2]

Ólöf's Story

I was born in Greenland, on the east coast. I am the youngest of eight children. My three sisters and four brothers are all living in Iceland. My father is living in Manitoba. My mother died in Iceland when I was sixteen years old.[3]

Snow-Houses

We lived near the sea-shore in Greenland. Our house was built of snow. It was round, perhaps sixteen feet across, and coming to a point at the top. It was lined with fur on all sides, and was carpeted with a double thickness of fur.

The way they lined the house was to take a skin of some animal, and hold it near a fire, which was in the centre of the room. When the skin was heated through, they took it and pressed it against the wall. In a short time, it stuck to the wall so tightly that it could not be pulled off without tearing the skin.

The door was a thick curtain of fur, hung over the doorway, by heating the upper part, and letting it stick fast to the wall. Outside of the door was a long, narrow passageway, just high enough for one of us little Esquimaux people to stand up straight in. That would be about high enough for a child six years old, in this country; and it was only wide enough for one person to go through at a time. If one wanted to go out, and another wanted to go in, at the same time, one would have to back out and let the other go first. This passageway was not straight; but turned to one side, so as not to let the wind blow in.

Our fireplace was in the centre of the house. The bottom was a large, flat stone, with other stones and whalebone put around the edge to keep the fire from getting out into the room. When we wanted to build a fire, we would put some whalebone and lean meat on the stone; then a little dry moss was put in, and then my father would take a flint and a whale's tooth, or some hard bone, and strike fire upon the moss. Sometimes he could do it easily, but sometimes it took a long while. After the fire started he would put some blubber upon it.

Although it was so very cold, we would often be without a fire, for what we made the fire of was what we had to live on, and we could not always afford to burn it. Our fire did not warm the room very much. It was mostly to give light, so that it might be a little more cheerful in the room. When we had no fire it was very dark.[4]

Staying Indoors

There was no chance to play around and romp inside the snow-house. We just had to sit with our arms folded and keep still. It was in this way that my arms came to have such a different shape from people's arms in this country. Where their muscle is large and strong, I have but very little; and instead of that, I have a large bunch of muscle on the upper side of my arms, and they are crooked, so that I can never straighten them. A doctor in Iceland once tried to straighten one arm by pulling, but he could not change it one bit; and it was very sore for a long time afterward and the muscles were swollen. But it was not so with my father and brothers. They went out to hunt and had more exercise and more pulling to do, and so their arms were straight.[5]

It was a great thing when the men would come home from a hunt, for then we would have a great deal to talk about:—how far they went, how cold it was, how they found the bear, or walrus, or seal, and who was most active and brave in killing it. Father would often say to mother, "Oh, how I wish you had been along, for we had such a nice drink of warm blood." The warm blood of a dying animal was considered the greatest luxury we could get, because we had not any cooked food at all. We ate it all frozen and raw, except when fresh from the animal. It was a great thing to strike the animal first with a spear, for the one who drew first blood was owner of the skin and was the boss of the whole job. They just had to cut it to suit him. The flesh was divided equally between all the hunters.[6]

Sometimes we used to get very tired in the dark snow-house, and then we would try a little amusement. Two of us would sit down on the fur carpet and look into one another's faces and *guess who was the prettiest.* We had to guess, for we had no looking-glass in which to see our own faces. The one whose face shone slickest with the grease was called the prettiest.[7]

If at any time we grew too tired of it all and ventured to romp and play, we were in danger of being punished. As there were no trees from which to cut switches there, they took a different way. When any child was naughty, mother would take a bone and she would put it into the fire and leave it there until it was hot enough for the grease to boil out. Then she would take it and slap that on her child and burn it. She was not particular where she burned her child, only she was careful not to touch the face.[8]

I can well remember what I got my last punishment for. I had been playing with my little brother inside the snow-house and I got mad at him, and so I threw him down and bit him on the back of the neck. Then mother heated a bone and burned me on the same place where I bit him. I got tired of that and didn't do that kind of a trick afterwards.[9]

Outdoors

But it was not always so that we had to stay in the snow-house. Once in a while father would come in and say it was not so cold as usual, and then we would have a chance to look round outside the snow-house. We never took a long walk. As nearly as I can remember, my father's house was on a low plain near the sea-shore. It sloped gently inland, and we could have seen a great way into the back country if it had not been for the great snowdrifts and masses of ice. There were some steep, jagged rocks in sight of our village, and during the long daytime enough of the snow would melt off to leave the rocks bare in a few places. On these bare spots we would find a kind of brown moss, which we gathered and dried to light our fires with.

We never saw anything green in Greenland, and I never could understand why they called it by that name.

When we looked out toward the ocean, we could not see very far, for even in the warmest season there was only a small space of open water, and beyond that the ice was all piled up in rough, broken masses.[10]

The great event in our family life, however, was the dog-sleigh ride. When father told us we could go, we came as near dancing and clapping our hands for joy as Esquimaux children ever did. But we did not have a fine cutter, with large horses and chiming bells. We did not even have an old-fashioned bobsled, in which young men and young women have such good times in your country.

Sometimes the sleigh would be made of a great wide piece of bone from the jaws of a whale, one end of which would be turned up like a runner. But more often it would be either a skin of some animal laid flat on the ground, or a great frozen fish cut in two at the back and then turned right over. I never saw such a fish in this country, or in Iceland, so I cannot tell what kind of fish it was.[11]

The Dogs

Our sleigh was drawn by dogs—sometimes six and sometimes ten or twelve. Each dog had a collar round his neck and a strip of reindeer hide tied into the collar and to the sleigh. When the dogs were well broken, they did not need any lines to guide them; but if they were not well trained, they had to have lines to control them. While we were getting ready to start, the dogs would jump about and whine and be as anxious to go as fiery horses in this country. The trained dogs would run forward and put their noses right into their collars without any trouble. When all was ready, away we went! It was great fun! The dogs could carry the sleigh faster than horses do in this country. Sometimes the sleigh was bumped and tumbled about a good deal on the rough ice, and once in a while it tipped over.

The dogs are about the size of shepherd dogs and have sharp pointed ears. They are very strong, and have heavy coats of long hair, which often drags upon the snow. They are of a dirty gray color.[12]

When my father had as many as ten or twelve dogs, he had a separate snow-house for them and kept them in that; but when he had lost or lent his dogs, so that he had only two or three, he would let them come into the snow-house with us. Our dogs had the same kind of food to live on that we had, and sometimes when food was scarce they had a hard time of it. They were never fed when they were going to start out for a sleigh ride, for then they would lie right down and refuse to move one step. But whenever we came back from a ride they were well fed.

Our dogs were very useful to us in other ways than drawing our sleighs, for they were very sharp and good to hunt. They helped us to kill the polar bear, and to find the seal and walrus.[13]

Winter and Summer

Now in order that you may understand our way of living better, I will explain that we have six months' night in Greenland, and during that time nothing is seen of the sun. The moon changes very much as it does here, and we have the light of the stars. Then most of the time the beautiful northern lights may be seen dancing and leaping about, with many colored rainbow beauties. The white snow is always on the ground, so that even when the moon and northern lights did not show, we could see to hunt round. Before and after the night time, there was about a month of twilight, and this was our finest time of the year. We had then the best chance to hunt.

In the long day we had the hardest time, for then the sun shone out so brightly that we would be made snow blind if we ventured far from home. The day was four months long, and if we did not have food enough stored away in an ice cave to last us through, we would be in great danger of starving.[14]

Polar Bear Hunting

The best time to hunt is when the ice breaks up. My people know when this is going to happen by the noise. There is a rumbling sound like distant thunder. Whoever hears that sound first goes from house to house and gives warning, so that all may be ready to join in the hunt. Then the hunters get their spears and let out their dogs, and hurry to the place where the sound is heard. The polar bear hears the sound also, and hastens to the place, for it is here that he, too, must make his living. This is the only time that Esquimaux ever dare to tackle a polar bear, for when he is going about alone and hungry he is very fierce and dangerous, but when the ice breaks up the bear goes straight for the sound. This grows louder and longer, until there is a mighty crash, louder than thunder, and great walls of ice are thrown high in the air, and a space of open water is to be seen. When the commotion has ceased, my people crowd along the edge of the water. They first look out for the bears, for they don't want him to catch any of their seals. They have some of their dogs loose in front of the sleigh, and some of them harnessed to it. When they come to the bear, he is busy watching for seal and pays very little attention to the hunters or their dogs. The loose dogs run up to him and begin to worry him. He chases some of them, and the others bite him behind. If he makes a rush at the hunters in their sleighs, the dog teams draw them swiftly away. The loose dogs keep on worrying the bear until he becomes furious with rage. Every little while a sweep of his huge paw lays one of his enemies on the snow, silent in death. A few minutes later, perhaps, another will be caught up in the powerful embrace of the great brute. The dogs crowd in and take hold wherever they can. The bear grows frantic in his struggles to punish his adversaries. At last he lies at full length panting upon the snow. Then it is that some hunter ventures to leave his dog-sled and try to kill him with a walrus tusk. No sooner is he sure that the animal is dying than he hastens to get a drink of warm blood. Then a long cut is made down the belly of the animal with the points of the walrus tusks and the skin is pulled and pushed off with their hands. All hands feast upon the warm grease that is inside the animal, and after that they divide the meat and take it home.[15]

The Ice

I will now explain that the breaking up of the ice I have told about is not from thawing. In the warmest time we ever saw in that part of Greenland where I come from, it never thawed enough to make the water run in streams. A few bare spots were melted off on the rocks and high points of land. Once in a while the snow would melt enough to drip a little, and form icicles, but not often. It was cold, cold, bitter cold, all the year round, and the people in this country can hardly have an idea of it, even in the coldest weather here. From this we see that there could be no chance for heat enough to make the thick ice break up by thawing. Have you ever seen a tub which was full of water frozen nearly solid? Then, perhaps, you remember that the middle was heaved up and cracked to pieces by the frost. This, I think, is what takes place in the northern seas, only on a far grander scale. A rumbling sound can be heard for some time before it really breaks up; but when it does come, there is an awful roar like loudest thunder, and great blocks of ice are lifted and piled one above another, until they are higher than the tops of the high buildings in this country. As it breaks up a good many times in the same place, these ice mountains are piled higher and higher, until they get so large we cannot see over them or round them at all. Each time the ice breaks up, there is an open space where the water is free from ice, and the walruses and seals come up to breathe. Sometimes a walrus will crawl away from this opening far enough for the hunters to head him off and kill him. The walrus is hard to kill, for he is so watchful, and there is no way to call him as they do the seal. But when killed he is quite a prize.[16]

Seal and Whale Hunting

In hunting the seal, they take a different plan. The seal is very fond of its young. The hunters will take advantage of this by lying flat on the ice and making a sound like the cry of a young seal. In this way they manage to call the old seal out on the ice. But even then it is not always easy to catch the seal, for it has a strong, flexible tail, by means of which it is able to throw itself a good many feet at a time, so that even when on the ice it sometimes gets away with its awkward rolls and flops and jumps. A seal is very active and always in motion.

Our greatest prize was the whale. Once in a while one would get entangled in the breaking ice so that it could not get away, and then everybody would be out to help or see the fun. A great many ropes of reindeer hide would be brought out and a great many spears stuck into the animal. Then the men would join together and try to pull the huge creature out of the water. Even with the help of all the dogs that could be used it was hard work, but they would manage it after a while. Then all would give a great shout and have great joy over the whale. One reason for rejoicing was that the whale had so much blubber. Blubber is the inside fat of the whale. There is a fine skin over it and it looks like tallow or leaf lard. It is quite hard in my country, but would melt down into what you would call whale oil in this country. After the whale is cut up we would have a great feast and eat all we could. Then, after taking the meat home we would spend a long time eating and sleeping.

It was only when the ice broke up and the people came together to hunt that they met one another. All the rest of the time the families stay in their own homes, and do not visit back and forth as your people do. The only exceptions are, when a man needs meat, or blubber, or a flint, and goes to borrow, or when a young man goes to steal his girl. There is no buying and selling, and no trading. Any one can get what he needs by asking for it, if it is in the village. The people try to treat each other as brothers and sisters.[17]

Marriage

I will now explain a strange custom among our people. When a young man gets to be about 25 years he is full grown and is considered to be of age. He then begins to think of beginning life for himself. It is a risky thing in my country to get a wife. A young man has to steal his girl out of her parents' snow-house and get her away into another. If he is caught trying to do this the girl's parents turn right on him and kill him. If he has not pluck enough to steal a girl for himself, he has to live alone, and when he goes to sleep he crawls head first into a fur sack. When he wants to get up he must crawl out backwards. I suppose he is what you would call an old bachelor.

A young man, who sees a girl he thinks he would like to have for a wife, makes a great many excuses to come to her father's snow-house. Sometimes he wants to borrow a flint, or blubber, or something else. If he comes without any excuse, the girl's parents tell him, "I know very well what you want; you want my girl, but you never shall get her." Then he gets kind of scared and runs off. But he sneaks round again pretty often. He thinks may be her parents will go out for a dog-sleigh ride, or may be they would lay them down to sleep some time. If he does get her out of the snow-house without being caught, the girl's parents send right back for him and think nobody is smarter than he is, and do all they can for him.

The reason a girl's parents want the young man to steal her is, that they want to find out whether he is willing to risk his life for his own girl or not. They think if he is not smart enough to steal a girl, he would not be smart enough to take care of her—kill a polar bear, so that she would have enough to live on.

There are not many old bachelors in my country, for if a man has not spunk enough to steal a girl he is looked down upon as a sort of soft, good-for-nothing fellow.[18]

Appearance and Cleanliness

Many people are disappointed when they see me, because I am not darker colored, with black hair. More of my people have light hair than dark, and we know that we are naturally a fair-skinned people, because when a baby is born in my country it is just as white as any American baby, and it has light hair and blue eyes. But the mother does not wash it with soft water and soap, as they do in this country, but she goes to work and greases it all over, and the child is never washed from the day he is born till the day he dies, if he remains in that country. The mother wraps her little one in the skin of a young seal, which has been made very soft by pounding and rubbing it on the ice. If the baby cries, the mother will not take it up and care for it, but she puts it in a corner and leaves it there until it stops crying, and then she takes it up and pets it. She can nurse it about a month. Then the mother will warm some blubber for it; but in a little while it must live just like the rest. She carries the baby in her hood, and does not expect it to learn to walk until between two and three years old. Then she makes a suit for it of young seal's fur. When the child becomes larger, say six or seven years old, a thicker suit is made of polar bear skin; and then little "Auska" feels as proud of his new clothes as "Our Charlie" does of his new boots, and the chubby "Roegnia" rejoices over her white suit as much as dainty Flora in her arctics and muff and fur collar. But Auska and Roegnia are dressed more nearly alike than Charlie and Flora. Men's clothes are just like the women's clothes; only a woman's coat comes down to a point and a man's coat is cut off square, and that is all the difference. They wear fur mittens and fur shoes.

I think it would be very nice for some ladies in this country, if they were to go to Greenland; for they would have no washing, no ironing, no scrubbing and no cooking to do. They don't even have to wash their faces or comb their hair. Esquimaux people have only the salt ocean water, and if they had soft, fresh water they dare not use it, for it would be like poison to their flesh when the thermometer was 60° or 70° below zero. So, when they eat, my people take a chunk of raw meat in one hand and a chunk of blubber in the other, and take a bite of each until it is eaten. Then they carefully rub the grease and fat all over their hands and face, and feel splendid afterwards.

The women have long hair, made dark by the smoke and grease. The men have long hair, also, and a thin, scattering beard over the face, which they never shave or trim, because they have no razor or shears.[19]

Deprivation

We had no church or court house, no school or factory, no doctor, lawyer or merchant, no money, jewelry or timepiece, not an axe, spade or hammer, no knife, fork or spoon, no bread, no cloth, no wood! I never saw as much wood in my country as would make one little match. For a needle we use the tooth of a fish; for thread the sinews of a reindeer.

Rich people were those who had a flint. Poor people had to go and borrow it when they wanted to light a fire. Common folks would sit down flat on the fur carpet, but "tony" people would get blocks of ice or snow and put in the snow-house and cover them with fur for seats. But it was only the *most toniest* people who did that kind of a trick.[20]

Religion

My people believe in good and bad spirits. They think there is a big Good Spirit and several small ones, and one big bad spirit and several small ones. They think if they tell a lie or do anything wrong, the bad spirit will come and hurt them some way. If a baby gets sick the mother does not do anything for it. She thinks a bad spirit has hold of her child, and will get her too if she helps it in any way. If baby dies she lays it away in the cold snow and leaves it without a tear. When a man is sick they carry him into a separate snow-house, and all they do to help him is to throw in a piece of poor meat which they do not care about themselves. If a woman is sick she is not taken from her snow-house, but is no better cared for. The only disease is something like consumption in this country. After an Esquimaux dies they drag him out and bury him in the snow, piling blocks of ice as high as they can above the grave. If he has not specially given his spear and flint and skins to some of his friends before he dies, then everything is buried with him, and the friends go home to think no more about him. They never speak of a departed friend, because they fancy it would annoy the spirit, which is supposed to be not far off.

When a man is first taken sick they do one thing for him, if he is not very bad. They gather round him and sing to the Good Spirit, in hopes that He will drive away the bad spirit. If the sick man recovers they think a great deal of him.[21]

Knowledge

Sometimes my father would tell us stories about his parents and grand parents, and then he would tell how they said that their parents told how long, long ago the first people had come from Norway. But no one knew what Norway was like. Some said it was a great house somewhere; some said it was the moon, and some said it was where the Good Spirit lived.

One thing had a great deal of interest for us all. When the sun shone out brightly at the beginning of the daytime it marked the first of the year, just as New Year's Day in this country. Then mother and father would bring out the sacks. Each one was made of a different kind of fur. Father had his, mother had hers, and each of the children had one. In each sack was a piece of bone for every first time that person had seen the sun. When ten bones were gathered they would tie them into a bundle for they had not words to count more than ten.[22]

Shipwrecked Sailors

In such a land I was born. In such a home was I brought up. In such pleasures I rejoiced, until there were about fourteen bones in my sack. Then something happened which changed my whole life. Six tall men came to our village. Our men were much frightened at first and did not know what to make of the giants. Some thought them bad spirits. But they were peaceable, and went hunting with our people and helped them, so that after a while they came to like one another. The strangers were Iceland fishermen. After they lived with us for more than a year, they were able to explain how they were shipwrecked in a storm, and how they got on the ice and walked on the ice till they came to Greenland. They told how much they wanted to get back to their families, and how much better country Iceland was. At last, three Esquimaux families told the Icelanders they would lend them their dogs and sleds if they would do them any good. And because they wanted their dogs back again they said they would go with them.[23]

Journey Across the Ice

So they started out. My father's family was the largest in the party, there being ten of us in all. Most Esquimaux families had only three or four children in them—sometimes only one child, and often none at all. I was a young and giddy thing then, and was glad to go. We traveled a long way down the coast, hunting as we went. Then we turned right out on to the ocean itself. On the way there were three polar bears killed and some seals and other animals, so that we had plenty to eat. I remember we would sometimes take something to eat when the sledges were flying over the ice with the dogs at full gallop. At intervals we fed the dogs, and they gathered closely round the sled and soon all were asleep. When we woke up we went on again. While on the ocean we often heard the sound of the ice breaking up, and would have to hurry away to escape being caught in the upheaval. We finally reached Iceland after being two months and some days on the way, according to the Icelanders' calculation, and having traveled about a thousand miles.

The people in Iceland were astonished to see us little people. They came to see us from a long distance. We were all weighed and measured. My father stood three feet five inches, and weighed 160 pounds. My mother was the same height woman that I am, and weighed 150. None of my brothers was quite so tall as my father, but they came near his weight. One of my sisters was only three feet two inches, and weighed 142. I weighed 136 pounds. Now I am three feet four inches high, and weigh 120.[24]

Schooling

The missionaries in Iceland took great interest in us, for they knew we were all heathens, and they said they would like to take us into their schools and educate us. So each family was taken into a different school. Our family was placed in the Lutheran school, and there I studied for five years. My teacher was a good and kind man. His name was Ion Thorderson. He was patient with me and helped me to learn; but some of the scholars were jealous of "the little thing" and made fun of me. For this they had to carry notes home to their parents, and this secured them a good whipping a-piece, so that they were heard to wish "that little thing" had never come into the school.

At first we lived several miles from the school, but we did not know anything about walking, in fact could not walk any distance, so they sent us on horseback. They used to tie me on so that I would not fall off. It was a funny sight to behold us eight little tots going to school.

I shall never forget the time when a kind friend gave me a pony. He was very gentle, and small enough so that by leading him along side a large stone I was able to climb upon his back. He would stand quietly and wait for me. I loved my pony and thought there was nothing in the world like him. But this long ride was very hard on us, and finally the teacher made arrangement so that we could live close to the school.

The school system was very different in some respects from American schools. The teacher was always the minister, and the school was connected with the church. A scholar had first to learn to read, and must keep at it until he could read better than the teacher. Then he was called upon to commit to memory large portions of history and of the Bible; and when he had learned them so well that he could repeat from beginning to end without the book, he was allowed to begin to write. He could not take pen in hand before that. After learning to write, he was taught figures; and after that I do not know what was done.

The teacher never laid a hand on the scholar in punishment. If he did anything wrong, a note was sent to his parents, and they flogged him soundly.[25]

Ash Bags

I enjoyed the life in Iceland, for I saw and learned so much that was new.

Some time in the spring there was a holiday, in which the young folks would cut up pranks, something like the tricks of April-fool Day here. The girls would try to fasten a small sack of ashes upon the clothing of the boys, and they, in return, would seek to place a pebble in the pockets of the girls, endeavoring to do it so slyly that the sack or pebble would be carried about all day without the one who bore it knowing anything about it.

One of these days, a girl tied a small sack into the beard of one of the men, while he was asleep, and he wore it all day before anyone told him, and then they had a great laugh at his expense. I thought I would try my hand at this, so I made a little sack and tucked it into the corner of a patch, which a big fellow wore upon his pants, the corner being ripped just enough to let the sack slip inside. I had great fun watching him all day, and when night came, he boasted that none of the girls had fooled him that day. "Oh, yes," said one of his companions, "the smallest girl in the house has fooled you badly." He felt pretty cheap when I pointed to the patch, and he found the sack sticking out so that he might have seen it easily.[26]

Icelandic Traditions

Picking up fuel was hard work, and took a great deal of time. They had but little wood [in Iceland], and no coal, so that it was necessary to gather the droppings of animals, and make great piles of this kind of stuff in the summer, so that it would be dry enough to burn in the winter.

If mice came about the houses and buildings in the fall, the Icelanders would fear a hard winter, and much damage to their sheep, for when the winter grew very severe, and the mice could get nothing else to eat, they would climb upon the sheep's backs, while they were lying close together in the sheds, and would burrow into the wool, back of the shoulder-blades, and eat the flesh, very often causing the death of the poor animals.

The Icelanders used sheep's milk a great deal, and I liked it. Sheep's milk is richer and sweeter than cow's milk. They used to put up a lot of milk in barrels, and put in some rennet, which would make it curdle into something like cottage cheese. This they would set aside for winter use, and were very fond of it. The family would be considered very poor who could not put up from eight to ten barrels of this food.

They sometimes, also, would churn mutton tallow, or whale oil, in the sheep's milk, and make a kind of butter. Whale oil makes a better butter than the tallow, and I think I would like it even yet.

While most people had dishes and knives and forks, it was not customary to set the table, unless there was company present. Each one had a cup for himself, made of wood with staves like a barrel, and curiously bound with whalebone hoops. They had handles upon them, but I do not know how fastened. A child's cup would hold about a quart, and a man's cup sometimes as much as three quarts. When each one had gotten his cup filled, he would take his place at any convenient spot in the room, on the bed, or anywhere, and proceed to empty the cup with great haste. We all had ravenous appetites, but did not always have enough to eat. We fared well when fish were plenty, but at other times a porridge made of Iceland moss and the curdled milk made up our fare.

Some seasons they can raise a few vegetables in Iceland, but this is not often. Of late years they cannot raise grain, although they used to raise good oats.[27]

The American Dream and Bereavement

One of the books that we had there was a history of America, and in that it said that money could be picked up off the streets, almost. I have since found it quite a difficulty. But that book put me into the notion of coming here. So when a colony of five hundred Icelanders were about to start for Manitoba, I got my father to come with them. He had just money enough to bring himself and one of his children, so he naturally chose his youngest and the one that was most anxious to come.

My mother died with consumption when we had been in Iceland for a year. I shall never forget the circumstances of her illness. I hated her, and turned from her just as we did in Greenland. She thought it was all right, and told me to keep away and to hate her, for fear the bad spirit would get me.

I said to my teacher one day: "I hate my mother."

"Why, my dear child, you should not do that."

"But I do hate her; she has a bad spirit in her, and Esquimaux people always hate their friends when they get bad spirits in them."

Tears ran down the good man's cheeks as he exclaimed, "Why, the dear child, she doesn't know anything!"

Then he took me upon his knee and began to explain that my mother did not have a bad spirit, but was sick. He dropped his school work entirely, and for three days devoted himself to explaining the Christian belief. Then he made me go to my mother and tell her all about it. My mother was glad—oh, so glad; and she died happy.

My four brothers and three sisters are in Iceland yet. I promised when I left that I would send for them, and I still hope to have them all with me.

We sailed in a ship from Iceland to Scotland. I cannot remember at what city we landed. From there I had my first railway ride, into England, and was much frightened by the noise and motion of the cars. Then we sailed to Quebec, and then came to Winnipeg. It took us five months and five days to come from Iceland to Manitoba.[28]

Delightful Details and a Woman in a Western Dress

The series of events in Ólöf's story remained unchanged through the years, but she often embellished her lectures with entertaining details. To further emphasize Eskimos' messiness she often described how, when she was handed soap for the first time after coming to Iceland, she thought it was something edible and took a big bite, chewed it vigorously, and found it quite tasty.[29] As Ólöf described in her biography, the hot summers in the United States did not suit her at all at first. She later amplified her story with a statement that in her home in the United States she had a special room, a sort of refrigerator, whose walls were covered with snow and ice. There she dwelled, lightly clad, during the summer months.[30] Initially Ólöf lectured in a white skin suit, and even had a dog with her on stage.[31] Once her career took off and she had become a respected and popular expert on Eskimo culture, she performed in beautiful Victorian gowns. A journalist at the *Freeborn County Standard* in Albert Lea, Minnesota, described Ólöf in her Victorian dress as follows:

> In an Eskimo's eyes she is probably handsome, but not so in an American sense. Her face is peculiar, and almost impossible to portray. Her hair, which she says when she left Greenland was black, is now almost golden. Her eyes are large and full of animation. Her usual attitude is with her chubby hands folded in front of her. . . . Her plump and robust figure was richly clad in red silk, close fitting, with train, the whole trimmed with lace. The ornaments consist of a heavy gold ring and watch guard ornamented with pendants. Her movements are easy and quite graceful, and her voice low, but clear and distinct. She was educated in Iceland, and speaks English very pleasingly.[32]

Judging by surviving photographs, Ólöf enjoyed dressing up and wearing jewelry, but her audience had mixed feelings about seeing an Eskimo wearing a Western dress. For example, Ólöf sorely disappointed her audience in Trenton, New Jersey, when she first appeared there clad in Western fashion. In order to make up for this she returned soon and promised to "not only tell of her life in the frozen North, but . . . appear in her native costume."[33] Ólöf solved this problem by donning a skin suit at the end of each lecture, but continued to deliver her lectures dressed up in an evening gown.[34]

No Longer a Dwarf

As is illuminated in later chapters, Ólöf's lie brought her a life of adventure and a great deal of fame that an immigrant dwarf woman with no education would never have had otherwise. But there was more at stake. Lying is taxing, and few people elect to do so without believing it will benefit them in some way.[35] It is clear that many things changed for the better in Ólöf's life after she disguised herself as an Eskimo.

One of the greatest changes, and probably the one she held most dear, was that in the eyes of others she was no longer a dwarf but a correctly built Eskimo woman.[36] She soon realized this and added a remark to her lectures, stating that among Eskimo women she was unusually tall.[37] This positive change in attitude towards her body probably played a significant part in Ólöf's decision to risk becoming an "Eskimo" for good.

The public's poor opinion of dwarves no longer fettered Ólöf, and she began to blossom. For the first time in her life she could develop talents and skills she had not been able to use as a dwarf. People no longer stared at her, the dwarf, and made fun of her, or looked past her and pretended not to see her. Now she was an interesting woman from a distant and exotic land, and she received positive attention wherever she went.

Ólöf's Body: Her Curse and Her Key to Fame

Ólöf's body was her curse, but through her lie she managed to overcome the limitations and constrictions that came with being a dwarf. Her small and disabled body became the key to her fame and success in the United States. The inspiration for Ólöf's disguise probably came from people's mistaken belief that, as an Icelander, she was naturally an Eskimo. Many Americans thought all Icelanders were Eskimos, and many Icelandic adults were asked whether they were Eskimos. Like Ólöf, they found this extremely annoying.[38]

Americans' belief that Iceland was inhabited by Eskimos shows how little they really knew about Iceland and Greenland. It is doubtful, however, that a fully grown Icelander could have played Ólöf's game for long and donned an Eskimo's disguise. The American public would have realized sooner or later that the person in question was not an Inuk. A typical Icelander of full stature would have been far too similar to Western people to sustain the deception for long.

Ólöf's Accent

Ólöf had another disability besides her physical stature, one that she shared with her fellow Icelandic immigrants: namely, she spoke English with an accent. Very few of the Icelanders who moved to North America in the nineteenth century spoke any English at all. Her father and stepmother were already middle-aged when they moved west, and they never gained full command of English. This was true of many other excellent men and women who, as a consequence, never lived up to their full potential in the new land.[39] But in Ólöf's case, her accent was to her advantage. Critics often mentioned it and claimed it gave Ólöf's lectures a unique and entertaining air. A critic in West Chester, Pennsylvania, wrote:

> Olof Krarer fairly captivated her audiences at the Normal yesterday afternoon and evening. The story of the life of the inhabitants of Greenland became doubly entertaining when related in the quaint broken English of this bright and witty little native of that frozen land.[40]

If Ólöf had been born a dwarf in the United States and had spoken unaccented English, she would hardly have been able to play the game she did.

Within a few years, Ólöf had earned her place among the most popular lecturers in the United States. The next chapter investigates what caused her lectures about Greenland's Eskimos to become as popular as they did.

The Race for the North Pole
and Ólöf's Popularity

Elisha Kent Kane, National Hero

It was no coincidence that Ólöf's lecturing career flourished concurrently with American explorers' race to become the first to reach the North Pole, led by engineer Robert E. Peary (1856–1920). The race was infused with patriotic pride, and Americans paid avid attention to the conquests in the Arctic. This passion comes closest to Americans' later fascination with the race to land a man on the moon, and to a great degree it explains Ólöf's success and popularity.[1]

Robert E. Peary was not the first American to interest his compatriots in the Arctic, however. A physician and an explorer by the name of Elisha Kent Kane (1820–57) was among the first to excite this interest when he embarked on his first Arctic expedition in 1849.

Elisha Kent Kane was born in Philadelphia in 1820, and was nine years older than Ólöf's father, Sölvi Sölvason. He came from a respected Philadelphia family and studied medicine at the University of Pennsylvania, but was an adventurer by nature and more interested in exploring the world than practicing medicine. When he was in his late twenties, he

Elisha Kent Kane, the first person to excite Americans' interest in the Arctic

decided to launch a search party to the Arctic and try to find the English explorer Sir John Franklin, who had vanished there in 1846 with his crew of 129 men. Sir John Franklin had been determined to find the Northwest Passage to the Pacific Ocean. He was less than successful, and disappeared together with all his men. Never before in the history of Arctic exploration had as many search parties been sent as went to find Sir John Franklin and his crew. From 1847 to 1855, nearly forty groups set out, and there was intense competition among them to be the first to find Franklin and his men.[2]

In 1849, Kane convinced a rich New York merchant, Henry Grinnell by name, to finance his expedition, but Kane's Grinnell expedition was fruitless, and he returned empty-handed to New York a year later.[3] He made another attempt soon thereafter, with the same results. Despite this fact, he was greeted as a national hero on his return to his hometown of Philadelphia.[4]

Kane's Writings

Elisha Kent Kane wrote two books about his expeditions. The former, entitled *The U.S. Grinnell Expedition in Search of Sir John Franklin*, was published in 1854. The latter, *Arctic Explorations*, appeared two years later, in 1856, the year Robert E. Peary was born. The publishers launched a massive advertisement campaign before the publication of the second book, and it sold 20,000 advance copies and became an overnight bestseller. *Arctic Explorations* became one of the most popular travelogues of the 1850s and could be found next to the Bible "in every American home."[5]

In *Arctic Explorations* Kane describes the lives of north Greenlanders in a lively and entertaining way. The tribe he encountered had never before had any contact with Westerners, and though they were childish and rambunctious in Kane's opinion, they were extremely helpful to him and his men. Kane and his men learned a great deal from the Greenlanders about living and thriving in the Arctic. Kane called them Polar Eskimos, and in the mind of Americans, Polar Eskimos from north Greenland became the only true Inuit. Ólöf later claimed to come from a similar part of Greenland.[6]

Kane's Death

After Kane completed his two books he went to London to meet Sir John Franklin's widow, intending to make yet another attempt to find Franklin and his crew. Nothing came of those plans. Kane became ill and went instead to Havana, Cuba, hoping that the island's mild climate would cure him. But this hope failed, for the thirty-seven-year-old Kane died in Havana in 1857, a year before Ólöf was born.

After Kane died, his body was moved in state from Cuba to his hometown of Philadelphia, which amply demonstrates the influence Kane's expeditions and writings about the Greenlanders had had on his fellow Americans. After an elaborate memorial service in Havana, his coffin was sent by ship to New Orleans, where it was placed aboard a steamboat on the Mississippi River and transported to Cincinnati, and thence by rail to Philadelphia. The procession traveled slowly, covering a distance of some 2,000 miles in about a month. Everywhere the coffin stopped, crowds gathered to pay their last respects to the fallen hero. Memorial services were held in New Orleans; in Louisville, Kentucky; Columbus, Ohio; and Baltimore; with a final service held in Philadelphia. A few years later, the ceremony served as a model for the funeral procession of President Lincoln.[7]

Robert E. Peary

After Kane's death, Americans continued to explore the Arctic. Americans' fascination with the north remained great, but there was little interest in expeditions during the Civil War. After the war ended, that interest was rekindled, peaking in 1887 when Robert E. Peary announced that he intended to be the first man to set foot on the North Pole.[8]

Robert E. Peary was born in 1856 in the town of Cresson, in Kane's home state of Pennsylvania. He was only two years Ólöf's senior. His parents were both of old English families from Maine but had moved to Cresson two years before Robert was born, and Peary's father and uncle started a cooperage in the town. The Peary family's stay in Cresson was to be short-lived, however, as Peary's father died of acute pneumonia when Robert was three years old. His mother, who had always been in poor health, decided to move with Robert back to her family in Maine. The young widow did not remarry, and dedicated her life entirely to raising and caring for her only son.[9]

Robert E. Peary

Peary was an energetic child, but his mother raised him like a girl and taught him to sew in the manner of fine ladies. When he played outside he had to wear a woman's hat to protect himself against the sun. The boys in the neighborhood were quick to catch on to this manner of dress and teased him for being like a girl. To make matters worse, Peary spoke with a lisp as a child.[10]

This experience, combined with Peary's lack of a male role model in his youth, made him determined to enhance his masculinity and courage. He dreamed of being a hero whose name was on every American's lips.[11] That dream was to come true.

First to the North Pole

Peary received his degree in civil engineering from Bowdoin College, Maine, in the spring of 1877, while Ólöf sat in quarantine in New Iceland. He worked for a while as an engineer for the United States Navy in Washington, D.C.[12] As a child, Peary was fascinated by Kane's expeditions and dreamed of exploring the Arctic. His interest in the North Pole was renewed in 1885 when he read a pamphlet by Swedish geologist and explorer Nils Adolf Erik Nordenskjold (1832–1901) about the latter's exploration of remote parts of Greenland. He became determined to be the first man to cross the Greenland ice cap, but before attempting the crossing he wanted to familiarize himself with the lay of the land. In the summer of 1886, he traveled with a Canadian whaling ship to Greenland with this objective in mind. He funded the journey with a loan of five hundred dollars from his mother.[13]

It came as a great shock to Peary when he learned a year later, in 1887, that the Norwegian explorer Fridtjof Nansen had been the first to cross the Greenland ice cap. Nansen crossed in the south, where the ice cap is smallest.[14] The disappointment did not deter Peary, however, but rather increased his determination to be the first man to reach the North Pole. He intended to start his journey on land, by crossing Greenland, as all previous attempts to reach the North Pole had been made by sea.

Peary devoted the next twenty-four years to exploring Greenland, while Ólöf simultaneously enjoyed a successful career as a lecturer and educator about the lives of Eskimos. Peary went on his first great expedition in 1891–92, and the second in 1893–95. He took shorter trips in the summers of 1896 and 1897, but from 1898 to 1908 he went on three long expeditions to the farthest reaches of north Greenland, staying for as

Setting out on a long dogsled journey

long as four continuous years in 1898–1902. Peary went on his last expedition in 1908, and the high point of his career came when he and his men reached the North Pole on April 6, 1909.[15]

Great Interest, Slim Offerings

Americans were very interested in Peary's North Pole expedition, paid close attention to every new development, and thirsted after news from the north, but he was a reticent writer and abhorred lecturing. Given the demand, information on the north was thus disproportionately limited.

Public interest in Peary's travels was quite apparent in 1893, when he had to step out of character and go on a lecture tour. Peary's expeditions were financed mostly by contributions from individuals, scientific foundations, and societies.[16] His attempts to raise funds for the 1893 expedition were not very successful, and out of necessity he decided to give lectures. In the fall of 1892, he turned to one of the best-known agents in the United States, J. B. Pond, and asked him to organize the tour. Pond was hesitant, believing that the time was too short, but Peary insisted and Pond agreed to work with him. Peary ended up giving 165 lectures in 103 days during the winter of 1893.

A bear defeated

Peary spoke in many of the same places as Ólöf, and filled every hall, with many prospective attendees being turned away at the door. The population of Elisha Kent Kane's hometown of Philadelphia showed by far the greatest interest in Arctic exploration and Greenlanders. Peary received an average of $150–$200 for each lecture, but in Philadelphia he received a generous $600 per lecture.[17] Ólöf was also extremely popular in the city, and it was there that she set her lecture record. She gave over eighty lectures on life in the Arctic there, more than in any other American city.[18]

Peary and Ólöf presented the Greenlanders in a similar fashion. Like Ólöf, Peary decorated the stage with objects from Greenland, and also brought along Greenlandic dogs and dogsleds he had brought home from one of his expeditions. Unlike Ólöf, however, Peary did not wear a skin suit on stage. He let his assistant, an African American man called Henson, wear such a suit instead, and Henson had to stand and sweat on stage while Peary spoke to the audience.

At the end of his tour, Peary's net income from his lectures was about

Josephine Peary with native women in north Greenland

$13,000, all of which went to fund his expedition. Pond later said that no other lecturer he had managed had been as successful as Peary. Such was the population's interest in the Arctic and the race for the North Pole.[19]

Josephine Peary and Her Three Books

Peary's lecture tour in 1893 was an exception in his career, as he was no great writer, published books about his travels rather late, and did little to satisfy the public's appetite for news from the north. Furthermore, he forbade his crew to speak in public about the expeditions. They were required to sign a confidentiality agreement and hand over their diaries to Peary at the end of each journey.[20] The books written by Peary's wife, Josephine, helped to mitigate this lack of information.

Peary married Josephine Diebitsch in 1888. Josephine was of German descent, a highly educated member of the upper class, born and raised in Washington, D.C. Shortly after their wedding, Peary announced—to the

Marie Peary (Snow Baby),
born in Greenland

shocked disapproval of most Americans—that all Greenland expeditions should have at least one woman aboard. He thought it was important that men be cared for by females while traveling, and maintained as well that women were just as capable of making such trips as men. In order to prove his point, he took Josephine along on the 1891–92 expedition, making her one of the first Western women to experience the harsh winters of north Greenland.[21]

Josephine liked Greenland and joined her husband's next expedition, during which they spent two years in Greenland between 1893 and 1895. When she left for Greenland the second time, she was pregnant with her first child. On September 12, 1893, she gave birth to a daughter who was given the name Marie Ahnighito. The birth of the daughter was of great interest to the locals, who flocked to the Pearys' home to see this white curiosity. Among them, the girl was never called anything but "Snow Baby."[22]

Unlike her husband, Josephine enjoyed writing and published three

Marie Peary with native friends

books about her life and experience in Greenland. In 1894 she published her diaries from her first year in Greenland, *My Arctic Journal.* Seven years later, in 1901, *The Snow Baby* was published. It was told from the perspective of the Pearys' daughter, Marie Ahnighito. Josephine's third and final book on Greenland, *Children of the Arctic,* also told from Marie's perspective, appeared in 1903. Marie, then six years old, spent fifteen months with her parents in Greenland in 1900–1901. Excerpts from her diaries were incorporated into the book.[23]

Josephine's books were accessible and sold well, providing the couple with a welcome source of income. While they were intended for readers of all ages, they became especially popular among American children, who read eagerly about the life of Inuit children and adults who often behaved like children. Josephine Peary's books satisfied the public's curiosity about the Arctic to some extent, but they were not enough. The populace was always eager for more, and Ólöf's lectures and biography met that need. By 1909, when Peary became the first Westerner to reach the North Pole, Ólöf had given her lecture more than two thousand times.[24]

The Textbook *Eskimo Stories*

Ólöf and Josephine Peary crossed paths in the textbook *Eskimo Stories*, published in Chicago in 1902. When the race for the North Pole grew more heated, Americans began to realize that victory at the Pole would be a momentous occasion in the history of the United States. Prominent educators realized that the public's knowledge of Arctic life and culture would have to be increased substantially. Around the turn of the twentieth century, Chicago publisher Rand McNally, then one of the largest publishers of textbooks in the United States, decided to release a special volume about Eskimos. The proposed book was intended to replace the few paragraphs devoted to Greenland and its inhabitants in American geography textbooks.[25]

A woman named Mary E. E. Smith, a teacher at the Jennings School in Chicago, was hired to write the book.[26] A gifted poet, she wrote the narrative in verse, relying on Josephine Peary's *My Arctic Journey* and *Children of the Cold*, a book published in 1899 by Frederick Schwatka, as her primary sources. Frederick Schwatka (1849–92), a physician who served as a lieutenant in the United States Army, went on a few Arctic expeditions, mostly to Alaska. His book described the lives and games of Inuit children in Alaska.[27]

The works of Josephine Peary and Frederick Schwatka were obviously reliable sources, but the publishers nonetheless wanted the only Eskimo in the United States, Olof Krarer, who was in fact living in their town of Chicago, to read through the manuscript and ensure that her people were being accurately described in the textbook-to-be. Ólöf did this with pleasure and made several comments, and it was decided to include a chapter from her own biography at the end of the book. In the book's introduction, its author, Mary E. E. Smith, wrote the following:

The author acknowledges her appreciation of the valuable suggestions made by Miss Olof Krarer, who read the book in manuscript, and whose interesting autobiography appears at the close of the volume under the title, "The Story of a Real Eskimo."[28]

In an introduction for teachers at the end of the book, Mary E. E. Smith recommended that teachers let their students commence their study of the lives of Eskimos by reading Ólöf's chapter, and then continue with the main text of the book, as Ólöf's chapter was unique in being written by a native Eskimo.[29]

Eskimo Stories became an extremely popular textbook and was taught in American elementary schools until the start of World War II.[30]

When *Eskimo Stories* was published in 1902, Ólöf had been living in Chicago for fourteen years. Let us now return to her adventurous life.

Chicago

The Slaytons and the Slayton Lyceum Bureau

Henry Lake Slayton walked quickly and confidently onto the platform of a Chicago railway station early one Sunday morning in 1888. His step had a rhythmic spring to it that betrayed his former occupation as a soldier. Slayton was tall, broad-shouldered, and sharply dressed in a dark, tailored suit and coat, the latter worn unbuttoned. His shoes were made of fine patent leather.

The few passengers who were about this early on a Sunday morning could hardly avoid casting a glance at him. He had thick, wavy chestnut-brown hair, a tall, round forehead, and a regal nose. His mustache was well groomed and his eyebrows bushy, and beneath them he had large, beautiful brown eyes that simultaneously conveyed kindness, firmness, a strong will, and a good sense of humor. It surprised no one when this man headed straight for the first-class cabin.

Slayton was the only passenger traveling first class this morning, as few members of the upper crust of society traveled this early on a holiday. He settled into his seat and glanced at his pocket watch. The train was scheduled to depart in ten minutes, at eight o'clock, and if all went according to plan he would arrive in time for the lecture that the Es-

*Henry Slayton, Ólöf's
employer and protector*

quimaux Lady, Olof Krarer, was scheduled to give at eight that evening. Slayton only rarely made trips of this sort nowadays. His agency, the Slayton Lyceum Bureau in Chicago, was one of the largest and most respected such organizations in the city, and was responsible for organizing tours and lectures for all of the most popular lecturers, artists, and entertainers in the United States.[1] Nonetheless, all good agents had to keep their eyes open, to predict developing interests and spot rising stars.

Slayton had strong suspicions that Americans' interest in the north would soon begin growing again. It had lain dormant during the Civil War, but the North Pole was still undefeated, and rumor had it that a Maine engineer by the name of Robert E. Peary had been exploring Greenland for the past two years, intending to be the first man to reach the Pole.

Slayton had soon set his sights on Olof Krarer, the only Eskimo in the United States. Her lectures on Greenland and the lives of Eskimos were by all accounts extremely popular, and after reading her biography he realized that he would have to act quickly and ascertain whether she were a suitable addition to his bureau's clientele.

Slayton arrived on time at the theater in downtown St. Paul.[2] The tickets were nearly sold out when his turn came at the ticket office, but he got the seat he wanted, the farthest one on the right in the last row, just by the exit. He always sat in that seat on occasions such as these, so he could slip out unnoticed if the lecturer wasn't good enough. This time, however, leaving was the farthest thing from his mind. He sat stock still for an hour and a half and would have stayed longer had the occasion called for it.

The curtain was drawn, revealing a stage decorated with white skins and objects from Greenland. And when tiny Olof Krarer took the stage, clad in white skins, the audience clapped instinctively and laughed with delight.[3] The laughter died down, however, when she stepped up to the pulpit and began to speak. She spoke with a strong accent that gave her lecture an exotic air, and listeners had to concentrate to understand her at first, but they soon became accustomed to her speech. The audience quickly became so captivated by Olof's story about life in the Arctic that complete silence reigned in the auditorium, punctuated from time to time by laughter and applause.

Slayton realized immediately that the woman in question was extraordinarily talented. Her delivery was extremely charming, and her flair for the dramatic was of a caliber usually associated with trained actors. She clearly had a gift for gab, and she injected a good deal of vitality into her descriptions of Eskimo life. Her stage presence was dignified and elegant, even though she was short and strangely built.

It seemed as though the applause would never die down after Olof finished her speech. But the audience's applause afterward didn't tell the whole story about the lecturer's abilities—this Slayton knew from past experience. Most important by far was the lecturer's ability to answer the audience's questions after the speech quickly and succinctly. Olof's performance in that respect was as exceptional as her lecture. People were extremely curious about Eskimo life and posed numerous questions. Some were easy, others difficult and challenging, but in all cases Olof answered them brilliantly. She was clearly very intelligent, this little Eskimo lady, there was no doubt about that.[4]

It was clear to Slayton that this was a rising star, and he acted accordingly. Immediately after the lecture, he contacted Ólöf's assistant, introduced himself, and told her what he wanted. The woman received him graciously; she was clearly tired of traveling and more than willing to place Ólöf in other hands. When Ólöf escaped the audience, she was introduced to Slayton and seemed pleased with his offer. Nonetheless, she said she wished to think it over, and promised to contact him soon. Shortly thereafter he received a letter from Ólöf, accepting his offer with pleasure. A few days later, the Esquimaux Lady, Olof Krarer, arrived by train in Chicago.

In 1936, Wendell Slayton, Henry Slayton's son, who was twelve years old when his father first met Ólöf, reminisced about this journey of his father's in a letter to Vilhjálmur Stefánsson:

> I recall my father Henry L. Slayton made a trip to Minnesota to meet Miss Krarer with a view of making a contract for her appearance under the management of the Slayton Lyceum Bureau. At that time she was lecturing on Greenland with bookings arranged by a personal manager. . . . She was glad to come under our management & we booked her for the next thirty years or until her eyesight failed & she had to give up platform work.[5]

The contract with the Slayton Lyceum Bureau changed Ólöf's life. Until then she had been a traveling lecturer, going from town to town and city to city with her assistant, who made reservations for her lectures at churches and town theaters. Now she had a permanent contract with one of the largest and most respected agencies in the Midwest and soon began lecturing at esteemed educational and cultural institutions. Furthermore, she became again a member of a family, eleven years after she left her family at Steinnes in New Iceland. Henry Slayton and his wife, Mina, made Ólöf a most generous offer. They invited her to move into their family home at 25 Waverly Place in the Near West Side, at that time one of Chicago's finest neighborhoods. Ólöf accepted the offer gratefully and lived with the Slayton family from that day forward.

The Slaytons' house was large and spacious, and when Ólöf moved in only four people lived there: Mina, Henry, their son, Wendell, and one maid. Adding a fifth member to the household was no trouble.[6]

As an Eskimo, Ólöf was unique in the United States, and would have caught the eye of many agents. By taking her into their home, the Slaytons guaranteed her fidelity to them.

So it happened that little Ólöf Sölvadóttir from Outer Langamýri in Húnavatnssýsla county, who as a child had never seen a group of houses larger than the village of Saudárkrókur, took up residence in Chicago, one of the largest and most vibrant cities in the United States. The best years of her life were soon to follow.

Henry Lake Slayton

Henry Lake Slayton, founder and principal owner of the Slayton Lyceum Bureau, was twelve years younger than Ólöf's father, Sölvi Sölvason. He was born in Woodstock, Vermont, on May 29, 1841, the oldest of the four children of Stephen D. Slayton and Lucy Maria Slayton, née Kendall. The Slayton family was of old Anglo-Saxon stock, descended from Captain Thomas Slayton, a Scotsman who came to Massachusetts in 1690.[7]

When Henry was four years old, the family moved to Lebanon, New Hampshire, where his father, "a man of rare intelligence," founded a knife factory that soon became a leader in the industry in New England. Henry's mother was an excellent wife and housewife, "one of those charming women whose lives are devoted to the happiness of those about them."[8]

After completing his compulsory education, Henry enrolled at the Kimball Union Academy, a secondary school in Meriden, New Hampshire. He studied there for three years and planned to continue on to Dartmouth University. But the outbreak of the Civil War changed his plans. Henry's father, Stephen Slayton, was a great opponent of slavery, and as a young man Henry had been influenced by his views.[9] Henry was twenty years old and not ready to become a soldier in 1861, when the Civil War began. Instead, he decided to study military science at Norwich Military Academy in Northfield, Vermont.[10] Upon completing his studies, he was hired by the State of New Hampshire to train volunteers for one year. When that contract was completed, he joined the army and became the first lieutenant of the Second Regiment of the United States Colored Infantry, one of the first armed units of African Americans in the United States Army. This unit soon gained a reputation for being one of the best trained in the army. It fought in Tallahassee, Las Tortugas, and Key West,

Florida. Its Confederate opponents "boasted of having orders to take no colored soldiers prisoner or white officers in colored regiments alive as prisoners of war, but to kill them at sight without quarter."[11]

After the war, Henry Slayton returned to New England and began studying law at the Albany Law School in New York State. He graduated with a law degree in 1867, the year Ólöf's mother died in an accident in Iceland. One of Henry's classmates was William McKinley, who served as president of the United States from 1897 to 1901 and was assassinated by an anarchist in Buffalo, New York.[12] Like his classmate McKinley, Henry supported the Republican Party and was active in politics, particularly during the run-up to presidential elections. He often wrote polarizing journal articles on various political topics.[13]

Henry Slayton in Chicago

After completing his law degree, Henry moved to Chicago, which was a rapidly growing city and popular among successful young New Englanders. When it was incorporated in 1837 it counted 4,179 inhabitants, but by the 1870s it was home to 1.2 million people and growing by leaps and bounds. Its swift growth can be attributed to its location at the outlet of the Chicago River from Lake Michigan, and it soon became an important center of transportation between the Northeast and the Midwest.[14]

Henry soon passed the bar examination in Illinois and began practicing criminal law. He was extremely sympathetic to the underdog, had become interested in the penal system as a law student, and was a "strong opponent" of the death penalty. He wrote several scholarly articles on the subject.[15] Like so many Chicagoans, Henry was badly hit by the fire of 1871. His office burned to the ground, he lost his entire library, and he barely escaped with his life. After this catastrophe, Henry was prepared to move away from the city. He accepted an offer from the governor of Texas and became superintendent of public schools for several counties in the state.[16]

In Texas, Henry founded schools for both black and white students on his own initiative. This effort earned him considerable animosity from the white population of Texas. Several schools for black children were set on fire, and Henry received death threats. "But he stuck to his post for two years, and after the free school system had triumphed he resigned and returned to Chicago."[17]

Henry and Mina's Marriage

After Henry resigned from his position in Texas, he spent a short period of time in his home state of New Hampshire. He soon moved back to Chicago and began practicing law again.[18] In March 1873, three years before Ólöf came to America, Henry married Mina E. Gregory, a woman of solid Anglo-Saxon family background like himself. Mina was the daughter of a Universalist pastor in Northfield, Vermont. She and Henry met when he was studying at Norwich Military Academy at the beginning of the Civil War.

Henry and Mina's marriage was characterized by a remarkable equality of education and elegance. Mina Slayton was exceptionally well educated in comparison with most ladies of her generation. She had a good singing voice and studied voice for a time at the New England Conservatory of Music in Boston. She was also a trained actress and elocutionist, having completed degrees in those fields from the Emerson School of Expression in Boston and the Comnack School in Evanston, Illinois. At the time of her marriage, she was completing a degree in elocution and dramatic interpretation of texts at the Murdoch School in Philadelphia. After she moved to Chicago, she furthered her education even more and took private lessons in elocution with a man named Walter Lyman.[19]

Mina Slayton

Only a few years before Mina began her career of public reading, women had been forbidden to express themselves publicly in speech or in writing, and it was very unusual that a woman could have gainful employment through elocution.

Advertisement from the Slayton Lyceum Bureau. "The Colored Ideals."

The Founding of the Slayton Lyceum Bureau

Before her marriage, Mina Slayton had worked as a singer and elocution-ist, and she wanted to continue with this work after she moved to Chicago. Henry decided to abandon his law career and become his wife's agent and manager. With that in mind, he founded the Slayton Lyceum Bureau in 1873. In so doing he fulfilled his "desire to give her the coveted opportunity to appear in the right way before the best people."[20] Mina Slayton was a very successful elocutionist. In the winter of 1873–74, the first winter the bureau was open, she gave twenty-five public readings in Chicago alone.[21]

In an advertisement pamphlet from the Slayton Lyceum Bureau, Mina was described as follows: "Among all the lady readers none have met with greater success, or given such universal satisfaction as Mrs. Slayton wherever she has appeared. . . . We will guarantee the best of satisfaction before any audience."[22] Shapely, tall, slender, and poised, Mina cut a striking figure on stage. Her long, thick hair was done up in Victorian style so that not a single lock fell on the tall, white collar of her dress. She had an open, handsome face; a moderately tall forehead; a long, curved nose; and thick, shapely lips. She had unusually beautiful eyes that radiated a gentle warmth.

Chicago, Railway Capital

This was before the advent of radio, films, music players, and television. People could read books and newspapers at home to entertain themselves, but electricity was not yet generally available in cities and towns, so people had limited light to read by. In a city like Chicago, the bulk of entertainment was to be had outside the home. People went to the circus, saw musicals and plays, and attended concerts, musicales, and lectures on various topics for their entertainment and education. The last three were primarily attended by wealthier, better-educated members of society. This was the target audience of the Slayton Lyceum Bureau, and in Chicago it was a large and a growing one.[23]

But Chicago offered another advantage to an agency such as Slayton's. The city was the hub of railway transport within the United States. From Chicago the rails extended in all directions, and consequently it was easy to send lecturers from Chicago to all the principal cities and towns in the country.[24] Ólöf, who was frightened when she first saw a train in Granton, Scotland, on her way from Iceland to America, soon became one of the Chicago railway companies' best patrons.

The Success of the Slayton Lyceum Bureau

The Slayton Lyceum Bureau started out as a small enterprise, but grew rapidly to become one of the largest and most respected agencies of its kind in the Midwest "and one of the largest and most successful in the world."[25] According to a description of Henry L. Slayton, he was particularly well suited to managing a business of this kind. A highly flattering paragraph from a book about the distinguished citizens of Chicago describes him as follows:

*This building housed the
Slayton Lyceum Bureau
in downtown Chicago.*

Henry L. Slayton . . . is possessed of that keen business ability, sound
judgment and spirit of enterprise, to which Chicago is so accustomed
and so much indebted. In his chosen field of labor he was the pioneer,
and from a small beginning and against obstacles of a discouraging
character, his tact, energy and perseverance have evolved a business
which is co-extensive with the limits of the country, and have made his
name familiar among the intelligent portion of the whole nation.
Gifted by nature with the sturdy qualities of mind and heart which
appear to be prominently characteristic of those who come from
New England, his success has been the legitimate result of a well
balanced organization, integrity of character and singleness of purpose. Having enjoyed both a military and legal education and practice, his training was of that methodical character, which has been
of signal benefit to him in conducting an enterprise which is the
very embodiment of systematic arrangement and management.

Thus peculiarly fitted for the undertaking of a complicated and delicate nature, the success of the Slayton Lyceum Bureau has been unmistakable, and the more brilliant because of the many failures of similar enterprises in the West, during the years that it has been steadily extending its influence.[26]

The company grew rapidly, as did the number of employees. The bureau's staff grew in numbers both at its office in Chicago and in the various towns and cities where its representatives set up quarters. In the company's name they sent lecturers, elocutionists, singers, and musical ensembles all over the United States.[27]

The Slayton Lyceum Bureau was initially housed in the Central Music Hall, which towered over Randolph and State Streets in downtown Chicago.[28] The office was later moved to 17 Van Buren Street, but when it was sold in 1909 it was housed in Steinway Hall, on the corner of Wabash Avenue and Jackson Boulevard in downtown Chicago.[29]

The Birth of Wendell Slayton

Henry came from a wealthy family, and when he and Mina were married they both held well-paying jobs. Shortly after their wedding, they purchased a stately two-story brick house at 25 Waverly Place on the Near West Side. Their house stood a short distance from Washington Boulevard, at that time one of the most spectacular boulevards in the city.[30]

Three years after Mina and Henry were married, on July 20, 1876, Mina gave birth to their first and only child, the son Wendell Philips, in her parents' home in Northfield, Vermont.[31] On that same day, the *Austria,* the ship that brought Ólöf to America, sailed through the mouth of the Gulf of Saint Lawrence and docked in Quebec City.[32] When Wendell was born, Mina worked as an elocutionist for the Slayton Lyceum Bureau, and she continued to do so until 1883. By that time the company was so large and successful that her services were no longer required.[33] Wendell was seven years old then, but five years later, when he was twelve years old, there was an unexpected addition to his family party: Olof Krarer, an Eskimo all the way from Greenland!

From Shanty to Palace

Ólöf's standard of living was completely transformed upon her arrival in Chicago. Many aspects of Chicago life came as a surprise to Ólöf, but others were more familiar. Like Winnipeg, Chicago was very much an immigrant city, and the rapid economic growth it experienced was founded on a steady influx of cheap immigrant labor. The first immigrants to Chicago came from Germany, Ireland, and Scandinavia. When Ólöf moved there in 1888, most of them came from eastern Europe and the Mediterranean.[34] Chicago's immigrants lived in slums that encircled the downtown area, in miserable timber and brick huts that had originally been intended for one or two families but now housed several times as many. According to calculations from 1894, the Polish neighborhood in western Chicago was more densely populated than the most crowded neighborhoods in Tokyo and Calcutta at the time.[35]

In between the houses were filthy factories where the immigrants worked, bars and gambling houses where they emptied their pockets, brothels, and "stockyards where death-bound cattle and sheep waited their turn."[36]

None of this took Ólöf by surprise. Her family had been among the poorest of immigrants in Winnipeg and had lived for a time in a shanty on the banks of the Red River, while her father and brothers worked as day laborers. But Chicago, like Winnipeg, also had a large population of wealthy citizens of Anglo-Saxon descent, who lived in expensive neighborhoods only a short distance from the immigrant slums. Ólöf was familiar with these neighborhoods as well, having worked as a maid in a few such homes in Winnipeg.

Ólöf was now living in a wealthy neighborhood once again, but her social status had been completely transformed. She was no longer a maid, but a full member of an upper-class American family. She was served by the family maid, Mary Herriman, who came from New York and, unlike Ólöf, spoke perfect English.[37] The difference between the Slayton family home and Ólöf's childhood home at Outer Langamýri could hardly have been greater. The farm at Outer Langamýri had been built from turf and rocks, with a kitchen, a pantry, hallways, and a *badstofa* that was the largest room in the house. There people spent their time when indoors, ate their food from an *askur* (a large, lidded wooden cup), worked, entertained themselves, and slept, often two or three in the same bed. Infants were born there, and there people died. There were one or two windows covered with a piece of stretched placenta or fish scales, as glass windows were not generally available at the time.[38]

The Slaytons' house was a large two-story brick house with a basement and an attic, with high ceilings and spacious rooms. The windows were large and the rooms airy and bright, the wooden floors covered with lush carpets. The house was well furnished: couches and chairs were upholstered in European fashion; tables, cabinets, and chests of drawers were decoratively carved; and crystal chandeliers hung from the ceilings.[39] A full wardrobe of tailor-made dresses, blouses, skirts, and shoes, all in the newest of fashions, awaited her. She certainly enjoyed sharing all her meals with the Slayton family, and it must have moved her to be waited upon by Mary Herriman.

At that time, all of the distinguished families in Chicago lived in the Near West Side, the Slaytons' neighborhood. A large fraction of the prominent players in turn-of-the-century Chicago public life grew up in this part of the city.[40] The streets there were broad, bright, and well tended, lined with trees and, in summer, with flowers as well. The finest clubs in the city were located here, as were the best churches, among them the Episcopal Cathedral of Saints Peter and Paul, the First Congregational Church, and the Union Park Congregational Church.[41]

It must have been quite a sight to see Mina and Henry Slayton out for a walk with Wendell and Ólöf on Sundays and on summer evenings, all clad in their finest. Surely they must have strolled now and again up to Silver Leaf Grove, "where there were soft breezes, good music and drinks that were soft or hard according to individual taste."[42] On other days they could have gone to Union Park or Jefferson Park, where Wendell could play with other children or sail his boat on one of the ponds.[43] Sometimes they were satisfied to roam the streets of the town, just to see and be seen.

As the years went by, other parts of the city began to encroach upon this upper-class neighborhood. The industrial areas of Chicago expanded westward from Lake Michigan, and townhouses were torn down and replaced by factories and warehouses. West of the neighborhood a large hospital,

Dr. Kokichi Morimoto, Tokyo, Japan, Illustrated lecture

July 19, 8 p. m.   Admission 25c.   Children 15c.

This distinguished Japanese lecturer and scholar has been engaged for his intensely interesting illustrated lecture on life in Japan. Dr. Morimoto is a professor in Johns Hopkins University, Baltimore, and was formerly professor in history in North Japan College, and was connected with the foreign office of the Japanese government. He is a forceful and interesting speaker, refined, witty and brilliant. It is a rare privilege to hear the wonderful history of Japan, and learn of the marvelous development of the Sunrise Kingdom, from the lips of a distinguished representative of that country. This lecture is profusely illustrated with unique motion pictures, and authorized Japanese views. Many of the illustrations are in colors and are the product of the best Japanese artist, the slides all being hand colored. "Japan and the Russo Japanese War," or "The Far East and the Far West," will be the illustrated lecture given. Nothing more instructive and interesting on the platform.

July 17, 2:30 p. m.

Admission 25c.

Children 15c.

Miss Olof Krarer, Esquimau Lecturer.

We are confident that our patrons will be pleased and delighted with the interesting and instructive lecture which will be delivered by the famous Esquimau lecturer, Miss Olof Krarer. Miss Krarer is an Esquimau 45 years old, 45 inches tall and weighs 100 pounds. She has been lecturing in America for fifteen years and has an excellent command of the English language. A clear, distinct voice with wonderful carrying capacity, she never fails to delight the large audiences which greet her. The story of her life, the strange customs of her homeland, her education by the missionaries is all more interesting than a fairy tale. We present Miss Krarer to the patrons of the Associated Chautauquas not as a freak or a curiosity but solely on her own merits as a lecturer.

July 11, 8 p. m.

Admission 25c.

Children 15c.

Chancellor M. A. Casey. Illustrated Lecture, "San Francisco In Earthquake and Fire."

Dr. Casey landed in San Francisco immediately after the first earthquake shock and personally experienced the subsequent shocks. He saw the first terrible effects of the earthquake, the start of the conflagration and the destruction of the city by fire. He worked for several days with the relief forces and was especially commended for his efforts by General Funston. The slides which were made for his lecture were especially made for the Associated Chautauquas from photos carefully selected by Dr. Casey. In this lecture the earthquake shock and the results are graphically described, the horrors of the fire, the dynamiting of the immense buildings and tragic, pathetic and humorous incidents which came under Dr. Casey's personal observation are related while the pictures add an addional attraction to this splendid lecture. No one should miss this great illustrated lecture, which is handled in masterful manner.

An advertisement for one of Ólöf's lectures for the Slayton Lyceum Bureau

Cook County Hospital, and a medical center were built. To the south, a community of immigrants and African Americans was growing rapidly.[44] The Near West Side became an oasis in the desert, and the constant presence of the slums must have been an unpleasant reminder to Ólöf of her origins and her position. Just one misstep, and she could find herself cast down from her present position and back to the "other side."

Another Successful Icelander in Chicago

Ólöf quickly became one of the most sought-after lecturers in the Slayton Lyceum Bureau. She was constantly traveling back and forth across the entire United States, telling people about her adventurous life in the Arctic. The audiences never seemed to get enough of this incredible tale, and Ólöf continued on her set path for several decades. But she was not the only Icelander living in Chicago at this time. In 1893, about a hundred of her compatriots lived in the city.[45] One of them was Hjörtur Thórdarson, who hailed from Húnavatnssýsla county, like Ólöf, and later became known as Chester Thordarson. Hjörtur, then five years old, moved with his family from Hrútafjördur to Wisconsin in 1873. His father died soon after they arrived, and the young widow, Hjörtur's mother, struggled to support her family. As a consequence, her children began working to support themselves as early as possible. Hjörtur's entire formal education amounted to a portion of two years in school, but he was very intelligent and imaginative and became a self-taught electrician. He also became a prolific inventor and filed over a thousand patents. His most famous invention was the "one-and-a-half-million volt transformer."[46]

Hjörtur married an Icelandic woman, Júlíana Fridriksdóttir, who was a seamstress and ran a large business in Chicago when they met. Júlíana encouraged her husband, and, with her help and executive experience, Hjörtur opened his own factory. At first he produced laboratory equipment, but he later expanded his range of merchandise. Hjörtur became an extremely wealthy man, with over 2,000 employees at the peak of his career.[47]

Hjörtur's story bears all the marks of the American Dream. It is the story of a poor boy who, by dint of hard work, rose to great heights in American society. Ólöf's story is a similar one, but it must be considered that the American path to success was not cut out for her, an uneducated immigrant woman who also was a dwarf. The only way for Ólöf to succeed was to outsmart the system that brought her fellow Icelander Hjörtur fame and fortune, and to lie her way to success.

Ólöf and Hjörtur never appear to have crossed paths. It is quite possible that he knew of Ólöf and was aware of her history, but if so he saw no reason to publicize it. Later in life, Ólöf herself was to work as an electrician like Hjörtur.

Slayton's Business Enterprises

The Chautauqua Movement for Continuing Education

In addition to organizing lecture and exhibition tours for individual lecturers and artists, the Slayton Lyceum Bureau planned entertainment fairs that lasted for a week or longer.

Just after the Slaytons founded their bureau, an adult education movement called the Chautauqua Movement spread like wildfire throughout the United States. The Slayton Lyceum Bureau owed much of its success to this movement, which drew its name from Lake Chautauqua in southwest New York State.[1] In the summer of 1874, a year after the Slayton Lyceum Bureau was founded, a Methodist priest gave a weeklong seminar for Sunday school teachers by Lake Chautauqua. The seminar was based around a series of lectures and soon became quite popular. By 1877, three years after it was first held, a total of 500 people had participated.[2]

Chautauqua assemblies soon evolved from seminars devoted solely to religious matters into courses on general matters of cultural and national interest, and similar lecture series, or "mini-Chautauquas," were set up in various cities and towns across the United States. Audiences flocked to these lectures, hungry for wholesome knowledge and entertainment.

Like the circus, the Chautauqua Movement depended on rail travel for its success. Lecturers and entertainers moved in groups by rail, from town to town and city to city, where they would dwell for a period of time while they lectured and entertained audiences. Among their ranks were some of the country's most important thinkers, scholars, and artists, all of whom presented cutting-edge work in their respective disciplines for the education and entertainment of their audiences.[3]

Also like the circus, the Chautauqua Movement was a unifying force in American society after the divisive impact of the Civil War. The same lectures were given, the same songs played and sung, the same stories told from east to west and from north to south.[4] The movement was as instrumental as the circuses in reinforcing the ideal of white supremacy, and with her account of Eskimos, Ólöf contributed diligently to that cause.

Around 1890, Chautauqua lecture series were offered in about two hundred cities and towns. They usually took place in large tents near a lake or in a woodland clearing to echo their origins at Lake Chautauqua. The festivities usually lasted a week, but in some places an entire month's worth of entertainment was available.[5] The Chautauqua week was the zenith of summer activities in many towns. It drew a crowd of citizens in their Sunday best, and in some localities workplaces would give their employees time off while it lasted.[6]

Lecture series like these required considerable preparation and organization. This work fell within the sphere of responsibility of agencies like the Slayton Bureau.

The Slayton Lyceum Bureau's Promotional Brochure

During his tenure as superintendent of public schools in Texas, Slayton published the weekly periodical *Corsicana* (1872–73).[7] This publishing experience proved quite useful, and soon after the founding of the Slayton Lyceum Bureau he began publishing an annual promotional brochure introducing the bureau's clients. This was the first publication of its kind in the United States, and Slayton started small, but soon the brochure became grand and elaborate, decorated with numerous pictures of stars and talented individuals.

The promotional brochure of the Slayton Lyceum Bureau contained the names of all of the important thinkers and artists of the day. By the time the bureau celebrated its thirtieth anniversary in 1903, it had organized over 65,000 lectures and concerts.[8]

The following paragraphs describe some of Slayton's various clients. Ólöf's parity with these people as an important client of the bureau provides some measure of her position in society at that time.

Lectures on Religion and Politics

Because the Chautauqua Movement was rooted in the Christian faith, lectures on religion were frequent and popular. Consequently, the Slayton Lyceum Bureau had some important theologians in its ranks. One of them was Father Francis L. Patton (1843–1932), professor of theology at Princeton Theological Seminary and later president of Princeton University. He lectured on topics related to doubt and questioning of the faith, and was well received wherever he went.[9]

Lectures on politics were also a permanent fixture on the lecture scene, and the Slayton Lyceum Bureau represented many respected politicians and specialists in policy and government. Among them was George R. Wendling, a lawyer educated at the University of Chicago. Wendling became a member of the Constitutional Committee of the State of Illinois at an early age and was voted the committee's greatest orator by an association of Illinois journalists. Among his lecture topics was the ideology of Voltaire.[10]

Senator and presidential candidate William Jennings Bryan, an acquaintance of Ólöf, also lectured for the Slayton Lyceum Bureau for a time. Bryan's "Cross of Gold" speech was always popular, but he also gave thunderous lectures on other topics of central concern to the American working classes at the time, and they were well attended.[11]

Women and Feminism

The Slaytons were extremely liberal-minded and ardently supported the feminist movement. Henry L. Slayton was an early supporter of women's suffrage, and as early as 1869, two years after he graduated from law school, he gave a public lecture on women's suffrage, delivered both in

Illinois and in New England.[12] It should come as no surprise, then, that among the Slayton Lyceum Bureau's first lecturers were the two most famous women's rights advocates in the United States: Susan B. Anthony and Elizabeth Cady Stanton.[13] From 1869 to 1881 the two women traveled constantly throughout the United States to promote various aspects of women's rights. After the Slaytons opened their bureau in 1873, they took over the task of organizing the duo's lectures in the Midwest.

Susan B. Anthony gave the lectures "Women Want Bread, Not Votes" and "The Homes of Single Women," as well as a speech on the equality of the sexes, which was only open to women. Elizabeth Cady Stanton covered a greater variety of topics than Anthony, giving lectures on young girls and boys, on household life and the role of the household in maintaining culture, and on women in the Bible. Like Anthony, Stanton also gave one talk intended for women only, the topic of which was social statistics.[14]

Other remarkable feminists worked under the auspices of the Slayton Lyceum Bureau, among them novelist Lille Devereux Blake (1835–1913), who was famous for her novel *Fettered for Life*, published in 1874. Blake's lectures centered on the emotional and social subjugation of women and the need to expand their rights.[15]

The United States' first female lawyer, Phoebe Couzins, also lectured for the Slaytons on the topics "A Few Mistakes in the Creation of Eve," "Women Without a Country," and "Women's Higher Education."[16] These pioneers paved the way for other women and enabled those who followed in their footsteps to earn a living from public reading and lecturing.

In order to avoid unilateralism in the debate on women's rights, the Slayton Lyceum Bureau sponsored one opponent of women's rights. This was the lawyer D. H. Pingrey, who had written a book in opposition to feminism and who gave the lectures "The Women's Kingdom" and "The Institutions of the United States." Those who organized lectures on women's rights were advised to invite Pingrey along when Stanton or Anthony lectured, so that both sides of the argument could be presented.[17]

Scientific and Technological Innovations

Many remarkable scientific discoveries were being made at this time. Technology advanced at a remarkable rate, and lectures on the newest scientific discoveries and technological innovations were very popular. Among the Slayton Lyceum Bureau's clients was a physics professor named W. C. Richards, who spoke on "The King of Chemicals: Oxygen," "The Queen of Chemicals: Water and Its Chemistry," and "Franklin's Kite and the Wonder of Electricity," to universal approval.[18]

Another lecturer in the technological sphere spoke only on one subject: Edison's gramophone.[19]

Literature, Art, and Music

Public reading of good literature was a prominent fixture in all lecture series, and Mina Slayton herself was the Slayton Lyceum Bureau's first representative in that arena. Throughout the years the bureau took many elocutionists and literary scholars under its wing, one of them a man by the name of Moses Coit Tyler. A faculty member at New York State's Cornell University, Tyler was the first man in the United States to hold a professorship in history. He was also one of the founders of the American Historical Association. Tyler was known for his research on old English ballads, which were popular among the American public but had received little attention by scholars in the past. Tyler gave lectures on these ballads, as well as the speaking on the comical side of the Revolutionary War.[20] Lectures on famous figures in American history were popular as well. A historian named Schuyler Colfax lectured only on Abraham Lincoln, but he was very popular and gave about two hundred lectures each year.[21]

Lectures on the visual arts were extremely popular, and the bureau didn't have to look far for experts on that subject. One of the most important art institutes in the United States, the Art Institute of Chicago, was a short distance away from the Slayton Bureau, and the institute's director, W. M. French, lectured for the bureau for many years. Motivated by a keen desire to bring art to the people, French gave accessible and entertaining talks on visual art. Among his topics were the magic of wax crayons and the artistry of drawing caricatures.[22]

Singing and music were also an important component of lecture series, and through the years the Slayton Lyceum Bureau had any number of singers and musicians on its register. Among them was the Hutchinson family, the oldest musical family group in the United States, who sang and played wonderfully. Another noteworthy ensemble was the Colored Jubilee Concert Company, a group composed only of African Americans who performed songs of joy and mourning that had originated among slaves on plantations in the South.[23] The Slayton Lyceum Bureau also worked with notable foreign musicians, such as the Norwegian violinist Ole Bull and the Hungarian violin prodigy Edouard Remenyi.[24]

Travelogues and Tales from Foreign Lands: Tank Lee

The Chautauqua lectures played an important part in establishing national unity among Americans after the divisive Civil War, in part by placing significant emphasis on important men and topics within the United States. Yet national unity cannot be created by only looking inward; it is also necessary to look beyond the borders of one's own country and investigate what differentiates it from other nations. Lectures about distant lands and life among exotic nations were extremely popular and well attended.[25]

At this time, world travel was the privilege of well-educated white men. The Slayton Lyceum Bureau organized lectures for a few such globetrotters. Among the most popular speakers was one G. W. W. Baily, who had lived in China for many years and was well acquainted with the life and culture of the Chinese. Among his offerings were lectures titled "The Geography, Population, Language, and Literature of the Chinese," "Chinese Religion," and "Government, Law, Jurisdiction, and Punishment in China."

Baily gave 150 to 200 lectures a year on average, his popularity due in large part to the fact that he appeared on stage disguised as a Chinese man, claimed his name was Tank Lee, and showed the audience a collection of Chinese treasures and works of art.[26] Audiences adored Tank Lee even though he was clearly an American and made no particular effort to hide the fact. Only a few foreigners from such exotic lands were well enough educated and spoke good enough English to be able to give public lectures about their homeland. Olof Krarer was thus unique in many respects. She was born and raised in Greenland, an Eskimo who described the culture and life of Eskimos firsthand. She also had a gift for storytelling and captivated her audiences with her accounts of adventures in remote Greenland and Iceland.

Ólöf's Popularity

"I remember the little Eskimo lady, Miss Krarer. . . . She was an excellent attraction who always made good with her audiences, and besides, she was a good box office feature," said S. Russell Bridges of Atlanta in a letter to Vilhjálmur Stefánsson in July 1938.[27]

Ólöf quickly became one of "the best known lecturers ever to have stepped on stage" and was particularly popular with scientific societies.[28] She was constantly traveling to speaking engagements and gave her lecture on the Arctic more than once in many cities. In her lecturing career, which spanned more than twenty years, she spoke about 2,500 times. She lectured nine times in New York, for instance, seven times in Brooklyn, and five times in Jersey City in New Jersey. She spoke three times in Syracuse, six times in Baltimore, five times in Aurora, Illinois, five times in Cleveland, three times in Mt. Pleasant, Iowa. She gave fourteen lectures in her home city of Chicago, but she set her record in Elisha Kent Kane's hometown of Philadelphia. Philadelphians never seemed to get enough tales from the Arctic, and invited Ólöf there eighty-three times.[29] Later in her career, Ólöf offered two new talks, one on missionary work in Iceland and another on the most remarkable things she had seen in America. Neither of them is believed to have been preserved.[30]

Ólöf, Better Than a Fallen Star

Ólöf's arrival attracted attention everywhere, and local newspapers often gave her glistening reviews praising her acuity, sense of humor, and narrative gifts.

The following example appeared in the *Brooklyn Daily Eagle:*

The hall of the Young Men's Christian Association was well filled last evening by an audience gathered to hear the lecture of Miss Olof Krarer, an Esquimau lady from the eastern shores of Greenland, her subject being "Greenland, or Life in the Frozen North." Miss Krarer

A Greenlandic love poem that Ólöf often sang

is the only Esquimau lady in the United States, and her lecture was unusually interesting. Not the least interesting feature of the entertainment was the little lady herself.[31]

The *Newark Evening News* had this to say:

An appreciative audience greeted Miss Olof Krarer, the Esquimau lecturer, at the Irvington rink last night. She is a pleasant-faced little woman, only three feet five inches in height and weighing 120 pounds, who left Greenland with a party of Icelanders.[32]

A journalist in Decatur, Illinois, praised Ólöf's sense of humor:

Olof has learned to speak English very well. She has quite an unusual appreciation of fun, and always enjoys telling of the hundred-and-one questions people are constantly firing at her.[33]

In Manchester, Iowa, the local newspaper's critic made the following observation on Ólöf's lecture:

The Lecture on Greenland by Miss Olof Krarer at the city hall last evening in aid of the Orphans' Home was one of the most interesting and instructive lectures ever heard in this city.[34]

A journalist in Vicksburg, Mississippi, wrote the following about Ólöf's lecture in that city:

> Miss Olof Krarer's picture of life from a Greenlander's standpoint afforded . . . a unique experience. . . . She is scarcely taller than a ten-year-old girl, a neat, trim, plump little woman, with very bright eyes, and a countenance that has nothing unfamiliar in its appearance. . . . Miss Krarer displayed much humor in her lecture and her naïve apology for the lack of a portion of the ordinary attire of a Greenland woman—the trousers—was very amusing. Hers is a plain, unvarnished story, that of a sensible, educated woman, depicting the terrible conditions of life around the North Pole. It was deeply interesting, however, and the audience frequently applauded her. . . . The lecture was given under the auspices of the Circle of the Silver Cross, King's Daughters, and was a financial success.[35]

A reporter for the *Star and Sentinel* in Gettysburg, Pennsylvania, said that "the little lady has a peculiar sense of humor, and during the closing portion of her lecture, answered all questions put to her, and often her replies were pointed with bright wit and a keen sense of the ridiculous."[36]

Ólöf's story of Eskimos' attitude towards hell was typical for her sense of humor. She said that

> the Christian ideas of heaven and hell would have to be modified before any attempt was made by missionaries to Christianize her people. Otherwise, she said, she was afraid that their fancy would be so captivated by the reputed temperature of the bad place that they would all want to go there at once.[37]

In March 1892, the following paragraph was published in the *New York Times:*

Miss Olaf [*sic*] Krarer delivered her lecture on "Greenland; or, Life in the Frozen North," last evening at the Second Reformed Presbyterian Church, in West Thirty-ninth Street. The lecture was for the benefit of the Indian missions and drew out a very fair audience. Miss Krarer is pretty well known to the general public, having been lecturing for something like four years.[38]

A reporter for the *Herald and Torch Light* in Hagerstown, Maryland, could barely contain his joy over Ólöf's presence in the United States. He said:

For a year or more there has been a "stranger within our gates," whose story of life in her native land is so fascinating and wonderful that had she dropped from some cold, starry planet in the Northern skies her presence would be hardly more marvelous.[39]

Olof Krarer's Influence

Ólöf's lectures and writings on the life and culture of Eskimos had far-reaching influence, and they were soon accepted as general knowledge of the Inuit among Americans. In November 1893, a teacher named Mrs. E. A. Carnahan from Coshocton, Ohio, gave the lecture titled "Getting a Start in School" at a teachers' conference in Zanesville, Ohio. In her lecture, Mrs. Carnahan presented her newly developed teaching methods. The lecture attracted such attention that it was published in its entirety in Coshocton's newspaper, the *Democratic Standard*, a week later.

Mrs. Carnahan said that teaching in elementary schools was almost entirely concerned with teaching children reading, writing, and arithmetic, and that this was of course important and good. However, teachers neglected to foster their students' imaginative and reasoning capabilities and their wish to explore and investigate their immediate surroundings. If these aspects were better developed, students would have a far easier time learning the fundamental subjects: reading, writing, and arithmetic.

She then described her teaching methods and said that the alphabet had come to life and become much more interesting when she had had her students make a work of art out of each letter. She had never seen

*Olof Krarer, a nobly
born aristocrat*

children happier than when they were allowed to investigate an insect in a bottle and observe its development and behavior through a magnifying glass. She also considered biographies an ideal medium with which to excite students' interest in the culture of foreign nations. Her students had a particular interest in hearing about "savages," especially the Inuit. She had them investigate sources and find out how Inuit children lived, what sorts of boats and sleds they owned, how they hunted, and in what kind of houses they lived. She then made Inuit dolls and sleds from cardboard, drawn by clay dogs, and finally she read for the students the biography of the little Esquimaux Lady, Olof Krarer. The children sat transfixed while she read Olof's story and were at a loss for words when they heard of Eskimo parents' cruel punishments.[40]

The textbook *Eskimo Stories* was published nine years after Mrs. Carnahan gave her lecture and was an extremely popular and widely read textbook. Vilhjálmur Stefánsson later leveled severe criticism at the Teachers' College at Columbia University in New York for promoting ideas about Greenlanders that were largely inspired by Ólöf. He asked one Miss Switzer, a teacher in the college, where these ideas originated. She investigated the matter and concluded that the ideas could be traced back to Ólöf's chapter in *Eskimo Stories*, which Miss Switzer had read in elementary school.[41]

It is rather ironic that Ólöf's assertions should have been valued so highly within the same university where one of the foremost experts in the field of Inuit studies, the anthropologist Franz Boas, conducted his research. His book *The Central Eskimo* was published in 1888, a year after Ólöf's biography was released.[42]

In 1910, *Harper's Bazaar* published an article on Eskimo courtship rituals and their treatment of the terminally ill. The author of the article was clearly well versed in Ólöf's biography. Newspapers across the country published fragments of these descriptions for their readers' entertainment, among them the *St. Petersburg Times* in St. Petersburg, Florida.[43]

A Nobly Born Aristocrat

Ólöf clearly earned herself a place among the most important lecturers in the United States, and was a respected authority on Eskimo culture and life. But what did Ólöf think of being in this company? How did she feel when thousands flocked to hear her speak in every important city and town in the United States, many of them more than once? What was her impression of stepping up to the podium at Cornell University or Indiana University? What was it like for her to sit down with Mary E. E. Smith, the author of *Eskimo Stories*, and give her advice on how best to improve the text of her book? Did she feel like a thief in Paradise, amused at her own cunning in garnering this place in a world where she did not belong? Or did Ólöf feel that she had finally earned the respect she deserved?

Diane Arbus, an American photographer famous for her photographs of people with physical and mental disabilities, has said that disabled people are the one true nobility, and that "there's a quality of legend about freaks." Healthy people, Arbus maintains, live in constant fear of getting into difficult situations and having to overcome severe challenges. Life with disability, on the other hand, is a constant struggle. Like protagonists in fairy tales, disabled people have solved all problems and overcome all challenges, and they possess the inner peace and dignity of aristocrats.[44]

We will never know with any certainty how Ólöf felt in the upper-class world that she lied her way into. But one thing is certain: Her appearance and manner were transformed when she moved from her time as a dwarf in the circus to her career as the only Eskimo on American soil. In pictures from that later period, Ólöf carries herself like an aristocrat of noble birth.

Liar, Liar

Was Ólöf a Compulsive Liar?

Ólöf wasn't just a liar; she was a liar of epic proportions. She lived most of her life, over fifty years, on lies, which inevitably gives rise to the question of whether she had some psychological disorder that might explain her behavior.

A difficult upbringing often causes individuals to resort compulsively to lies in order to attract attention and avoid trouble. As is discussed in earlier chapters of this book, financial and emotional insecurity were ever-present in Ólöf's childhood home. Her parents had continuous financial difficulties, and her father, Sölvi Sölvason, was a womanizing reveler who had an affair with the household maid. Ólöf's mother left the household and the family fell apart. Ólöf was sent to a foster home with strangers at the tender age of nine, and her mother died in an accident three years later. From that point onward, there was no woman left alive in Ólöf's nuclear family who could provide her with emotional safety and security. Being a dwarf can hardly have improved these already dire circumstances.

In view of Ólöf's childhood experiences, it does not seem improbable that the seeds of a personality disorder may have been sown in her breast at an early age. Close scrutiny of her behavior certainly reveals some of the symptoms of the type of personality disorder that emerges as excessive self-absorption. Like Ólöf, individuals who suffer from this disorder have often been neglected emotionally as children.[1] They are highly egocentric and demand constant attention and adulation. They have low self-esteem and long to lead a better and more exciting life.[2] In order to cast a favorable light on themselves and win the respect of others, these individuals often compose very convincing and powerful autobiographies cunningly intertwining facts and lies, dramas in which they themselves are the protagonists and their adventures run the gamut: tragedy in childhood, famous relatives, heroism in warfare, abuse at the hands of enemies, and degrees from respected universities.[3]

No descriptions of Ólöf as a child have survived, but it is probable that she suffered from an inferiority complex. Ólöf's life in Iceland was monotonous and dull, and her active imagination probably drove her to dream about a better life elsewhere. There are no indications, however, that she composed fabulous lies to attract people's attention and adoration as a child. Ólöf's family emphasized that she was not the lying kind. Quite the contrary: They said that Ólöf, who was of "more than average" intelligence, had always been a good, virtuous, and honest girl.[4] It seems that it was not until she came to America and discovered the magical power of lying that Ólöf took it into her service and composed her incredible autobiography. Thus it was an urge for self-preservation, a desire for a better life, and her courage and audacity, rather than an unhealthy compulsion, that prompted her to lie.

Ólöf was also very sensitive and quickly determined where the wind was blowing and what opportunities there were for a woman like herself. Stories of the Inuit were extremely popular among Americans at this time, but the individuals who knew their culture and had experienced their way of life could be counted on the fingers of one hand. Ólöf sensed the call of the times, donned her disguise as the Esquimaux Lady, Olof Krarer, and began to entertain Americans with bizarre stories of her life and relatives in northernmost Greenland.

Another indication that Ólöf was not a compulsive liar is the fact that her story remained consistent for so long. Compulsive liars are often self-destructive; they change their lie and add to it when challenged or when listeners point out inconsistencies in their story, thereby revealing themselves to be liars.[5]

This happened to both Archie Belaney (1888–1938), who masqueraded as Grey Owl, and Sylvester Long (1890–1932), known as Buffalo Child Long Lance. Both men contradicted themselves often and were publicly suspected of fraud more than once. Both were alcoholics, spent their lives in continuous flight, and died young. Long Lance committed suicide at age forty-two, and Grey Owl died when he was fifty.[6] Ólöf, on the other hand, had an unwavering thirst for life. She did everything in her power to remain on the path to success that her lies had opened up for her, she never contradicted herself, and she lived to the age of nearly seventy-seven.

Still, Ólöf's life was not without fear, and she had to take various precautions to prevent being exposed.

Ólöf's Memory

When Ólöf first disguised herself as an Eskimo, she discovered a way to improve her station in life dramatically. Still, it must have been clear to her from the beginning that she was in constant danger of being caught in the act. To prevent such a calamity, she took numerous precautions and employed a variety of clever tricks.

A good liar has to have a good memory to ensure that he sticks to the same story, as a small change to the lie can be his downfall.[7] Ólöf had a mind like a steel trap, and her story changed very little through the years. Three versions of her story are preserved. The first and the most detailed is the biography recorded by Albert S. Post and published in 1887. A second, shorter version was published in *Eskimo Stories.* It was published in 1902 and deals only with Ólöf's life in Greenland. A young, up-and-coming writer from New York, John Schoolcraft by name, recorded the third version in 1921. Schoolcraft met Ólöf in Battle Creek, Michigan, where she lived at that time, and was so enchanted with her story that he decided to record it for publication.[8]

Important Changes to the Story

The principal changes that Ólöf made to her story were numerical. In the first version of her biography she said that six Icelandic fishermen were stranded near her village, but in the 1921 version there are only two. In the first version Ólöf claims to have been fourteen when she left her homeland, but in the final version she is sixteen. In the first version Ólöf describes having had a major growth spurt after coming to Iceland, but says she still never reached her father's height. In 1921, however, she describes the growth spurt as having been so powerful that she surpassed her father.[9]

Ólöf also made a few substantive changes to her story. The most important one concerned the fate of her family and her move to America with her father. In the first version of her biography, Ólöf said that her mother had died of tuberculosis shortly after arriving in Iceland. Ólöf and her father had then left for America, and her seven siblings now waited in Iceland for a chance to join them. In the 1921 version, she maintains that her mother and siblings all died after arrival in Iceland because they couldn't adapt to the climate. To save Ólöf and her father from the same fate, Icelandic missionaries had entrusted them to a group of Icelanders who were going to Canada.[10]

This change to Ólöf's story is quite interesting, since by this point she must have been seriously concerned that she might be exposed. By 1921, transportation between Iceland and North America was vastly improved over what it had been in 1887, when her biography was first published. It is as if Ólöf feared that some enterprising individual might go to Iceland and try to find her relatives. The safest option was to put her entire family six feet under.

The modifications to her story occurred over a long period of time, and apart from the changes to her family's fate, they tended to center on numerical details of the sort that audiences rarely memorize.

Eskimos' Dirtiness and Skin Color

Many other things could have led to Ólöf's being exposed, including her appearance and build. She had dirty blonde hair, blue eyes, and fair skin.

Four Inuit women with their children

In most people's eyes, "savages" like the Inuit were dark-haired and dark-skinned. Ólöf could have employed the same method as the Englishman Grey Owl, who dyed his hair black and his skin brown in order to look like a Native American. But as has already been described, Ólöf played a more daring game. She kept her appearance unchanged and boldly told audiences that Eskimos were fair-skinned by nature. This came as quite a shock to her listeners, who considered fair hair and blue eyes to be one of the principal characteristics of people of Germanic and Anglo-Saxon descent. But Ólöf was quick to set things right with her audiences, adding that although Eskimos were naturally fair, they were also born and bred to a messy way of life, and their dirtiness made them dark after all.

Ólöf's description of Eskimos' dirtiness was in all respects consistent with other published descriptions at this time. In *Children of the Cold*, Frederick Schwatka describes Inuit children as follows:

> Most of the Eskimo children have red cheeks, despite the dark hue of their faces, and though they are rarely free from dirt. Yet, the chil-

dren's faces are generally neater than those of the "grown-up" people, many of whom look really horrible, as they never wash their faces.[11]

In her books about Greenland, Josephine Peary also frequently made reference to the Greenlanders' poor hygiene. According to her they never bathed and smelled downright horrible.[12] They never cleaned their houses, and the smell of rot wafted out the doors. Mrs. Peary went much farther than Ólöf in her descriptions of Greenlanders' dirtiness and appearance. At one point, she described them as "the queerest, dirtiest-looking individuals I had ever seen. Clad entirely in furs, they reminded me more of monkeys than of human beings."[13]

In the textbook *Eskimo Stories*, author Mary E. E. Smith dedicates one chapter to Eskimos' lack of hygiene. The chapter is entitled "No Soap, No Towels, No Water." As is mentioned earlier, the book was written primarily in verse, and this chapter's poem contains the assertion that Eskimo children are born with nearly white skin, but because of a lack of soap and water in the Arctic they never bathe. Within a short period of time, their faces then become dark from grease and dirt. If children in Western countries had neither water nor soap nor towels, they would meet the same fate. At the end of the poem, Mary E. E. Smith instructs her American pupils to imagine what it would be like to be an Eskimo. The verse is as follows:

Suppose we were you,
And you were we.
But oh! how dreadful
That would be!
If we were you,
And you were we,
Then we the unwashed
Folks would be![14]

In view of all this, it is no wonder that people didn't doubt Ólöf's explanations of Eskimos' fair-skinned appearance, as she was the only Eskimo who had ever taken a bath. A reporter in Detroit was completely convinced of the veracity of Ólöf's tale even though she looked quite a bit like the German-born maids he met daily on the streets of Detroit.[15]

Childrearing and Stature

Ólöf had short and knotted arms, which are a particular symptom of her kind of dwarfism. She was aware that audience members who knew something about dwarfism would realize this. As a consequence, she needed a good explanation for her strange arms, and she chose to blame the cruel childrearing methods of the Eskimos. Ólöf said that Eskimo children were rarely permitted to play and had to sit on the floor with their arms crossed day in and day out, all year round. Here Ólöf was skating on thin ice, as the games of Inuit children were described in detail in most books about the natives of the Arctic. In his best-selling *Arctic Explorations* from 1856, Elisha Kent Kane describes his surprise and delight at seeing Inuit children play:

Strange that these famine-pinched wanderers of the ice should rejoice in sports and playthings like the children of our own smiling sky, and that parents should fashion for them toy sledges, and harpoons, and nets, miniature emblems of a life of suffering and peril! how strange this joyous merriment under the monitory shadow of these jagged ice-cliffs! My spirit was oppressed as I imagined the possibility of tarrying longer in these frozen regions; but it was ordinary life with these other children of the same Creator, and they were playing as unconcerned as the birds that circled above our heads.[16]

An Inuit family by a "tupik" or summer tent

Frederick Schwatka's *Children of the Cold* also devotes an entire chapter to detailed descriptions of the games and toys of the Inuk boy Borea.[17]

Ólöf was doubtless familiar with these descriptions; however, like a good liar, she didn't let them influence her but stuck to her story and found that it didn't cause her problems. Quite the contrary: Her short and knotted arms were considered a unique example of the mutual influence of nature and nurture on the evolution of man. A journalist in Mt. Pleasant, Iowa, had the following to say about Ólöf after hearing her lecture:

> As a psychological study, the little lady from Greenland . . . is proba-
> bly unexcelled on this continent; and as a study in heredity or the
> influence of vocation and environment for successive generations
> upon the body she is equally so.[18]

Ólöf: Eskimo and Icelander

Ólöf employed another remarkably clever trick to secure her position, for she presented herself as not only an Eskimo but an Icelander as well. She was born and raised in Greenland, and her body bore witness to that. But although she was a teenager when she left Greenland, she didn't reach adulthood until she was in Iceland. Eskimos were eternal children of sorts, illiterate and unable to count past ten. In Iceland Ólöf converted to Christianity, went to school, and learned to read, write, and speak fluent Icelandic. There she also learned general courtesy and cleanliness. The story of her time in Iceland also enabled Ólöf to use her given name. She told audiences that Eskimos only gave their children one name, like Westerners gave animals. Her Greenlandic name had been Olavar, which sounded like Ólöf, and so she was baptized as Ólöf in Iceland. Her father's Greenlandic name had been Krauker, which was changed to Krarer in Icelandic fashion and which Ólöf adopted as her surname. Her father had also been given the name Sölvi in Iceland, which meant "saved," so in Iceland her name had been Ólöf Sölvadóttir.[19] This enabled Ólöf to keep using her original name even though it was Nordic. In this way she avoided the danger of accidentally revealing her true name, a mistake that has brought many a liar to his knees.

This aspect of the story probably appeased Ólöf's conscience also. The lie did contain a grain of truth, after all, and by incorporating her Icelandic experience into her history she avoided having to hide her Icelandic origins. Instead she could take pride in her Icelandic heritage. This explains why Ólöf's career as a liar ran as smooth a course as it did. She often sang a short Icelandic song at the end of her speech and told her audience that she intended to go back for a visit soon. She never returned to Iceland.

Ignorance, Racism, Naïveté

There is no contesting the fact that Ólöf's tale was an enormous lie, and it will always be difficult to answer to any degree of satisfaction the inevitable question: Why did none of the thousands of Americans who heard her speak realize as much? Americans' ignorance of Inuit customs and life certainly played an important part. But it was not only ignorance that governed Americans' gullibility; there were darker forces at work. A good liar wins his audience's trust by playing to their prejudices and their fear of others.[20] And Ólöf played her act to perfection, pandering to Americans' prejudices against primitive, exotic nations.

The conclusion of the Civil War and the immigration of large groups of people from southern and eastern Europe threatened the position of the white American middle class. Ólöf's description of the savage behavior of the Eskimos was a good reminder to Americans to be wary of foreign nationals and simultaneously affirmed the superiority of the white race and of Western civilization. In her lectures, respectable Americans could breathe easier for a moment and bask in their superiority and that of their country. It was clear from Ólöf's manner of speaking and her convictions that she agreed with her audience about the superiority of the white man, and this should be no surprise. She herself had little in common with Eskimos, being descended from Nordic Vikings.

At the end of her lecture, Ólöf reminded her audience of the bounty of America, saying:

Americans, I think you do not realize your blessings in this great land of plenty, where you have so many fine things. Even here, I often see

Inuit in summer garb

sad faces, and hear words of discontent. Sometimes I am a little dis-
contented myself, when I see something I want, and think I cannot,
or ought not to, have it. But I soon get over that feeling when I remember my home in the frozen north, where we sat still through the
weary hours, shivering with the cold, choked by the smoke, and often
almost perishing with hunger.[21]

Then she added:

If I was to go back to my race of people, I would not be able to tell
them about what I see and hear in this country. They have not the
language to express the thought. They have seen nothing like a sewing
machine, or a piano. They have no materials to enable them to make
machines. They never saw a painting or a drawing. Their wild, rude
songs is all they have that is anything like music. They have no idea of
a book. They eat when they're hungry, and sleep when they're sleepy.
They are happy and contented *when they don't know any better.*[22]

It is clear that ignorance, gullibility, and Americans' ideas of their own
worth ensured Ólöf's success, but their naïveté was another contributor.

A man named William H. Stout attended Ólöf's lecture three times while he was a student at Indiana University in Bloomington. He said he couldn't recall a single voice of suspicion as to her origins, and that "college students then were not given to as much doubt as to the genuineness of people as they are now."[23]

The Slaytons Kept Quiet

Although the American public never suspected Ólöf, there was a group of people who assuredly knew the truth about her origins, but fortunately for her, these people stood to benefit from keeping quiet. First among these people were the Slaytons. When they hired Ólöf she was already famous as the only Eskimo in the United States, and they took her into their home in good faith that she actually was an Inuk. Soon after Ólöf moved in with them, they must have realized that she was not an Inuk but a Western dwarf.

Indications of this can be found in the Slayton Lyceum Bureau's introductory materials about Ólöf. In order to emphasize that she was a true Eskimo, she was said to have difficulty tolerating great heat and to have suffered greatly in the summertime when she first came to America. But the winters were easy for her, and on the coldest winter days she could go lightly clad on long excursions without feeling cold, while her traveling companions were bundled up in full winter clothing and still nearly froze to death.[24] It hardly needs mentioning that the bureau never discussed its other clients' physical fitness or tolerance of heat and cold.

Ólöf's small stature was also mentioned, and the fact that the Inuit were a short people was emphasized heavily. This seems to have been done in order to refute preemptively any suggestions that she was just an ordinary dwarf. The bureau's introduction of Ólöf also emphasized that she was extremely gifted and intelligent, neither of which characteristics were commonly associated with strange beings such as dwarves. A further part of the description ran as follows:

> At the close of her lecture any one in the audience is at liberty to ask her any proper questions concerning her life and native country.

Some of the ablest legal talent in the country have taken advantage of this privilege, but Miss Krarer is always equal to every occasion and emergency.[25]

The Slaytons also went to great lengths to protect Ólöf and reduce the probability that she might be exposed. They personally oversaw her bookings and organized her travels. Amy M. Weiskopf, who worked in Slayton's office, wrote in a letter to Vilhjálmur Stefánsson that she had never been aware of anything suspicious about Ólöf, but that hers might not be the most revealing testimony:

> I do not recall having heard at any time during my association with the Slayton Lyceum Bureau any suggestion or intimation that Miss Krarer was not an Eskimo. However, had there been, I would have been unable to form any opinion myself as I did not know Miss Krarer personally, as she came into the office not more then [sic] two or three times in the entire five years I was with the Slayton Bureau. All her business was transacted through the Slaytons, at whose home she lived.[26]

Mr. and Mrs. Slayton were respectable and honest citizens, and one must wonder why they didn't throw Ólöf out of their house as soon as they discovered the truth about her origins, but chose instead to help her cover her tracks and continue the deception. At this point they must have come to care for Ólöf and sympathize with her in her isolation and disability. They probably admired her intrepidity and courage as well. However, another probable reason is that Ólöf was an extremely popular and successful lecturer, and Americans couldn't seem to have their fill of stories from the Arctic. Ólöf was thus a source of considerable income for the bureau, and this was not something the Slaytons were eager to sacrifice. But the Slaytons' absolute faith in Ólöf's cunning and skills probably cemented their convictions. Ólöf may sometimes have had stage fright before her lectures, but once on stage she stood her ground and never let the Slaytons down.

The Pearys Also Knew and Said Nothing

Ólöf and Robert Peary were nearly the same age, Ólöf born in 1858 and Peary in 1856. Ólöf's lecturing career coincided almost exactly with the height of Peary's fame, and his expeditions to Greenland and the race for the North Pole stoked the fires of Ólöf's popularity.

Documents from Peary's possession number in the thousands and are spread among several document repositories, but are mostly unclassified and unregistered, and it is not known at this point whether or what kind of references to Ólöf might lie hidden there.

As is described earlier, Robert Peary tried his utmost to control the flow of information from Greenland at this time. All those who joined his expeditions had to sign a written statement pledging that they would never divulge anything about the expeditions, either orally or in writing. At the end of the journey they were required to turn their diaries over to him.[27]

Peary made these stipulations in part because he wanted to maintain a pristine image of his expeditions, which were generally perceived as a complete success.[28] No shadow was permitted to fall on them, as that might discourage individuals and institutions from supporting future expeditions. A further factor was Peary's refusal to accept public funds for his expeditions, as he felt that this would limit his freedom as an explorer.

Peary wanted sole possession of any income from books, articles, and lectures about his Arctic explorations. But he was a poor writer and disliked public speaking, and only as a last resort did he have recourse to these activities as a source of income.[29] In 1893, when he was forced to give lectures in order to raise funds, Peary spoke in many of the same cities as Ólöf. Many of her fans were certainly in the audience.

Although there is no documented evidence that Josephine and Robert Peary knew of Ólöf, it is highly unlikely that they were completely unaware of the Esquimaux Lady with the mousy brown hair and the blue eyes. She lectured about life in Greenland in all of the most important cities and towns of the United States, and her lectures were discussed in all of the principal newspapers in the country. They must have heard her mentioned, especially considering that the textbook *Eskimo Stories* by

Mary E. E. Smith, published by Rand McNally in 1902, was based largely on Josephine Peary's book *My Arctic Journal*. *Eskimo Stories* also contained a chapter on Ólöf's life, including her claim that Eskimos' sedentary lifestyle made their arms so short and knotted, and that all Eskimos were pale and blue-eyed at birth but became dark because they never bathed. It is possible that the Pearys never read Ólöf's chapter in the book, but they should at least have been aware that she couldn't be a true Inuk, because her skin color—one of the characteristics of her appearance that captured audiences' attention the most—was frequently mentioned in newspaper articles about her.

The Pearys had dwelled in Greenland for extended periods of time. They had intimate contact with Greenlanders, men and women alike, and were quite familiar with their build and skin color. A group of native women often came into the Pearys' home in Greenland, where they sat, scantily clad, and sewed skin clothes for the Pearys and their companions. Many of Peary's assistants were Greenlanders, and he himself had a love affair with an Inuk woman by the name of Ahlikasingwah. They had two sons together: Anaukaq, born in 1900; and Kali, born in 1906.[30] The Pearys were thus well aware that Inuit women were not blonde and fair-skinned, and that their arms were neither short nor knotted.

Like Ólöf, Josephine frequently discussed Greenlanders' lack of personal hygiene, but she knew full well that even if a Greenlander washed his hair every day it would never turn blond. In 1895, the Pearys took a young girl home with them from Greenland, and she lived in their home in the United States for a year. The girl had seldom bathed in her life, and found it difficult to accustom herself to washing her hair regularly. Her appearance was certainly improved by the regular baths, but her hair stayed just as dark as before.[31]

Ólöf's lectures were no threat to Peary's fame and success, however—quite the contrary, they supported his cause. Peary's Arctic explorations weren't intended solely to conquer distant lands and prove the superiority and courage of Americans.[32] They were also meant to improve the life and conditions of Greenlanders, who had survived in dismal conditions at the edges of the Earth for centuries. Ólöf's lecture demonstrated that their culture and living conditions were vastly inferior to those of West-

Ahlikasingwah, Robert E. Peary's lover and the mother of two of his children. The color of her skin and her physical appearance were clearly very different from Ólöf's.

erners. But Ólöf's success and popularity in the United States also testified to the transformative power of Western culture for primitive nations. In Peary's opinion, his arrival in Greenland improved the Greenlanders' living conditions. In the book *Secrets of Polar Travel*, he describes the improvements his arrival brought to their society:

> Conditions are now different among these people. Instead of lacking every accessory and appliance of civilization, every man and boy owns his canoe; there is an ample supply of cutlery, knives, hatchets, saws, cooking-utensils, and needles. All the men have their own repeating-rifles and breech-loading shot-guns and plenty of ammunition, and every hunter has wood for his sledge, his lance, his harpoon, and his seal spear. As a result of owning better weapons, the condition of the whole tribe has improved. The efficiency of the hunters is double what it used to be, thus insuring a more abundant food-supply and better clothing. Warmly clad and well fed, they can meet more easily with hardships which are their daily lot.[33]

Robert Peary, No Stranger to Hyperbole

There may be one further explanation for Robert Peary's decision not to expose Ólöf: He himself was far from innocent of stretching the truth. Because he relied on private contributions from individuals and institutions to fund his expeditions, he had always to keep his supporters hopeful and didn't hesitate to exaggerate his successes. According to Peary, his Arctic expeditions were a continuous victory march, and he rarely mentioned accidents, mistakes, and difficulties. He also provided incorrect destination coordinates on occasion and claimed that his expeditions had gone farther than they actually had.[34]

Peary was far from being the only one of his colleagues who did this. Exaggeration was common practice among explorers at the time, and there was a tacit agreement among them to remain quiet about inaccuracies in their fellow explorers' exploits. If they exposed their colleagues today, they might find themselves exposed tomorrow, and so it was better to remain silent.[35] And why, we might ask, wouldn't Peary have wanted to protect Ólöf in the same way that his colleagues protected him? Weren't they both working for the same Arctic cause and doing it immeasurable good, each in his own way?

Three Meteors and Six Greenlanders

Ólöf's unique status and importance as an Eskimo in the United States is perhaps best highlighted by the story of the six Greenlanders whom Robert Peary brought back from Greenland in 1897. In Greenland, Peary had heard of three meteors that had landed not far from the village of Cape York, where he had lived for a time. These meteors had been the villagers' principal source of iron for centuries and were called "The Woman," "The Dog," and "The Tent," the last being the largest of the three.

In 1895, Peary was once again in financial difficulties. He decided to bring the meteors back to the United States for fund-raising purposes, show them to the public, and then sell them to a scientific institution. Peary and his assistants managed to loosen "The Woman" and "The Dog" in their first attempt. Two years later, in 1897, they finally succeeded

The Inuk girl Aviaq and boy Minik came with Peary's ship, Hope, *to New York in 1897. Aviaq died within a year of arrival.*

in removing the largest and heaviest stone, "The Tent," and loading it into Peary's ship, the *Hope*. There it joined various other spoils, such as the bodies of several recently deceased Greenlanders, some of whom were old friends of Peary's whom he disinterred and brought along just before he cast off for home. He intended to sell the bodies to the American Museum of Natural History in New York for research.[36]

Also on board, however, were six Greenlanders who were very much alive: three men, one woman, and two children. Peary meant to deliver them, like the bodies, to scientists at the Museum of Natural History. There they were to dwell for a year while a team led by the anthropologist Franz Boas studied their culture and physiology.[37]

When *Hope* docked in Brooklyn, Peary disembarked the same day and headed home. But the day after the ship arrived, an exhibition of the meteor "The Tent" and the six Greenlanders was opened on board. In two days, twenty thousand New Yorkers paid the entrance fee to see the meteor and the skin-clad Greenlanders.[38]

When the show was over, the Greenlanders were placed in the care of employees of New York's American Museum of Natural History, and they were installed in a storeroom in the building's basement. The population of New York hadn't had enough of these strange creatures, however. They flocked to the museum and stared down into the Inuits' room through grilles in the floor. But the excitement ended abruptly when all the Greenlanders fell ill with pneumonia and were hospitalized. Within a year, four of them had died. One man recovered and returned to Greenland.[39] A boy by the name of Minik survived the ordeal and was placed in foster care with an American family. He later returned to Greenland but was unable to take root there, returned to the United States, and had a miserable life. His biography may be read in the book *Give Me My Father's Body: The Life of Minik, the New York Eskimo* by Kenn Harper.

This story clearly demonstrates how important it was to Peary to keep the American public's interest in Greenland and Greenlanders alive. His efforts weren't always successful, as the story of the six Greenlanders shows. Thus the healthy and active Esquimaux Lady, Olof Krarer, was a unique creature in America. She kept people's interest in the Arctic alive with her frequent lectures. So why make a fuss about the fact that she wasn't a true Inuk and didn't always tell the truth?

Icelanders' Silence in America: Sympathy and Shame

The Pearys' silence was extremely convenient for Ólöf, but there was another group of people who knew the truth about her and chose to remain silent: the Icelandic immigrant community. Their silence may be attributed partly to sympathy. They felt sorry for this dwarf woman and didn't wish to cause her to lose her means of employment. And they were also amused that a woman like Ólöf could live a good life by telling lies about Eskimos to Americans. But there was another, more important motive behind their silence: the shame that such a woman should be one of their own.

The Icelandic immigrants in America were no hicks. Granted, they had lived under the tyranny of the Danes for centuries and were a poor and undeveloped nation. But that did not change their origins or their culture: They were descended from nobly born Vikings who fled the tyranny of King Harald Fair-Hair in Norway and founded a free state in Iceland. Their language and culture were unique, as the Sagas of the Icelanders demonstrated. In the minds of many Icelanders, emigrating to America was a way to escape authoritarian Danish rule, and the founding of a republic in New Iceland a continuation of the Viking settlement of Iceland a thousand years earlier.[40] Icelanders in North America never looked on themselves as a minority group, but soon perceived themselves as the equals of other Americans of Anglo-Saxon descent.[41]

The Icelanders in America cared a great deal about their reputation in American society and could not abide any besmirching of their collective honor. The dwarf Ólöf did not conform to the ideal of the dignified Icelandic woman in any way, and the fact that she was a consummate liar made matters even worse. Therefore the best solution was to remain completely silent about her. Indeed, she vanished from Icelandic society soon enough, and was far from their territory when she began giving her lectures.

The West Icelanders usually paid close attention to their compatriots' successes in America and bragged about their good fortune in the newspapers and periodicals that circulated within the community. But Ólöf's name is nowhere to be found on the pages of these journals, and in the thousands of West Icelandic letters researched by writer Bödvar Gudmundsson, she is never mentioned.[42] The silence about her among Icelanders is near absolute.

There was one exception however. On March 5, 1892, the editor of the *Free Press* in Manitoba published an inquiry by a reader who was asking if it was really possible to walk on ice from Greenland to Iceland. The reader had read Olof's biography and being somewhat ignorant about geography wanted to know for sure if this was the case. An Icelander by the name of Jón Ólafsson, the editor of the Icelandic newspaper in Winnipeg, *Heimskringla*, obviously outraged by Olof's lies, responded immediately by a letter to the editor of the *Free Press* titled "A Greenland Yarn." There he stated:

> Sir,—You ask for information in this morning issue of your esteemed paper, about the possibility of walking over the ice from Greenland to Iceland. Now, Sir, I boast of being the best informed man in this country in all general matters regarding my native country, Iceland. And I most positively assure you, that the possibility of walking over the ice from Greenland to Iceland is exactly the same as walking from Manitoba to the moon over the rays of the rainbow. And this simply because the ocean between Iceland and Greenland never freezes over. . . . There has never come a Greenlander to Iceland. . . . A Greenlander simply has never been seen in that country. Miss Olof Krarer is simply a fraud.[43]

Mr. Olafsson's revelation that Olof was a fraud had no consequences for Olof's career. The news never made it across the border, and the Icelandic community remained silent like the grave.

But Icelanders weren't perfect, after all, and not all Icelandic black sheep disappeared as conveniently as Ólöf. When the behavior of Icelanders in America threatened their reputation, they joined forces in spite of interior conflicts and disagreements and defended their honor, all as one. This is well demonstrated in the case of Ingólfur Ingólfsson, a convicted murderer who was sentenced to death in Edmonton, Alberta, in 1924 for a crime he committed in a small town in Saskatchewan.[44] Ingólfur came to Canada in the year 1900, soon fell out of touch with society, and took a job as a migrant worker.[45] In 1924 he showed up penniless in a small town in Saskatchewan and ran into an old acquaintance, a Scottish farmer by the name of Hugh MacDermott. MacDermott hired Ingólfur as a day worker, and in the evenings the two friends often drank together at the town tavern. One evening, after the two of them had drunk quite a bit, they got into a fight over money matters and Ingólfur grew alarmingly loud. The tavern owner decided to call the police. When the police officers arrived, they ordered Ingólfur to leave town immediately, which he did. But his employer vanished as well, and a few days later his neighbors began wondering about his whereabouts and found him dead in the town well, clad in the same raincoat he had been wearing that night in the tavern.

Suspicion fell on Ingólfur, and he was soon found in Battlefield, a small town about 250 miles away. He had plenty of money and a few valuables from MacDermott's farm on his person. Ingólfur was charged with murder and found guilty. In accordance with the law, the case was appealed to the Supreme Court of Alberta, where the judgment was upheld and Ingólfur sentenced to death. His hanging was to take place three months later, in February 1925.

When news of Ingólfur's fate reached the ears of more successful Icelanders in Canada, it was decided immediately that the hanging must not take place. His execution would be a blight on the honor and reputation of Icelanders in the entirety of North America, so the courts' decision would have to be overturned. Time was short, and so a collection was started. Soon the Icelanders had amassed enough money to hire a good lawyer of Icelandic descent who managed to convince the authorities to reopen the case.

Ingólfur was a thief, of that there was no question, but he had not been proven guilty of murder. There were no witnesses to MacDermott's death, and no conclusive evidence was found to incriminate Ingólfur. This logic was effective, and the death sentence was commuted to a sentence of life imprisonment for robbery. Ingólfur's life was spared and the honor of the Icelandic community salvaged, if not entirely saved. The Icelanders still had difficulty accepting a convict as one of their own, and tried once more to intervene on Ingólfur's behalf. They collected still more money, hired another lawyer of Icelandic descent, and charged him with proving that Ingólfur was insane. This would make him immune on grounds of mental incapacity and would mean that he belonged in an insane asylum rather than in prison.

The lawyer did his best, but although Ingólfur was certainly somewhat crazy at times, he was far from insane. As it turned out, he was quite happy in prison and had no desire to move into the company of psychiatric patients.[46]

The story of Ingólfur Ingólfsson is recounted here because it increases our understanding of the West Icelanders' silence about Ólöf's life and work: Icelanders were fine, upstanding people, and in their ranks there should be neither liars nor murderers.

St. Petersburg, Florida

The Sale of the Slayton Lyceum Bureau

The Slayton Lyceum Bureau was founded in 1873. It was one of the first of its kind in Chicago and quickly became the largest and most respected such agency in the city. As time went on, however, the agencies grew in number. Competition increased, and by the turn of the century the Slayton Lyceum Bureau began to lose ground. Henry L. Slayton was growing older and his health was beginning to fail. But he was not yet ready to sell the bureau and retire. Instead he hired a young man who had a good reputation as an agent, Charles L. Wagner by name, to reinvigorate the business.[1]

Charles L. Wagner was born and raised in Shelbyville, a small town in Illinois. From an early age he listened to lecturers and entertainers who visited his town. Wagner was an enterprising young man, and together with a friend he started organizing lecture series in Shelbyville. The duo managed to attract such speakers as Helen Potter, Susan B. Anthony, Joseph Cook, and Col. Copeland, but the latter became so popular that he soon returned and gave another lecture in Shelbyville. Wagner and his friend made a tidy profit from these lectures, and Col. Copeland became a good friend of theirs. He encouraged them to continue in their business and helped them convince other respected lecturers to come to Shelbyville. One of these was the famous agnostic Robert G. Ingersoll, who lectured on the life of Abraham Lincoln with great success. Ingersoll liked Wagner so much that he made him his agent for the entire Midwest. Wagner managed Ingersoll's lectures until the latter died in 1899.[2]

Charles L. Wagner soon attracted a great deal of attention, comparable to that received by Major Pond in his time, when he founded the oldest and most respected bureau in the United States, the Redpath Bureau in Boston. Wagner was ambitious, intrepid, and daring, had considerable business acumen, and did well by his clients. Henry L. Slayton soon realized that Wagner was the ideal man to revitalize the Slayton Bureau. He hired him as a secretary and made him co-owner.

The Slayton Lyceum Bureau came back to life under Wagner's direction. He attracted many new talented individuals and brought back others who had been registered with Slayton but moved elsewhere.[3] The bureau began turning a healthy profit before long, and Wagner invested the profits in railway company stock on behalf of Henry and his son, Wendell. When he did so, he paid "cash for the entire amount," which was considered a remarkable feat at a time when many agencies were fighting to stay afloat.[4] The Slayton Lyceum Bureau was now in good hands, which was very convenient, as Henry and Mina Slayton spent the winters of 1904–8 in California on the instruction of their doctor. Henry was in poor health and had difficulty tolerating the harsh Chicago winters.[5]

In 1908, when the Slayton Bureau was flourishing, it was decided to sell the company. They did not have to wait long for a buyer. As soon as news got out that the bureau was for sale, the Redpath Bureau in Boston made an offer that Henry, Wendell, and Charles L. Wagner accepted. The sale of Slayton's company was finalized on Ólöf's fifty-first birthday, February 15, 1909.[6] This was probably pure coincidence, but Ólöf had certainly contributed amply to the company's success through the years. After selling the bureau, the Slaytons moved with Ólöf to St. Petersburg, Florida, where they were also very successful.

By this point in time, Wendell, the Slaytons' only son, was a divorced father of two. His ex-wife lived in Battle Creek, Michigan, with their two children, a daughter named Novella and a son, Philip.[7] But Wendell decided to join his parents and Ólöf and moved to St. Petersburg.

St. Petersburg, a Green Oasis

St. Petersburg is beautifully situated on the southernmost tip of the Pinellas Peninsula, midway between Tampa Bay and the Gulf of Mexico and about 270 miles south of Jacksonville. The town is like an island between the two bays, and as a result the climate there is much more temperate than elsewhere in Florida, especially in winter. Warm winds from the two bodies of water keep average temperatures between 62 and 68 degrees Fahrenheit, and in April and May they range between 71 and 75 degrees. It does not rain heavily in winter, with January being the wettest month at 21.3 inches of rain, and April the driest, at 11.8 inches.[8] St. Petersburg is located on the former site of a small fishing village, and fishing remains one of its principal industries.[9] The city is richly vegetated with a vast variety of trees, bushes, and flowering plants, and many kinds of fruit trees provide its residents with fruit all year round.[10] Birdlife in St. Petersburg is quite varied, and many exotic birds can be seen in flight, including white and brown pelicans, herons, ibises, and storks.[11]

The city's beauty and rich vegetation undoubtedly made a great impact on Ólöf, and it is quite possible to imagine her thinking to herself that she had arrived in Paradise itself.

Hotel Management

Henry L. Slayton's age and deteriorating health had been the primary incentives behind the sale of the bureau and the family's move to Florida. Yet Henry had no intention of retiring. He had been in Florida during the Civil War, was familiar with its natural beauty and mild climate, and saw the business opportunities entailed in Florida's probable future as a winter destination for northerners.[12]

Shortly after the Slaytons arrived in St. Petersburg, they began hunting for a piece of property in the city where they could build a hotel with apartments for potential winter guests. On March 31, 1909, exactly six weeks after the sale of the Slayton Lyceum Bureau in Chicago, the Slayton family purchased two plots of land at 255 Second Street in northern St. Petersburg. The location was ideal, on the northwest corner just past Williams Park, which was the heart of the city for decades.[13]

The Slaytons' business acumen was laudable, and they were well attuned to the changing times. They founded their agency just as the Chautauqua Movement raged through the country like wildfire. They moved to St. Petersburg and purchased property in town to build a winter hotel in 1909, the same year the first train of winter guests came south from New York.[14]

St. Petersburg, a Modern City

St. Petersburg was a young city. It was incorporated in 1888, the year the Slaytons hired Ólöf. As in Chicago, this coincided with the arrival of the railway network, and the train station in St. Petersburg was opened the same year the city was founded. The main advocate of bringing the railroad to the city was a Russian immigrant and entrepreneur Pyotr Alexeievich Dementyev, who took the name Peter Demens (1850–1919). Demens gave the city its name and chose the name of his home city in Russia, St. Petersburg.[15]

A gentle climate and easy railway access were important reasons for the city's popularity as a winter destination. But these factors alone were not sufficient to transform a small fishing town into a popular tourist resort. The winter guests wanted to enjoy every modern comfort, and the St. Petersburg authorities did everything in their power to make the city as modern as possible. The city was soon wired for electricity and telephone access, a telegraph center was built, and newspapers were published regularly. Good banks and business services were established, houses had plumbing installed, and streets were paved, enabling cars to drive easily through town.[16] A good garbage collection system was soon established, and strict health and hygiene rules were set. The city's streets and squares were unusually tidy and clean.[17]

Henry L. Slayton's Death and Seven Gables

Henry L. Slayton had been in poor health for many years, and about a year after the family moved to St. Petersburg he died unexpectedly at the home of his friend S. S. Sowen, who lived in Chicago. Slayton had been on business in his old home city when he caught a bad cold and took to his bed in his friend's home, where he died suddenly on June 9, 1910, at the age of sixty-nine.[18] Slayton's death was a serious blow for the family and could have marked the end of their business enterprises in St. Petersburg, but this proved not to be the case.

The roles of the sexes were very clearly defined in St. Petersburg. At that time, women could neither vote nor hold public office. They were meant to dedicate their lives to their household and children, and housewives were held in high esteem.[19] But Mina had followed her own path her entire life, and after her husband's death she didn't show the least hesitation. Her experience with business was long and rich. She had been the principal driving force behind the founding of the Slayton Lyceum Bureau and had been involved in its operation from the start, first as an elocutionist and later as the woman "behind her husband." Their son, Wendell, having grown up with the family business, possessed substantial business experience as well. Mother and son also had Ólöf on their side, and she pursued any job she took on with dedication. After Henry's death, Mina therefore continued undeterred with the construction of the winter resort.

The first section of the hotel was finished in 1913, just as the first organized winter trips came to St. Petersburg from the Midwest. The Atlantic Coast Lines railway company brought 200 sun-worshipping winter guests from Ohio and Indiana that year. A year later such trips became a part of the railway schedule, and winter guest trains arrived regularly throughout the winter, with an average of 1,500 passengers on board.[20] The Slaytons named the hotel Seven Gables for this distinctive feature of its architecture.

One of the Most Popular Hotels in Town

The population of St. Petersburg grew rapidly. In 1910, a year after the Slaytons and Ólöf moved there, the town's inhabitants numbered 4,127. Ten years later the population stood at 14,237, having grown by 245 percent. Only eleven other cities in the United States expanded as swiftly as St. Petersburg over this period. During the busiest part of the winter, the city was home to over 80,000 people.[21]

Seven Gables

Hotel rooms and rental apartments were in great demand, and Seven Gables soon became one of the most popular hotels in the town. It was extremely well situated next to Williams Park, and the guests at Seven Gables didn't even have to cross the street to enjoy all the park's pleasures. A husband and wife who were regular guests at Seven Gables for many winters and rented an apartment facing the park reminisced years later about how much they had enjoyed living there. They could sit by an open window and listen to a concert in the park, which was alive with excitement, and watch the goings-on below.[22]

The City of Sun, Youth, and Health

St. Petersburg soon earned itself the nickname "Sunshine City," and winter guests were promised that the city was governed by happiness itself and that everyone there was in the best of health. The city's climate and natural surroundings were said to possess great healing power, and respected physicians throughout the United States advised their patients, especially those suffering from lethargy and nervous complaints, to go to St. Petersburg to improve their health. Asthma, arthritis, and related diseases were also supposed to be completely cured by a stay there.[23]

The city was said to be particularly agreeable to older people, because in St. Petersburg time slowed down and continuous sunshine made people younger and lengthened the span of their years.[24] But the Sunshine City was first and foremost a city of youth, home of the young and energetic. Young people could be seen amusing themselves wherever one looked.[25]

The joy and contentment weren't self-perpetuating, however, and the city authorities and hotel owners had to ensure that the winter guests had plenty to keep them amused. All sorts of entertainment were available in the wintertime, and the offerings were comparable to the very best in the great cities of the United States. The city boasted an art club, a library, many theaters, auditoriums, and concert halls. There were also twelve churches in St. Petersburg.

From the turn of the twentieth century to the end of the 1920s, a series of lectures in the spirit of the Chautauqua Movement was held in St. Petersburg in late February or early March each year. The Chautauqua week was one of the main cultural events of the year and attracted the city's residents and winter guests, as well as people from nearby towns.[26] Many respected and popular lecturers and entertainers came to St. Petersburg during this week. Among them was senator and presidential candidate William Jennings Bryan, Ólöf's colleague and a former client and acquaintance of the Slayton family.[27]

Guests also amused themselves out of doors and could choose from among many athletic clubs, such as a sailing club, a tennis club, and a roque club. Roque was an American version of the English croquet. Croquet was very popular in America in the latter half of the nineteenth century. At the turn of the century, tennis became fashionable, croquet's popularity waned, and the game was close to dying out. A group of young men in Norwich, Connecticut, simplified the rules, dropped the first and the last letters of its name, and called the game roque instead of croquet. Roque soon became quite popular throughout the United States and was a sensation in St. Petersburg in 1912, when the city's roque club was founded. Every winter, thousands gathered in Williams Park to watch roque tournaments.[28] The city also had a few golf courses and golf clubs. Fishing was popular, as was sailing, and people could spend days at the beach, sunbathing and swimming in the warm ocean.[29]

St. Petersburg, City of the White

Not everyone was intended to enjoy the splendors of the Sunshine City. St. Petersburg had a large African American population, which lived in the southern part of the city. The African Americans constituted the bulk of the city's workforce and commuted daily to northern St. Petersburg for work. They were strictly forbidden to spend time there outside of working hours and were forbidden entry to all shops, clubs, gardens, and other public places in the northern part of town. After the workday was over, they had to leave as quickly as they could.[30]

Like the African Americans, Ólöf was considered to be of a different race than the city's white citizens, but her exotic origins did her no disservice. She was known throughout the city as Olof the Eskimo, but she had cast off almost all trappings of her origins.[31] She was fair-skinned, dressed according to the newest fashions, and carried herself in all respects like one of the upper-class women in town. Only her short stature and knotted arms suggested that she was of a different race than they. But that didn't bother anyone—at least not to begin with.

Wendell's Business

After the first stage of Seven Gables was completed, Wendell Slayton wanted to try his hand at other kinds of business. In 1915 he opened Florida Fruitland Realty, a real estate office that sold land for construction projects, at 428 Central Avenue, the main shopping street in St. Petersburg.[32] The real estate office was unsuccessful and soon closed. Three years later, in 1918, Wendell made another attempt at starting his own business. He founded St. Petersburg Business College at 341 Central Avenue, offering secretarial education and other subjects.[33] Wendell did not have his parents' knack for business, however, and the college closed within a year. From then on he dedicated himself completely to running Seven Gables and found plenty there to occupy him. In the years that followed, several apartment buildings were added to the property, and by 1928 they had reached a total of seven buildings containing forty-two apartments.[34] Mina, Wendell, and Ólöf lived in a spacious apartment in a house at the back of the property.[35]

Ólöf in St. Petersburg with a young friend. They are standing on the same step.

Ólöf: Esquimaux Lady Turned Electrician

After the Slayton Lyceum Bureau was sold and Ólöf moved to St. Petersburg, she continued giving lectures on Arctic life for the Alkahest Bureau for a time. The Alkahest Bureau had its headquarters in Atlanta, Georgia, and organized lectures in the South. The bureau was partnered with the Redpath Bureau, which had bought the Slayton Lyceum Bureau in Chicago.[36] Ólöf lectured mostly in the South, but there is no documented evidence that she gave her lecture in St. Petersburg.

Between her lecture tours, Ólöf worked at Seven Gables. The hotel had a large number of African American employees.[37] Ólöf did not perform ordinary tasks at the hotel, but studied electricity and laid and maintained the electrical wiring in the Seven Gables apartments.[38] In between lecturing and working as an electrician, Ólöf had plenty of time

Ólöf in front of Seven Gables. The years in St. Petersburg were some of the best of her life.

and ample opportunity to enjoy the leisure activities in St. Petersburg. She only needed to cross the street to be in the center of the city's social life in Williams Park. There she could meet people of all ages, women and men, and converse with them about topics of mutual interest. She could also join in games, try her hand at chess or whist, throw horseshoes, bowl, or watch young men compete at roque.

When Ólöf had had enough of games, she could sit by the musicians' stage and listen to the twenty-four-member orchestra that performed twice a day during the winter months.[39] She could then go down to the beach, take a seat in the hot sand, and enjoy the ocean breeze, stop by an ice cream store on the way home, rest on one of the famous green benches of St. Petersburg, which lined all of the main streets in town, and chat with her neighbors.[40]

In photographs from this time, Ólöf radiates joy and contentment, and the years in St. Petersburg were doubtless some of the best in her life. But nothing lasts forever, as Ólöf had discovered when still a child, and her ten years of paradise in St. Petersburg were soon to end in an abrupt and unexpected fashion.

Huldah Slayton

On October 5, 1918, Wendell Slayton married his second wife, a woman named Huldah Janssen from Davenport, Iowa.[41] Thirteen years younger than Wendell, Huldah was thirty years old at the time of their marriage. She was a strikingly beautiful woman, blonde and blue-eyed, tall, slender, and graceful.[42] She was an ambitious modern woman and had been an accomplished athlete during her youth in Davenport. After the onset of World War I, there was no man left at the high school in Davenport who could coach the school's football team, so Huldah took the position. During her stint as coach, practice was held indoors so that as few people as possible would find out that the team was being coached by a woman and not a man.[43] Shortly thereafter, Huldah moved to Chicago, where one of her places of employment was Hull House, a service center for poor immigrants.[44] Wendell and Huldah were married in Davenport, but after the wedding they settled in St. Petersburg, where she soon became one of the most prominent women in the city. Few causes were beneath her interest.

She was president of the charitable Interlock Club, and was president and sat on the Summer Activity Board of the St. Petersburg Woman's Club from 1927 to 1930. As president of the Woman's Club, Huldah oversaw the building of its $35,000 clubhouse.[45] She was also president of the eighth division of the Florida Federation of Women's Clubs and was a member of all the most important charities in St. Petersburg.[46]

Huldah and Ólöf

After she and Wendell were married, Huldah moved into Wendell, Mina, and Ólöf's home at Seven Gables. As Ólöf said herself later in her life, Huldah couldn't stand having this little woman in the household, and Ólöf's life soon became miserable.[47] She finally realized that she would have to leave the family and was placed in the household of Irving Stone, a wealthy industrialist, and his wife, Harriet, in Battle Creek, Michigan. The Stones had lived in St. Petersburg for a time and were friends of the Slayton family and Ólöf.[48] In addition to the couple, their grown daughter, Ethel, lived in the household, and in a census from 1920, Olof the Eskimo is registered as the Stone family's maid.[49]

It is difficult to say why Ólöf was not allowed to remain in St. Petersburg. By this time, in 1919, she had lived there for ten years, was well known in society, and should easily have been able to find a place to stay in the city. But Huldah couldn't stand Ólöf, and if Ólöf had remained in St. Petersburg she would probably have been a frequent guest in the Slayton household. This is probably a partial explanation of her expulsion from the city. But there may have been more at work here. It is not unlikely that Huldah soon discovered that Ólöf was not an Inuk but rather a Nordic dwarf. She would have realized that her in-laws had lived a good life off this woman's lies.

Ólöf, Mina, and Wendell had lived with the lie for more than thirty years and had grown accustomed to it. Huldah was probably more acutely aware than they that the danger of Ólöf's being exposed was always present, and she seems to have been unable to live with the tension accompanying such a risk. If the truth were to come to light, the Slayton family's reputation would suffer greatly for it, and the only way to avoid such a calamity was to get Ólöf out of town. Mina and Wendell knew their own guilt and probably had no choice but to send Ólöf to Battle Creek to guarantee the happiness of the married couple and preserve peace in the household.

Mina and Wendell had obviously become fond of Ólöf, who was over sixty years old by this point in time. They were concerned about her welfare, and it was no coincidence that they found her a place in Battle Creek, which was home to Wendell's ex-wife and two children, Philip and Novella. They knew Ólöf and surely kept an eye on her while she lived in Battle Creek.[50]

The Circle Closes

Huldah's arrival in the household almost certainly brought back painful childhood memories for Ólöf. When she was a little girl, the arrival of a new woman, Soffía Eyjólfsdóttir, in her home resulted in her parents' divorce and the disintegration of her family. Huldah's arrival had a similar impact on Ólöf's life, and while she must have been glad to escape Hul-dah's dominion, she was not happy to leave the household. Ólöf had lived with the Slayton family for half her life, or thirty-one years. Mina and Wendell were the only living souls who were near and dear to her. Her move to Battle Creek was tantamount to eviction.

Ólöf's life had now come full circle. She began her career in America as a maid, but rose like Cinderella from the ashes and conquered the kingdom with the power of her lies. There she reigned as one of the most popular lecturers on Eskimo culture for decades, and shared her audi-ences with some of the nation's most prominent scholars and artists. She earned a good income for herself and the Slayton family and lived a life of ease and contentment. But Huldah probably discovered that Ólöf was a liar and wouldn't relent until she had been sent back to the ashes in the far north of the country. So now, just as in the beginning, Ólöf stood on a stool and washed dishes for other people.

This experience was doubtless among the most difficult that Ólöf en-dured after she came to America. As an Eskimo, she had lived such a suc-cessful life that she probably forgot how insecure a life built on lies really is. But now she feared nothing more than being exposed. In order to pre-vent this possibility, she frequently repeated her story about how lying was an unknown phenomenon in Greenland, and Eskimos didn't know how to lie. It surprised her greatly, she said, that Americans, despite be-longing to such a cultured and developed nation, should lie. It later be-came a turn of phrase in the Stone family to say "This is Greenland" when someone wished to emphasize his or her sincerity.[51]

Ólöf also felt a continual need to repeat her story about life in Green-land and the adventurous journey to Iceland, reciting it for anyone who would listen. One of her listeners was the budding young writer from New York, John Schoolcraft, who met Ólöf when he was visiting his sis-ter in Battle Creek in 1921. Schoolcraft was so charmed by the story that he recorded it with the intention of preparing it for publication. His record was never published but served an important purpose nonetheless, as it was to result in the discovery of Ólöf's deception years later.[52]

It is testimony to Ólöf's conviction and skill as a storyteller that John Schoolcraft was so convinced by her story. But the story was no longer being told by a respected and popular lecturer of Eskimo descent. It was told by a desperate dwarf woman from Iceland who had been backed up against a wall by her lies and lived in constant fear of being discovered and cast out of society, alone and abandoned.

Alice Slayton

After Ólöf left St. Petersburg, the Slayton family's success continued. When World War I ended, the stream of travelers to St. Petersburg grew even more. Seven Gables expanded, with the number of apartments reaching forty-two in 1928.

In 1922, three years after Ólöf left the Slayton family home, Huldah and Wendell had their only child, Alice, who was the apple of her parents' and grandmother's eye.[53]

The Seven Gables business was booming, and Huldah was indefatigable in building the family reputation around town. In 1924, when Alice was just past two years old, the family held a roque contest in the little girl's name, and the winner was awarded the Alice Slayton Cup.

The Alice Slayton roque competition was held in early spring, lasted for a few days, and was very well attended. The city's newspapers paid close attention to it, and the *St. Petersburg Times* published the following piece on the finals:

> The seventh and final contest in the Alice Slayton cup series for 1924 was played on Saturday afternoon in the presence of a record crowd of enthusiastic fans. The contenders, William Edgar ("Scotchy") Thompson, of Brownsburg, Ind., and Edward George Krug, Rochester, N.Y., had each won three games—this brought the battlers to a final testing of their roque accomplishments. . . . "Scotchy" glided . . . to a win. Following the finish of the final contest the cup was formally presented to the winner. Little Miss Alice Slayton, the winsome daughter was present and called upon to confer honors upon the champion. So the little lady toddled out on the marled arena and with a smile that had a full column speech of sweetness and mischief in it daintily handed the cup to "Scotchy" and "Scotchy" smiled back his grateful regards.

It was a charmingly pretty episode. The little princess was given an ovation, the immense assembly standing—the gentlemen with hats removed.[54]

It was very much in the spirit of St. Petersburg to champion the young, beautiful, and mischievous Alice Slayton, whose blonde hair and blue eyes made her the very image of her mother. Alice's star continued to shine in St. Petersburg, and in her senior year of high school she was named the Class of '39's "most attractive" female student.[55]

The Wall Street Stock Market Crash

Alice Slayton lived in prosperity for the first few years of her life, but when she was four years old her family's fortunes began to change. In late August 1926, a hurricane tore through southern Florida, making a lasting impact on the state's economy.[56] St. Petersburg suffered less than many other cities in south Florida, but the Slayton family was hit hard by the hurricane. Shingles from the roof of the church across from Seven Gables were blown into the largest house on their property, damaging the roof and walls. After the incident, the Slayton family renovated the house, but the project was expensive and they had to draw on their savings to fund it. The family's financial situation took yet another turn for the worse three years later, when the Wall Street stock market crashed, wiping out nearly all their assets.[57]

The golden years of St. Petersburg were soon over. The wealthy northerners who had come there regularly in the wintertime, living high and spending carelessly, soon stopped coming. Many of them, too, had lost all their investments in the Wall Street collapse.[58] The Slayton family fought to stay afloat for the next two years and tried to keep Seven Gables running, but to no avail. In 1931 they lost the hotel to a man from Maine by the name of Bernard Gibbs. Gibbs leased the business to Wendell, and the family continued to live in the apartment at Seven Gables.[59]

Mina Slayton's Death

By this time, Mina Slayton's health had deteriorated sharply. She spent long hours in bed, and on September 19, 1932, eight days after her eighty-third birthday, she died in her home at Seven Gables after a difficult illness.[60] At the time of her death, Mina had lived in St. Petersburg for twenty-three years. An obituary appearing in the *St. Petersburg Times* the following day bore the headline "Year's Illness Ends in Death of Mrs. Slayton." Wendell, Huldah, Alice, and Wendell's two children from his previous marriage, Philip and Novella, both living in Battle Creek, were named as Mina's next of kin. No mention was made of Ólöf, although she had lived in Mina's home for thirty-one years. The funeral was held two days later, on September 21, 1932, at the Universalist Church on Mirror Lake Drive in St. Petersburg.[61]

The business at Seven Gables was doing poorly, and shortly after Mina's death Wendell and Huldah stopped running the hotel. Their marriage was suffering as well, and they divorced soon thereafter. Wendell moved back to Chicago, but Huldah and Alice remained in St. Petersburg, and Huldah supported them by working as a supervisor in a local rental apartment complex. Huldah died unexpectedly in April 1939 at only fifty-one years of age, just over a month before Alice graduated from high school. After her mother's death, Alice went to live with her maternal uncle, Walter A. Janssen, in Washington, D.C.[62]

After the Slayton family lost Seven Gables, the hotel was bought and sold a few times, but was finally razed to the ground in the summer of 1964. Thus vanished the last traces of the Slayton family's activities in St. Petersburg.[63]

Ólöf's Wealth

The Slaytons were extremely wealthy for most of their lives, but Ólöf's own financial situation is much less clear. The rumor among her Icelandic relatives was that she was very rich but extremely stingy and refused to share her wealth with others.[64]

Income taxes were not levied in the United States until 1913,[65] so it is difficult to document Ólöf's personal income while she worked for the Slayton Lyceum Bureau. She worked for the Slaytons for twenty-one continuous years, from 1888 until the bureau was sold in 1909. Ólöf earned a sizable income, but there are various indications that she had limited control over the money she earned.

Ólöf's disability made it difficult for her to live on her own and take care of herself. When she was hired by the Slaytons in Chicago, she could have lived on her own, hired an assistant, as she had done up until then, and used her income to pay her assistant and take care of her own needs. Instead, she accepted the Slaytons' offer and moved into their home at 25 Waverly Place. She was accustomed to such an arrangement, as she had lived in her employers' homes in both Iceland and Winnipeg.

Because Ólöf lived with the Slaytons, her financial situation was different than if she had lived on her own and received a negotiated salary. In official documents, she was defined as a boarder in the Slayton family's household.[66] It is quite unlikely that the Slaytons kept precise records of their expenses on Ólöf's behalf, subtracted them from her salary, and paid her the difference. It seems far more probable that she was treated as a member of their family, that she didn't simply work as a lecturer but was employed by the "family company," and that the distinction between her own interests and those of the Slaytons simply ceased to exist. Mr. and Mrs. Slayton were probably more like parents than employers to Ólöf, managing her finances and providing her with everything she needed and money for personal use. But a generous portion of the money Ólöf brought in over the course of a year probably went straight into the collective funds of the family and the company.

Ólöf had worked as a lecturer before the Slaytons hired her, and she knew full well that she was a substantial source of income for them. Everything seems to indicate that the Slaytons treated her accordingly. They took extremely good care of her and spared no expense in making her life as comfortable and pleasant as possible. The Slaytons were no less concerned than Ólöf herself that she be content, healthy, and industrious.

Ólöf seems to have been satisfied with her position with the Slayton family, but she probably realized that she couldn't make too many demands of them. She had lied her way into their household, and most likely they discovered the truth about her heritage shortly after she moved in with them. Fortunately for her, however, they decided not to turn her out of the house but trusted her and believed in her ability to keep up the act. Such faith was probably immensely precious to Ólöf. She had grown up in abject poverty and suffered emotional neglect, but now she was the center of the Slaytons' attention and concern. Last but not least, they gave her an opportunity to develop her storytelling and acting talents —and as Napoleon supposedly said, human happiness lies in the ability to develop and use one's talents to their full extent.[67] And under the Slaytons' protection, Ólöf rose to fame and fortune.

When the Slayton Lyceum Bureau was sold in 1909, the business was doing extremely well. It was sold for $60,000 dollars, the equivalent of about $1.3 million in today's currency.[68] This sum was divided equally among the owners of the bureau: Henry L. Slayton, Wendell Slayton, and Charles Wagner.[69] Henry and Mina Slayton took the profits of the sale and invested them in the construction of Seven Gables. Rumor had it that Ólöf invested a considerable sum of money in Seven Gables and had a vested interest in its success.[70]

It is quite possible that Slayton valued Ólöf's financial contributions to the company and considered her a co-owner of Seven Gables, but there is no legal evidence that she was a co-owner. Documents pertaining to the purchase of lots in St. Petersburg and records of loans and asset transfers concerning the Seven Gables business bear the names of Henry, Mina, and Wendell, and later Huldah. Nowhere is Ólöf's name mentioned.[71] But regardless of Ólöf's legal status vis-à-vis Seven Gables, she clearly put considerable effort into the business, even learning an electrician's trade in order to maintain its wiring.

For the first five years after Ólöf moved to St. Petersburg, she traveled in the South and gave lectures for the Alkahest Bureau in Atlanta. That income probably fell directly to her, and she may have put some of this money aside for her old age. She does not appear to have been in financial difficulty during the last years of her life, and there were resources available to pay for the years she spent in a nursing home and for her funeral.

The Death of Miss Krarer,
Eskimo and Former Lecturer

Ólöf's Last Years

Ólöf lived and worked in the Stones' home for eight years, from 1919 to 1927, but then her health and her eyesight began to fail, and she became largely unable to work. As the Stones were growing older themselves, it was clear that Ólöf could no longer live with them.

Although Mina and Wendell had sent Ólöf away from their own home, they still cared about her, and they helped the Stones find her a new home. Ólöf was placed with old friends of the Slaytons, the Edmunds family, who lived at 187 Lake Avenue in Benton Harbor, a popular summer community on Lake Michigan. Ólöf knew the Edmunds family from her time in Chicago, was far closer to them than to the Stones, and was more contented living there.[1]

The Edmunds family consisted of Edwin Edmunds, age fifty-three, vice president and chief financial officer of the Fidelity Insurance Company in Benton Harbor; his wife, Fanny, also fifty-three years old; and their son, Dix, a twenty-one-year-old student. The 1930 census lists Olof "Krayer," an Eskimo born in Greenland, as a maid in the household, but it is unlikely that she would have been much help.[2]

The Baptist Retirement Home in Maywood, Illinois, where Ólöf spent the last years of her life. It was then called Baptist Old People's Home.

After five years in the Edmunds household, Ólöf had become so sickly that she needed constant care. She was then placed in a nursing home for women, Baptist Old People's Home, a small and tidy establishment at 315 Pine Street in Maywood.[3] The Chicago suburb of Maywood, "Village of Eternal Light," was incorporated in 1881 and was still a small country town when Ólöf arrived there.

Wendell Slayton was living in Chicago at the time and was instrumental in getting Ólöf placed in the nursing home. His happiest days were now past. An only child, he had been his parents' favorite, had wanted for nothing growing up, and had worked for the family company most of his life. Now both his parents were dead and the family fortune gone, he was divorced for a second time, and he had severed all ties to Huldah and his daughter Alice.[4] He lived alone in a guesthouse, Hotel Lorraine[5] in downtown Chicago, and by this point in his life, Ólöf was one of very few people who were close to him. She had moved into his home when he was twelve years old, and they had lived under the same roof, with short interruptions, for over thirty years. It is clear that he wanted to do everything he could to ensure her comfort in the last years of her life. When she died he had a dignified funeral held for her.

Ólöf's Death and Funeral

Ólöf died of intestinal cancer on January 31, 1935, fifteen days before her seventy-seventh birthday, after having lived in the Baptist Old People's Home for two years and nine months.[6] She was born an Icelander in Iceland but died an Eskimo in America.

When Ólöf died she had not given a public lecture for about twenty years. Yet she was not forgotten, and the day after she died, the following report of her death appeared in the *Chicago Tribune*, the largest and most respected newspaper in Chicago:

MISS KRARER, ESKIMO, ONCE LECTURER, DIES

Miss Olof Krarer, 76 years old, an Eskimo woman who was born in northern Greenland and was 14 years old before she ever saw a white man, died yesterday in the Baptist Old People's home, 315 Pine avenue, Maywood.

For many years after coming to the United States miss Krarer was with a lecture bureau. She traveled about this country speaking on Greenland and its people. She was in this work thirty years before retiring.

Miss Krarer was only 46 inches tall, and said that the tallest man of her tribe was scarcely more than 4 feet in height. None of the tribe even knew that white men existed until a party of six Icelanders was shipwrecked sixty-two years ago near the Eskimo colony in Greenland, she said.

Funeral services will be held for Miss Krarer tomorrow at 201 Lake street, Maywood. Burial will be in the Oakridge cemetery.[7]

Ólöf's funeral was held on February 2, 1935, at Paul W. Senne's funeral parlor at 201 Lake Street, Maywood, a few blocks from the nursing home where Ólöf spent her last years. Dr. Frederick Franklin Shannon, a respected and popular minister at the People's Church in Chicago, officiated. In attendance were Wendell Slayton, the Edmunds family, and

Here lies Ólöf Sölvadóttir from Outer Langamýri as the Esquimaux Lady, Olof Krarer

probably others among Ólöf's acquaintances and friends from her years in Chicago and in the nursing home.[8]

Ólöf was buried in the Oakridge Cemetery at Roosevelt Road in Hillside, another suburb of Chicago southwest of Maywood. Her grave is in the southernmost, sunniest part of the cemetery, adorned with a simple, sober tombstone. Ólöf Sölvadóttir from Outer Langamýri lies there in the well-labeled grave of the Esquimaux Lady, Olof Krarer.

Funeral Director Paul W. Senne and Ólöf's Death Certificate

Wendell Slayton was not the only person at Ólöf's funeral who knew that she wasn't an Inuk but a Western dwarf. The funeral director, Paul W. Senne, had discovered the truth when Ólöf's body was placed in his care. But he was obviously aware that this was a sensitive matter and didn't care to create controversy at the time. He accepted the information on Ólöf's death certificate, which was filled out by Mrs. J. E. Replinger, the chief administrator of the nursing home, and recorded Ólöf's race as "Eskimo."

But Paul W. Senne was not entirely comfortable with this deception. A month after Ólöf's death he sent a correction to the Cook County Census Bureau with a correction of Item 4 on the death certificate, the race of the deceased. The original entry, "Eskimo," was changed to read "White."[9]

It was doubtless Paul W. Senne's honesty and conscientiousness that drove him to correct Ólöf's death certificate. But it is tempting to imag-

Ólöf's death certificate, where she is registered as an Eskimo. The certificate notes her date of birth as April 22 rather than February 15. In her last years, Ólöf feared few things more than that she might be exposed as a liar. It is possible that she gave a false date of birth as a precaution to make tracing her origins more difficult.

Paul W. Senne's correction of Ólöf's death certificate. She was now no longer an Eskimo in public documents, but white.

ine an additional motive. Ólöf was well known as an Eskimo, and it is probable that somebody would find out the truth about her origins sooner or later and draw attention to the false records. If this should happen, Senne's failure to recognize the difference between the body of an Inuk and a white dwarf would be a black mark on his reputation. His correction of Ólöf's death certificate protected him from such a loss of face.

Ólöf's deception was revealed a year after her death. But Paul W. Senne had no reason to fear for his honor, any more than the others who chose to remain silent about Ólöf. The exposure was kept quiet, and the next chapter investigates the reasons why.

Ólöf the Black Sheep

As is mentioned earlier in this book, the West Icelanders remained completely silent about Ólöf. Although they paid close attention to their compatriots' successes in America and bragged about their achievements in journals and newspapers, no reference to Ólöf appears in their pages.

After Ólöf left on her adventures, she remained in contact with her family, but in later years she gave the correspondence up entirely. Thorstina Jackson wrote to Ólöf's relatives and old acquaintances in Winnipeg to collect information about her for Vilhjálmur Stefánsson, but by that time, nobody knew where she was.[10] Ultimately, however, news of Ólöf's death did reach Icelanders in Winnipeg. At that time Ólafur S. Thorgeirsson published an annual Icelandic-language *Almanak* in Winnipeg, and each volume contained a column listing all known deaths of Icelanders in Canada and the United States. The announcement contained the name of the deceased and an account of his or her family heritage, origins, and place of residence and employment.

The announcement of Ólöf's death seems to have troubled the publisher somewhat. He clearly knew that Ólöf was an Icelander by heritage, had moved west with her people, and as such was part of Icelanders' colonial history in America. But she had brought shame to Icelanders in America with her lies. Thus it was not desirable to draw attention to her name. One possibility was to omit her name entirely, but this seems to have been contrary to the *Almanak* publisher's code of ethics. He chose to announce Ólöf's death but eliminate all personal information about her.

The announcement simply reads "Ólöf, woman, 76 years old."[11] Her family heritage and place of birth are not mentioned, her patronym was eliminated, and not a word was devoted to her life and work. In the eyes of the West Icelanders, Ólöf was clearly no man's child, her life a blank, and no memories associated with it.

According to Torfi Sveinsson, grandson of Helga, Ólöf's eldest sister, Ólöf's family and next of kin were extremely dissatisfied with her deception and avoided speaking of it. In Torfi's opinion, they were probably quite relieved that no more was made of Ólöf in the entry in the *Almanak*, as she was a source of shame to the family.[12]

Ólöf Exposed

Ólöf and Vilhjálmur Stefánsson

Being a successful liar is no mean feat. All liars, good or bad, need to have luck on their side. But everyone's luck runs out eventually. Most liars are eventually found out, and this was the case for Ólöf as well.[1] It was the famous Icelandic-born explorer Vilhjálmur Stefánsson who exposed Ólöf a year after her death.

Vilhjálmur was twenty-one years younger than Ólöf, born in New Iceland in 1879, two years after Ólöf left her home at Steinnes in New Iceland and went to Winnipeg to work. Vilhjálmur and Ólöf never met, but Ólöf knew his parents and older siblings. They made the crossing from Iceland to Canada on the same ship in 1876. Vilhjálmur's family, like Ólöf's, had originally intended to settle in Nova Scotia but ended up in New Iceland. Vilhjálmur heard stories of Ólöf as a child but had paid little heed to them. After he became an explorer, however, her name came to his attention on two occasions. The first was in connection with his discovery of a fair-skinned Inuit community on the north coast of Canada.[2]

Vilhjálmur Stefánsson and the Blond Eskimos

In 1908–12, Vilhjálmur spent four continuous years in the Arctic. He lived for a time among the Copper Inuit on the Minto Inlet on Victoria Island, off the north coast of Canada. The Copper Inuit are so called because of the beautiful copper artifacts they created. They had not communicated at all with Westerners, had no knowledge of firearms, and hunted with finely crafted bows and arrows. What made them particu-

Vilhjálmur Stefánsson
circa 1936

larly remarkable in Vilhjálmur's eyes was the fact that they were fair-skinned, and that among them there were people whose eye color and complexion indicated that they were "anything from one-quarter to three-quarters European." As the Copper Inuit had not communicated with Westerners in recent times, Vilhjálmur concluded that their fair appearance was due to interbreeding with Norse Vikings.[3]

The story behind Vilhjálmur's theory is as follows: As a student at Harvard University in Cambridge, he visited Iceland, where he heard the story of the Icelandic colony in Greenland* and became fascinated by its mysterious disappearance. He wrote an article on the fate of the Icelanders in Greenland, and it was published in *American Anthropologist* in 1906. The article was entitled "The Icelandic Colony in Greenland," and in it Vilhjálmur con-

---

*Translator's note: Norse settlement of Greenland began with the exile of Erik the Red (Eiríkur raudi) from Iceland in 982 CE. A few years later, a fleet of Icelandic ships joined him in Greenland, and over time two Norse settlements developed in South Greenland, called the Eastern and the Western Settlements, respectively. The Western Settlement was abandoned by the mid-fourteenth century, and the last confirmed reports of Norsemen in Greenland are from the early 1400s. An Icelandic ship landed in Greenland in 1540 and found no trace of the Norse community. To this day it remains uncertain how the colony died out; disease, the harshness of the climate, and strife with the Inuit have all been hypothesized.

cluded that the Icelandic colonists had died out. In his opinion, the Icelanders were less fit than the Greenlanders for living off the land and
therefore lost in competition with them. He did not think the Icelanders
and the Greenlanders had assimilated, as Greenlandic culture bore no
marks of Norse influence. Only one word in their language was shared:
kind, the word for sheep.[4]

After encountering the Copper Inuit, Vilhjálmur revised his position
and concluded that the Icelanders had not died out but that they had survived by assimilating into Greenlandic society. Their descendants had
then moved from Greenland to north Canada, where their heritage could
be observed in the blond Eskimos.[5] Vilhjálmur wrote to a close Canadian
friend, John Marvor, to inform him of his discovery. Part of the letter
was published in the *New York Times* in the fall of 1911, and the news of the
blond Eskimos did not garner much attention. But a year later, on September 9, 1912, a journalist with the *Seattle Daily Times* made the story
front-page news. The story of Vilhjálmur's discovery of the blond Eskimos, whom he believed to be descendants of Erik the Red, now spread
around the globe. Before long, explorers and scholars were engaged in intense debates about the validity of the theory.[6]

The Norwegian explorers Fridtjof Nansen and Roald Amundsen
criticized Vilhjálmur harshly. Nansen said Vilhjálmur was a trickster, but
Amundsen went farther and asserted that Vilhjálmur's conclusions were
"nonsense" and "a figment of the imagination." William Curtis Farrabee,
a respected professor of anthropology at Harvard, who knew Vilhjálmur
from his years as a student there, issued a statement to the effect that the
university's anthropology department had limited confidence in him as a
scientist.[7]

But Vilhjálmur also had his supporters. One of them was a professor
at Cornell University who wrote a letter to the *New York Times,* claiming
that Vilhjálmur's theory was far from ludicrous. He himself had had the
remarkable experience of meeting a blonde and blue-eyed Eskimo from
Greenland, Olaf [*sic*] Krarer by name. She had given a lecture about Arctic life at Cornell, and afterward he had hosted a party in her honor in his
home.[8]

An article appearing in the *Washington Post* on Sunday, March 16, 1913,
bore the headline: "Blond Eskimos Discovered Long Before Stefansson

Copper Inuit

Found the Tribe." The article begins by stating that there was no reason to make such a fuss about Vilhjálmur Stefánsson's discovery of blond Eskimos and his theory that native Greenlanders and Vikings had interbred. Vilhjálmur had not discovered anything new, and Viking-Greenlander assimilation was an obvious fact. If Americans just had a slightly better memory, they would have remembered the little blond, blue-eyed beauty, the Eskimo Olof Krarer.

Ólöf, who was described as unusually well educated for an Eskimo woman, had come to the United States and lived there long enough to learn good English. She had then become a respected and popular lecturer, traveled about the United States, and given lectures on her native Greenland. Anyone who doubted the veracity of this news was advised to read a six-page article about the blonde Eskimo woman in the journal *St. Nicholas*. The article had been published in August 1890, more than twenty years before Vilhjálmur Stefánsson made his contested discovery.[9]

Vilhjálmur could easily have exposed Ólöf at this time, but he elected to keep his own counsel. A desire to protect her may have played some part in his decision. But why should he expose her when she constituted a valuable piece of evidence in support of his theory about the blond Eskimos? It would not have improved Vilhjálmur's standing to expose Ólöf at that time. His reputation as a scientist had been undermined by his declarations about the Norse descent of the blond Eskimos. Exposing Ólöf would not only have revealed that she was simply a Western dwarf, but also that she was of Icelandic descent like Vilhjálmur himself. This could have led people to question whether lying was in all Icelanders' blood. The best choice, for the time being, was to remain silent.

Vilhjálmur's discovery of the blond Eskimos attracted worldwide attention, and this particular piece of news almost certainly reached Ólöf in Florida. We will never know her reaction to it, but Vilhjálmur's discovery was a double-edged sword for her. While it strengthened her position in the eyes of those who believed Vilhjálmur's theories, it also invited danger from the opposing faction. Those who doubted Vilhjálmur's theory might begin to doubt that the blue-eyed Esquimaux Lady, Olof Krarer, was actually a true Inuk. Still and all, this discovery by Vilhjálmur appears not to have made any impact on Ólöf's life in the paradise of St. Petersburg.

Ólöf Exposed

Ten years later, in 1922, Ólöf's name came to Vilhjálmur's attention a second time. He was then living in New York, and, like Ólöf, he made his living in part by giving Chautauqua lectures about his expeditions in the Arctic. Vilhjálmur employed a young secretary named Dorothy Daggett. One evening, Miss Daggett had dinner at the home of some friends, where she met John Schoolcraft, the writer who had been enthralled by Ólöf's story when he had met her in Battle Creek, Michigan. Schoolcraft told Miss Daggett that he was planning to publish the biography of this remarkable Eskimo, but she found something suspicious about his tale and recommended that he have Vilhjálmur proofread the biography before publishing it.

Schoolcraft took Dorothy Daggett's advice. Vilhjálmur immediately saw what was afoot and advised Schoolcraft not to publish the story. Schoolcraft's meeting with Miss Daggett was not entirely fruitless, however, as the two were later married.[10] Schoolcraft decided against publishing the story, but the manuscript is preserved in the library of Dartmouth College.

Thorstina Jackson

After this experience, Vilhjálmur was determined to expose Ólöf. He began by collecting information on her and engaged a West Icelandic scholar, Thorstina Jackson, to help him with his research. Together they contacted Ólöf's family, who agreed to provide information about her on the condition that nothing be published until after her death.[11] Ólöf died early in 1935, and Vilhjálmur did not sit idly by. The following year he published his book *Adventures in Error*, which contained an article on Ólöf.

Adventures in Error comprises eight essays. In writing the book, Vilhjálmur's concern was not only to correct people's misconceptions about the Inuit, but also to correct other misinformation that people believed blindly. The pickings were far from slim. One essay concerned false notions about childrearing. Another demonstrated that wolves do not travel in packs but in families, and a third stated that reaching the North Pole was not nearly as difficult as many believed. One article was harshly critical of Canadian geography textbooks, which Vilhjálmur considered to give a completely inaccurate picture of weather in the Arctic, as he had found that it snowed far less there than in southern Canada. The last essay in the book was a critique of Americans' gullibility. The American journalist H. L. Mencken had written a satirical story about how the first bathtub was brought to America. Americans had swallowed his story whole, and his article was now referenced as a scientific source document in American historical journals. Sandwiched in between these last two articles was Vilhjálmur's report about Ólöf, exposing her monumental lies. The title of the article is simply "Olof Krarer," and his discussion of her career reveals both anger and sarcasm. He repeatedly refers to her as "pathetic."[12]

In his article, Vilhjálmur traces Ólöf's family heritage and career. It includes a chapter from John Schoolcraft's biography and Ólöf's chapter from *Eskimo Stories*, the latter of which offended him particularly. Vilhjálmur had spent long years in Arctic Canada and considered it his calling to dispel Western misconceptions about the Arctic and its inhabitants. But it was difficult to defeat such prejudices when millions of schoolchildren in the United States were required to read *Eskimo Stories*. *Eskimo Stories* was still a popular textbook, and American elementary school teachers heeded the advice of its author, Mary E. E. Smith. They had their students begin by reading Ólöf's chapter, as its author was a "native Eskimo." Thus millions of American children received Ólöf's story as incontrovertible fact. Most of them read little about the Inuit later in life, and believed Ólöf's lies for the rest of their lives.

The Critics' Silence

When Vilhjálmur and Thorstina Jackson began collecting information on Ólöf, they hoped the exposé would attract widespread attention.[13] On the contrary, their revelation was met with silence. *Adventures in Error* was well received in general and was covered in several important newspapers and one scientific journal.[14] But none of the critics saw fit to mention Ólöf by name or discuss her thirty-year career as one of the most respected and popular lecturers on Eskimo culture in the United States.

A few critics discussed Ólöf and her lies about the Inuit indirectly. M. Persis Johnson wrote a review of *Adventures in Error* for the *Boston Evening Transcript*, praising the book and describing Vilhjálmur as intelligent, rational, and possessed of a subtle sense of humor. He added that many storytellers and even historians had taken advantage of ignorance about the Inuit, describing them as strange creatures who lived in houses made of snow on a long, narrow, snow-covered spit of land, living on raw meat and fish oil. This was all wrong, Johnson said: Only a small minority of the Inuit had ever seen a house made of snow, let alone lived in one.[15] An anonymous critic for the *Springfield Daily Republic* also referred to Ólöf indirectly when he emphasized that Inuit mothers did not carry their children in a hood on their back, nor did the Inuit live in houses made of snow.[16]

The longest and most detailed review of Vilhjálmur's book was published in *Isis*, the journal of the History of Science Society. The author of the article was George Sarton (1884–1956). Sarton was the founding father of the history of science in America, held the first professorship in the discipline, and taught at Harvard University.[17] Vilhjálmur and George Sarton were good friends, and for a time Vilhjálmur served as president of the History of Science Society, an honor that he considered the greatest of his life.[18] Sarton's article about Vilhjálmur's book opens as follows:

> I would like to call the attention of our readers to this volume because of its great methodological value. The burden of it is to illustrate the persistence of error and its cultivation not only by ignorant people but by many others who ought to know better. The explanation is laziness and inertia, as well as the love of standardized stories. Most of the stories discussed relate to arctic conditions which the author knows so well, and about which false facts or false deductions continue to flourish in spite of the explorers' efforts to correct them. I can readily sympathize with the author's anger because the situation is very much the same in my own field.[19]

Sarton went on to discuss some of the accepted "facts" about Greenlanders, for instance, that they lived in snow houses and drank fish oil instead of water, and that mothers carried their children in hoods on their backs. He did not mention Ólöf by name, even though she was one of the principal architects of the dissemination of falsehoods about the Inuit. At the end of the article, he states his intention to have his students at Harvard read Vilhjálmur's book because it would encourage critical thought and teach students constant vigilance and a healthy skepticism, even toward respected specialists. He then adds that "authorities, it should be remembered, are authorities only in their own field and even then it is just as well to examine their credentials and to make sure that any particular statement of theirs is deliberate."[20]

Given the three decades Ólöf spent as a leading expert on the subject of Greenlandic culture, these words were certainly a timely reminder.

Why Did the Critics Keep Silent?

Why is it that not one single critic felt compelled to discuss Ólöf and her career spanning several decades? Was it so unremarkable that it didn't even deserve mention? Or had the Great Depression made Americans immune to con artists and fraud?

The answer to both of these questions is no. Ólöf's career as a dwarf passing as an Eskimo is unique. Her life was a dream come true for those who disguised themselves as members of another race. She had financial security, lived and socialized with the upper class, and unlike most such disguised characters, managed to keep her secret and live a relatively stable life.

Neither had the Great Depression dissipated people's interest in such trickery. This became quite clear when Grey Owl died in 1938, two years after Ólöf was exposed. Grey Owl was revealed as a fraud immediately after his death, and news of his trickery traveled like wildfire through Europe and America.[21] The fact that he died at the peak of his career partially explains the interest in his death and the subsequent discovery. Ólöf, on the other hand, had been out of the public eye for over two decades when she died, which explains in part why Vilhjálmur's exposé attracted less attention than the revelation about Grey Owl. But there were other, more important factors: Grey Owl's and Ólöf's differing heritage, sex, and message.

Grey Owl was a well-born and well-educated Englishman, tall, graceful, and imposing. Native Americans were heavily romanticized during this period in American history, and white Americans believed they could learn a great deal from their philosophical outlook and way of life. Grey Owl had championed Native Americans' ideas about the sanctity of nature and animals; he advocated a noble cause and fought for animal protection and conservation.

He had also rebelled against the rigid constraints of British society, which was a sure way of winning the approval of Americans, who had fought for and won their independence from the British. Grey Owl had followed a time-honed American tradition of disguising himself as Native American in order to fight the oppression of the British ruling powers: The rebels who orchestrated the Boston Tea Party in 1773 disguised themselves as Mohawk Indians.[22]

In general, the news that Grey Owl had been an Englishman born and bred was well received, and many found it downright amusing. Eight of the largest newspapers in Canada, from Calgary to Ottawa, published articles—all very positive—about Grey Owl. In an *Ottawa Citizen* editorial from April 23, 1938, he was described as a genius whose works were not in the least devalued by his not having been a true American Indian. On the contrary, his impact on conservation would be even greater for his having disguised himself. "His attainments as a writer and naturalist will survive and when in later years our children's children are told of the strange masquerade—if it was a masquerade—their wonder and their appreciation will grow. He is assured a place in the annals of his adopted country."[23]

An article on Grey Owl's deception appeared on April 20, 1938, in *The Tribune*, one of Winnipeg's leading newspapers, under the title "Fun to Be Fooled." Like the editor of *Ottawa Citizen*, the author was convinced that Grey Owl would never have been so successful a conservationist had he not disguised himself as Native American, for "it is an odd commentary, but true enough, that many people will not listen to simple truths except when uttered by exotic personalities."[24] This journalist's assertion certainly applies to Ólöf. If she had not disguised herself as an Eskimo, it is unlikely that anyone would have lent an ear to her stories and adventures.

Grey Owl was a handsome man from a good family background who fought for a worthy cause, and it is hard not to laud his effort and audacity. The same cannot be said of Ólöf. She was an Icelandic commoner, completely uneducated, and a dwarf besides. The picture Ólöf painted of Eskimos was very crude, dark, and exaggerated.

At this time, Westerners' attitudes toward the peoples of the Arctic were changing. After the disasters of World War I, the Arctic and the Inuit took on a romantic glow that Vilhjálmur Stefánsson did his best to accentuate. The Inuit were no longer considered inferior to white men, but superior to them in morality and kindness. In many people's minds, the Arctic was a refuge, free from the corruption of the civilized world.[25]

Ólöf's career also cast a dark shadow on the American people and made their gullibility, ignorance, and racism painfully clear. Critics of Vilhjálmur's book were probably shocked to think that Ólöf was able to convince the American public that all Inuit were short, stout, and fair-skinned, and had knotted arms. The year 1922 saw the premiere of American explorer Robert J. Flaherty's (1884–1951) documentary about the Inuit, *Nanook of the North*. The film, which documented the lives of the Inuit in northern Canada, immediately received a great deal of attention and went on to become one of the most enduring documentaries in history.[26] *Nanook of the North* showed clearly that the natives of the North had nothing in common with Ólöf as far as their appearance went.

Critics of Vilhjálmur's book must also have wondered why nobody said a word in protest when Ólöf asserted that the Icelandic sailors and three Inuit families crossed the ice between Greenland and Iceland on sleds. A quick glance at a map would reveal this to be completely impossible.

Public discourse by critics about Vilhjálmur's exposé would have brought a great deal of embarrassment to the American people at that time. Ólöf's existence and career were an inconvenient fact, and there is only one good way of dealing with such inconveniences: smother them with silence.[27] Thus it should not be surprising that critics chose to keep quiet about Ólöf's feat and do their best to prevent Ólöf Sölvadóttir from Outer Langamýri from entering the annals of America's most famous deceivers.

But the memory of the Esquimaux Lady, Olof Krarer, lived on for years among the American people. On October 8, 1890, Ólöf had given a wildly successful talk in Gettysburg, Pennsylvania. The lecture was so well attended that she was invited to return less than a month later. Fifty years after Ólöf lectured in Gettysburg, her visit was mentioned twice in the *Gettysburg Times* in a column devoted to the main events in town life a half century earlier.[28]

When Ólöf's visit was remembered in the *Gettysburg Times*, four years had passed since the publication of Vilhjálmur's article. The news of her exposure had not yet reached Gettysburg.

Ólöf, Pride of a Nation

Although Americans remained silent about Ólöf's endeavors, at least one Icelander was very proud of them. This was Sigurdur Nordal, professor of Icelandic and comparative literature at the University of Iceland and

Sigurdur Nordal, Ólöf's admirer. The picture is taken around the time he gave his radio broadcast on Ólöf.

a good friend of Vilhjálmur Stefánsson. In 1945, Sigurdur gave a radio broadcast about Ólöf, based on Vilhjálmur's essay, on the Icelandic National Broadcasting Service.[29]

Sigurdur opened his broadcast by observing that, while Icelanders pay close attention to their compatriots' success overseas, they had as yet paid little heed to the successes of one Ólöf Sölvadóttir. However, Ólöf deserved no less attention than other successful Icelanders, Sigurdur continued, for if her case were scrutinized closely, her success in disguise in America was no less—and perhaps even greater—than the successes of many who were eulogized.

Sigurdur was very proud of Ólöf, the dwarf from Outer Langamýri, and much amused by her. He described her rise to fame and noted that her family heritage had stood her in good stead. Her paternal grandfather, Sölvi Sveinsson, and her father, Sölvi Sölvason, had both been gifted poets, and her father had also had quite a caustic sense of humor. Ólöf's first cousin, Gísli Ólafsson, the son of Ólöf's sister Helga, was also a gifted poet and an accomplished actor and mimic. Sigurdur had seen Gísli's "first large public performance here in Reykjavík" and not only appreciated his talent for poetry and mimicry, but also admired this farm boy's audacity and fearlessness while performing in front of a crowd in the capital city. He never faltered or stumbled on stage and appeared so at home that it seemed he had been an actor all his life. "It is not unreasonable to think," Sigurdur continued, "that Ólöf was gifted with considerable acting ability, a good sense of humor and a taste for irony," as well as being blessed with a lively imagination.[30]

In Sigurdur's opinion, it was not only Ólöf's immediate family but also her Icelandic heritage that contributed to her success and her stellar performance. He said:

I give myself leave to doubt that it would have been easy to find a completely self-educated country woman among immigrants from other countries, even a dwarf gifted with Ólöf's natural intelligence, who could have stepped into her shoes. Her demeanor, self-assuredness, and humor display specific traits of an old culture, which gave her an advantage over people in the pubescent stage of education and judgment. I think Ólöf brought great honor to the simple but unique Icelandic country upbringing of earlier times, for she certainly did not engage in her deception without reason, and it made nobody any stupider than he was before.[31]

Little Iceland and Big America

Vilhjálmur Stefánsson's book containing the article about Ólöf was published in 1936, some nine years before Sigurdur Nordal gave his broadcast. It is tempting to guess that Sigurdur chose this time to tell Ólöf's story in order to inspire Icelanders to believe in themselves. In 1944, a year before he gave his address about Ólöf, Icelanders had founded a republic after an independence struggle with Denmark that had lasted several decades. The United States had maintained a military presence in Iceland for four years, and the arrival of the troops had ushered in a new phase in Icelandic history. Iceland had been rapidly transformed from a stagnant farming community to a modern, urban society. Many Icelanders feared for the fate of their young republic and worried that the country would soon fall under the control of the United States. But Ólöf's story demonstrated clearly that they had nothing to fear. The little dwarf nation would always hold its own against the immature and ill-informed giant population west of the Atlantic.

Conclusion

The preceding chapters give an account of the dwarf woman Ólöf Sölvadóttir, who was born at Outer Langamýri in Húnavatnssýsla county, Iceland, in 1858, but who died as the Esquimaux Lady, Olof Krarer, in Maywood, Illinois, in 1935.

Ólöf was born into an agrarian society in Iceland in the mid-nineteenth century, a society that had barely changed for centuries. In her youth, she could look forward to one future: a life as a farm servant. But then wonders began occurring, not in Iceland but on the new continent in the west, North America, and they would transform Ólöf's prospects.

In Ólöf's youth, the United States fought a long and bloody civil war to determine whether slaves should be granted freedom. The battle was between the northern Union, which wished to free the slaves, and the southern Confederacy, whose best interests were protected by the status quo. One of the Union's freedom fighters was a young, promising man by the name of Henry L. Slayton, who was later Ólöf's employer and protector over a period of many years.

As history bears witness, the Union was victorious and African Americans were granted freedom. But the authorities soon realized that the country needed to expand its workforce substantially. The governments of Canada and the United States also wished to settle their vast western territories fully, a task requiring millions of people. Therefore they sounded the call east across the ocean, asking people to come and help. And come they did. They streamed in tens of thousands to the promised land, thankful to be able to cast off the centuries-old yoke of their homeland and start a new and better life in a new country. This call reached Iceland, and Ólöf's family was among fifteen thousand Icelanders who heeded it.

Immigrants were not the only ones who were on the move following the Civil War. Young, educated people from respected families in the oldest states in the United States longed for a new life far from home just as much as the immigrants did. Henry and Mina Slayton were among their number, and the city of Chicago was their promised land. With sheer diligence, they succeeded in founding a lecture bureau that entertained and educated the American public for decades, and Ólöf was one of their most loyal employees.

At this time, not only was America opening to the world, but the world was opening to America, and Americans explored foreign territories as never before. One frontier was particularly enchanting to them: the Arctic. The quality of the land might be lacking, but there was the elusive North Pole. No white man had ever set foot on the North Pole, which effectively made it still undiscovered. And in its vicinity lived a strange group of people, the Eskimos. The American Robert E. Peary, who was only two years older than Ólöf, was entranced at an early age by tales of the Arctic. As a young man, he became determined to be the first man to reach the North Pole. The American populace supported his efforts wholeheartedly and paid close attention to his Arctic adventures and the news he brought back of its strange inhabitants.

Ólöf Sölvadóttir was no less ambitious than the Slaytons and Robert Peary. Like them, she had big dreams about her future in the new land. But few avenues were open to a dwarf woman from Iceland—or so it seemed at first glance. Her highest possible attainment was to exhibit herself as a circus curiosity, which, in many people's opinion, was even more demeaning than being a servant. But then Ólöf Sölvadóttir had a unique opportunity. Most Americans didn't know any better than to believe that there must be Eskimos in a country named after ice. Eskimos figured prominently in people's imagination, and Ólöf was frequently asked whether she was one. Tired of the perceived insult of being associated with so low a race as the Eskimos, Ólöf decided that offense was the best defense. She accepted the good priest's offer to lecture, donned her disguise as Olof Krarer, the Esquimaux Lady, and began telling strange stories about the lives of the Eskimos. She played this role until her dying day.

Who Was the Guiltiest Party?

Thus far I have avoided passing moral judgment on Ólöf's actions, but one question remains unanswered: Who was the guiltiest party? Was it society, which confined people like Ólöf to the sidelines from the start? Or was it Ólöf, who deceived society on her own initiative? Ólöf was a liar; that is indisputable. She falsified her background and her biography. She then used this story in order to deceive tens of thousands of Americans and con them out of their money. A Christian value system would judge this behavior as wrong, and she and her agents could easily have been sued in court for what she did. But were society's views on disabled people any more just? People with disabilities were told from the outset that they were good for little or nothing, and they were condemned to the lowest ranks of society. Ólöf was unusually gifted, but only through lies could she foster her many talents and show what she was made of. Who can begrudge her that?

The deception was greatly advantageous to Ólöf and changed her life. And as Sigurdur Nordal put it so succinctly, her lies "made nobody any stupider than he was before."

Ólöf's career and her success were unique. Not many uneducated immigrant women earned themselves a place among the ranks of the most important educators in the United States and gave lectures on foreign cultures. Ólöf's countrymen, however, were not proud of her success. They were ashamed of her lies and kept completely silent about her. In their minds, she hardly even existed. Yet few Icelandic immigrants held Iceland's banner as high aloft in North America as Ólöf did.

Americans adored and respected her. Years passed before they discovered that she had lied to them. When they realized later that an uneducated Icelandic dwarf had deceived them, they were so ashamed that they, too, kept their silence. Consequently, Olof Krarer, the Esquimaux Lady, kept her reputation pristine. This was doubtless Ólöf's dearest wish, and as so often before, her wish came true.

On Source Materials

Diaries and letters are usually the principal source materials for biographies such as this one. These sources generally contain personal information about the subject of the biography. In letters and diaries, people often express opinions and feelings they never reveal elsewhere.

Preservation of the letters and diaries of commoners has never been a priority, and such documents are rarely found in libraries and archives. No diaries or letters belonging to Ólöf or her next of kin have been found; they have probably been destroyed. It is also likely that once Ólöf started her masquerade, she took care to keep all documents about herself away from prying eyes.

The lack of primary sources about Ólöf herself limited the scope of this work to some extent. Fortunately, there proved to be no dearth of sources about Ólöf, her family and contemporaries, her work, and her entire life history, both in Iceland and in America.

The principal sources in Iceland were parish records, censuses, property descriptions, and annals. When Vilhjálmur Stefánsson researched his report on Ólöf, he contacted a number of people with the assistance of Thorstina Jackson. Together they corresponded with Ólöf's friends and family in Canada and the United States, as well as Americans who encountered Ólöf after she donned her disguise as Olof Krarer. These letters are preserved in Vilhjálmur's records at Dartmouth College Library in Hanover, New Hampshire. I acquired copies of them, as well as some pictures of Ólöf that Vilhjálmur tracked down. I then turned to further sources in the United States about Ólöf, the Slayton family, and others with whom they interacted. These sources included newspapers, books, journals, and censuses.

The Slayton Lyceum Bureau published a lavish annual catalog presenting its clients. A few editions of this publication are preserved in the Chicago Public Library. The bureau also published a special brochure about Ólöf, which contained information about her work and excerpts from critical responses to her lectures. I also found articles about Ólöf in American newspapers, but my coverage of these sources was far from exhaustive. Only one American newspaper, the *New York Times*, has compiled a registry of all articles published and all individuals mentioned in its pages. Ólöf lectured in countless towns and cities, and her lectures were almost always reported on in local news. It would have taken far more time than I had available to comb through every imaginable publication.

I also relied on scholarly and biographical works about the most important American explorers of the age. Ólöf's fame was based almost exclusively on Americans' enduring fascination with the Arctic and the race for the North Pole.

The Slayton Lyceum Bureau was sold to the Redpath Bureau in Boston. When it went out of business in 1930, all of its documents were donated to the University of Iowa Libraries in Iowa City. Among these documents was the contract for the sale of the Slayton Lyceum Bureau, of which I obtained a copy.

There is nobody left alive who knew Ólöf personally, but I contacted Alice Slayton Mundorff, the Slaytons' granddaughter, who is now quite old and lives in Southern California. Ólöf had left Alice's family before she was born, and her only memory of Ólöf was of hearing the story of her adventurous journey across the ice as a child. However, Alice Slayton gave me important information about the fate of her family and its last years in St. Petersburg. She also provided me with photographs of her grandmother Mina and her mother, Huldah.

In Iceland, I contacted Torfi Sveinsson from Saudárkrókur (d. 2004), the grandson of Ólöf's eldest sister, Helga. Torfi told me stories about Ólöf that had circulated in her family in Iceland. He told me as well of the two different accounts of the death of Solveig, Ólöf's mother. Torfi was also the one who provided me with the poem Sölvi wrote when his courtship with Solveig was at its peak.

Last but not least, I found Ólöf's biography, recorded by Albert S.

Post and published in 1887. It is an invaluable testament to Ólöf's creativity and shows clearly why she became so popular. These sources *luckily* enabled me to develop a fairly comprehensive picture of Ólöf and her adventurous life.

Thanks

Every story has a story. The story behind the book about the dwarf Ólöf the Eskimo begins with Jóhann Pétursson, who was known in Iceland as Jóhann the Giant. I had devoted many years to researching Icelandic national identity and Icelandic masculinity, and in 1998 I wanted to continue on that path. I considered Jóhann's life and work an ideal project. I therefore contacted Gudrún Eggertsdóttir, librarian at the National and University Library of Iceland, and asked her to investigate what materials the library had concerning Jóhann. She responded quickly and thoroughly, as always, and I would like to thank her sincerely for that and for all the help and friendship she has given me throughout the years.

The library turned out not to have much material related to Jóhann in its possession, and Gudrún therefore contacted the Dalvík Museum, where Jóhann's documents and belongings are preserved. They were reluctant to provide us with any information for reasons that soon became clear: Another person was in the process of creating a documentary film and a book about Jóhann, so my work was clearly superfluous.

In the meantime, Professor of Icelandic Literature Dagný Kristjánsdóttir gave me a copy of Sigurdur Nordal's 1945 radio broadcast on Ólöf, a special printing of which had been in her parents' possession. Dagný considered Ólöf an entertaining example of a woman who had worked in an American circus, like Jóhann, but who had been a dwarf rather than a giant. I was immediately fascinated by Ólöf's story and realized that the dream project had fallen into my lap. I told Dagný of my decision to write about Ólöf, and from that point on she was one of my most loyal supporters. She proofread my grant applications to the Icelandic Centre for Research and provided continual encouragement. I eventually received a two-year grant from the Icelandic Centre for Research, for which I would like to extend my heartfelt thanks. Dagný also proofread the manuscript of the book and made extremely helpful and useful comments, and I wish to thank her warmly for everything.

I would also like to thank Philip Cronenwett, who heads the department of the Dartmouth College Library where Vilhjálmur Stefánsson's documents are kept. He responded quickly and efficiently to my request for sources on Ólöf from Vilhjálmur's documents. Nelson Gerrard, a Canadian of Icelandic heritage who has written about the settlers of New Iceland, provided me with invaluable information about Ólöf's family in its first years in the new country, and I thank him for his contribution. My best thanks also go to Renee Choe-Winter, who searched the documents of the Redpath Bureau for me at the University of Iowa Libraries.

Carol Gibbes, formerly a librarian in the anthropology collection at the University of California, Santa Barbara, and her successor, Lorna Lueck, both helped me find previously unknown materials about Ólöf, and I send them my best of thanks. I would also like to thank David Lawson at the University of California, Santa Barbara, and José Antonio Martinez Aroza at the University of Granada, Spain, for all their help with the illustrations in the book.

My first field trip in the course of my research was to Seattle, Washington, in 2001. By lucky coincidence, an old schoolmate and good friend, Erna Indridadóttir, was studying there at the time. Erna took me to explore Ballard, where Ólöf's father, Sölvi; his partner, Soffía; and Ólöf's siblings Ingibjörg and Arnljótur settled in 1893, and I learned a great deal about their life in Ballard. Erna also helped me to locate Sölvi's unmarked grave, which we found after an extensive search, and I thank her sincerely for all her help and for unforgettable days in Seattle.

Ólöf spent most of her life in Chicago, and I contacted the Chicago Public Library and the Chicago Historical Society early in my research. My queries were received most graciously; the employees showed great interest in the work and sent me copies of all documents they could find concerning the Slayton Lyceum Bureau and its owners. I later traveled to Chicago to compile further sources, and the employees of both organizations were remarkably helpful and provided excellent service, for which I thank them. I would also like to thank Lena Hallgrímsdóttir and Einar Steinsson, who guided me through Ólöf's old upper-class neighborhood in Chicago, the Near West Side, and helped me find the street where she lived. This neighborhood has been deeply impoverished for many years now and is just beginning to rise out of poverty again. I also thank Gunnar Ólafur Hansson and Suzanne Gessner for helping me to find the home of Henry Slayton's friend near the University of Chicago, where Slayton died unexpectedly in June 1910.

I also wish to thank Júlía Kristmundsdóttir Perrus, who lived in St. Petersburg, Florida, and her husband, Dean Perrus, for their hospitality and all their help. Júlía searched for documents on the investments and enterprises of the Slayton family in St. Petersburg and enabled me to get straight to work at the county library when I visited that beautiful city in the early spring of 2003. Júlía had also contacted members of the St. Petersburg Historical Society, who greeted me most cordially and helped me find important documents and old photographs. The employees at the St. Petersburg Public Library were also extremely helpful. I wish to extend my sincerest thanks to all these excellent people.

I owe a special debt of gratitude to Alice Slayton Mundorff, the Slaytons' granddaughter, who gave me invaluable information about the fate of her family, information that was nowhere to be found in business records and documents. She also sent me photographs of her mother, Huldah, and her grandmother Mina.

Naturally, a great deal of my research took place in Iceland, mostly in the National and University Library. I would like to thank its staff for all their helpfulness and flexibility through the years. I also spent a considerable amount of time at the National Archives of Iceland and would like to thank the staff there, especially archivist Jón Torfason, for all their assistance. Not only did Jón point out documents to me that I would never have thought to consult, but he proofread the first chapter of the book for me. Jón was born and bred in Húnavatnssýsla county, just like Ólöf, and takes a keen interest in the county's history. He corrected a number of minor errors concerning the farms and their locations, and his input was of the kind that is invaluable to any researcher. He also gave me good advice about referencing sources.

To Torfi Sveinsson (1919–2004) of Saudárkrókur, Ólöf's grand-nephew, I extend special thanks for poems and stories from Ólöf's family. I would also like to thank Ásdís Sigurdardóttir and Ósk Ólöf Sigur-dardóttir, both descendants of Helga Sölvadóttir, who provided me with useful information about Ólöf's family heritage. I thank Sigurdur An-tonsson for procuring a drawing of his grandfather, Gísli Ólafsson, by artist Jóhannes Kjarval. Thanks are due also to Björg Einarsdóttir, Böd-var Gudmundsson, Erla Hulda Halldórsdóttir, Helga Stefánsdóttir, Helga Ögmundardóttir, Hulda Sigurborg Sigtryggsdóttir, Inga Huld Hákonardóttir, and Sigurdur Gylfi Magnússon for pointing out useful sources and sharing important information regarding the project. Fur-thermore, I would like to thank my mother, Sigrídur Gudbrandsdóttir, for valuable suggestions for improvements on the text of this book. I also thank Thorsteinn Thorsteinsson for proofreading the conclusion and the chapter on source materials.

Halldór Gudmundsson, who was head of Edda Publishing, publish-ers of the original version in Icelandic, when my contract for the book was finalized, deserves thanks for his support, as does Kristinn Hall-grímsson, my attorney and my brother-in-law, who put the finishing touches to the contract on my behalf during my absence. I would also like to thank Ólöf Eldjárn, the Icelandic original's editor, for a smooth and enjoyable collaborative effort; Sigrídur Rögnvaldsdóttir and Páll Valsson from the publishing house Mál og menning, for valuable com-ments and suggestions; and Uggi Jónsson for proofreading and useful suggestions.

My good friend, anthropologist Sigrídur Dúna Kristmundsdóttir, followed this project from the start. She proofread a few versions of the manuscript and made suggestions for improvements, drawing on her vast experience in such matters. For that, she receives my sincerest thanks. Hrafnhildur Schram, editor of the illustrations for the book, deserves particular thanks. Not only did she choose pictures and procure them, but she has given me exceptional support and friendship through the years. Last, I would like to thank my nearest and dearest for everything.

My husband, Björn Birnir, read every version of the manuscript and made numerous suggestions and comments. My two children, Hallfríður Björk and Einar Björn, showed me exceptional patience. Without their unstinting support and encouragement, the book about "that brilliant woman," as my son Einar Björn described Ólöf, would never have been written.

Inga Dóra Björnsdóttir

Notes

Inuk—Greenlander—Eskimo

1. Wendell H. Oswalt, *Eskimo Explorers*, 22.
2. Ann Fiendrup-Riordan, *Eskimo Essays*, 5.
3. Gísli Pálsson, *Travelling Passions*, 321.

Prologue

1. Albert S. Post, *Olof Krarer*, 14.
2. Albert S. Post, *Olof Krarer*, 18.
3. Albert S. Post, *Olof Krarer*, 18.
4. Vilhjálmur Stefánsson, *Adventures in Error*, 270.
5. Robert W. Cherney, introduction to *The Cross of Gold* by William Jennings Bryan, 2–3; John Tapia, *Circuit Chautauqua*, 5.
6. Robert W. Cherney, introduction to *The Cross of Gold* by William Jennings Bryan, 9–10.
7. William Jennings Bryan, *The Cross of Gold*, 28.
8. Robert W. Cherney, introduction to *The Cross of Gold* by William Jennings Bryan, 12.
9. Janet M. Davis, *The Circus Age*, 220.
10. John Tapia, *Circuit Chautauqua*, 58–59.

Iceland—Youth

1. Björn Bjarnason, *The Annals of Brandsstadir* (in Icelandic), 210; Rev. Pjetur Gudmundsson, *Annals of the 19th Century*, vol. 3, *1857–1869* (in Icelandic), 30.
2. Helga Thórarinsdóttir, *History of the Icelandic Midwives' Association 1919–1979* (in Icelandic); Jón Thórdarson, "Audkúla and Svínavatn Parishes, 1857," (in Icelandic), 1:95.
3. National Archives of Iceland, "Parish Service Records 1816–1866" (in Ice-

landic), 192; Bjarni Jónasson, "Perspectives on Svínavatn District, continued" (in Icelandic), 81.

4. National Archives of Iceland, "Parish Service Records 1816–1866" (in Icelandic), 1.

5. Veronique Dasen, *Dwarfs in Ancient Egypt and Greece*, 8; Joan Ablon, *Living with Difference*, 4–6.

6. Björn Bjarnason, *The Annals of Brandsstadir* (in Icelandic), 213.

7. National Archives of Iceland, "Parish Service Records 1816–1866" (in Icelandic), 195; National Archives of Iceland, "Parish Service Records for Svínavatn District 1816–1866" (in Icelandic); Bjarni Jónasson, "Perspectives on Svínavatn District, continued" (in Icelandic), 81; Björn Bjarnason, *The Annals of Brandsstadir* (in Icelandic), 214.

8. Bjarni Jónasson, "Perspectives on Svínavatn District, continued" (in Icelandic), 80–81.

9. Bjarni Jónasson, "Perspectives on Svínavatn District, continued" (in Icelandic), 86.

10. A letter from Magna Magnúsdóttir, in Bjarni Jónasson, "Perspectives on Svínavatn District, continued" (in Icelandic), 87.

11. Jónas B. Bjarnason, "History of the Svínavatn District Agricultural Society" (in Icelandic), 17.

12. National Archives of Iceland, "Census in a Reading Room 1840" (in Icelandic), 225.

13. Bjarni Jónasson, "Perspectives on Svínavatn District, continued" (in Icelandic), 81.

14. National Archives of Iceland, "Census in a Reading Room 1840" (in Icelandic), 226; Páll Kolka, *Father's Fields* (in Icelandic), 152.

15. National Archives of Iceland, "Parish Service Records 1816–1866" (in Icelandic).

16. National Archives of Iceland, "Parish Service Records 1816–1866" (in Icelandic).

17. Thorstina S. Jackson, *A History of Icelanders in North Dakota* (in Icelandic), 275.

18. Pétur Sigurdsson, "Three Farmers in Bólstadarhlíd District in the 19th Century" (in Icelandic), 82.

19. Pétur Sigurdsson, "Three Farmers in Bólstadarhlíd District in the 19th Century" (in Icelandic), 82.

20. Pétur Sigurdsson, "Three Farmers in Bólstadarhlíd District in the 19th Century" (in Icelandic), 82.

21. Torfi Sveinsson, interview, May 2002.

22. Sölvi Sölvason, according to Torfi Sveinsson of Saudárkrókur, grandson of Helga Sölvadóttir, Ólöf's eldest sister, from an interview, May 2002.

23. National Archives of Iceland, "Parish Service Records 1817–1867" (in Icelandic), 195.

24. National Archives of Iceland, "Parish Service Records 1816–1866" (in Icelandic), 84.

25. National Archives of Iceland, "Parish Service Records 1816–1866" (in Icelandic), 61; Gudmundur Sigurdur Jóhannsson and Magnús Björnsson, *A Genealogy of East Húnavatnssýsla County* (in Icelandic), 4:1314.

26. Joan Ablon, *Little People in America*, 1, 29.

27. Gudmundur Hálfdanarson, "Social Development in 19th-Century Iceland" (in Icelandic), 10.

28. Gudmundur Hálfdanarson, "Children—Poor Man's Principal?" (in Icelandic), 122.

29. Albert S. Post, *Olof Krarer*, 21.

30. Albert S. Post, *Olof Krarer*, 21–22.

31. Joan Ablom, *Little People in America*, 22, 13–30.

32. Scholar Sander L. Gilman maintains that a definition of normalcy includes being able to go out in public and be left alone. See Gilman, *Creating Beauty to Cure the Soul*, 146.

33. Sigurdur Nordal, *An Epistle on Ólöf Sölvadóttir* (in Icelandic), 10.

34. Albert S. Post, *Olof Krarer*, 19.

35. Joan Ablon, *Living with Difference*, 47–54.

36. Sigurdur Nordal, *An Epistle on Ólöf Sölvadóttir* (in Icelandic), 33.

37. Björn Thorsteinsson and Bergsteinn Jónsson, *A History of Iceland to the Present Day* (in Icelandic), 314.

38. National Archives of Iceland, "Parish Service Records, 1867–1817" (in Icelandic).

39. National Archives of Iceland, "Parish Census, 1866–1891" (in Icelandic), 65.

40. Björn Thorsteinsson and Bergsteinn Jónsson, *A History of Iceland to the Present Day* (in Icelandic), 314; Gunnlaugur Haraldsson, *Physicians in Iceland* (in Icelandic), 15.

41. Gudmundur Hálfdanarson, "Children—Poor Man's Principal?" (in Icelandic), 13–14.

42. Adalsteinn Eiríksson, *The Women's School in Reykjavík, 1874–1974* (in Icelandic), 96.

43. Joan Ablon, *Little People in America*, 21; *Miss Olof Krarer*, Slayton Lyceum Bureau Special Publication.

44. Gísli Gunnarsson, *Fertility and Nuptiality in Iceland's Demographic History*, 8.

45. Sigurdur Gudjónsson, "Abolition of Labor Bondage and the Liberalism Movement" (in Icelandic), 12–13.

46. National Archives of Iceland, "Parish Service Records, 1816–1866" (in Icelandic); National Archives of Iceland, "Parish Service Records, 1867–1917" (in Icelandic).

47. National Archives of Iceland, "Parish Census, 1866–1891" (in Icelandic), 4.

48. *The Annals of Brandsstadir* (in Icelandic), Manuscript Lbs. 2283, 58.

49. National Archives of Iceland, "Parish Census, 1866–1891" (in Icelandic), 4.

50. National Archives of Iceland, "Parish Service Records, 1816–1866" (in Icelandic); National Archives of Iceland, "Parish Service Records 1817–1867" (in Icelandic), 72.

51. Cf. a summary of Icelandic women's legal status in Sigrídur Th. Erlendsdóttir, "Changes in the Legal Standing of Icelandic Women in the 20th Century" (in Icelandic); Már Jónsson, "Woman Forgive Men's Adultery" (in Icelandic), 70–78.

52. National Archives of Iceland, "Húnavatnssýsla County, xVIII, 3. Property Transactions, 1846–1877" (in Icelandic), 554–55.

53. National Archives of Iceland, "Parish Census, 1866–1891" (in Icelandic), 40.

54. National Archives of Iceland, "Parish Census, 1866–1891" (in Icelandic), 34, 36, 40, 41.

55. National Archives of Iceland, "Parish Census, 1866–1891" (in Icelandic), 50, 59–60, 69.

56. National Archives of Iceland, "Parish Service Records, 1816–1866"; National Archives of Iceland, "Parish Service Records 1817–1917"(in Icelandic), 46, 55, 65.

57. National Archives of Iceland, "Parish Census, 1860–1884" (in Icelandic), 160.

58. National Archives of Iceland, "Parish Service Records, 1867–1917" (in Icelandic), 173.

59. National Archives of Iceland, "Parish Census, 1860–1884" (in Icelandic), 160.

60. Pétur Sigurdsson, "Three Farmers in Bólstadarhlíd District in the 19th Century" (in Icelandic), 82.

61. National Archives of Iceland, "Parish Service Records, 1867–1917" (in Icelandic), 219.

62. Pétur Sigurdsson, "Three Farmers in Bólstadarhlíd District in the 19th Century" (in Icelandic), 82.

63. Gudmundur Hálfdanarson, "Social Development in 19th-Century Iceland" (in Icelandic), 20–27.

64. Gudmundur Hálfdanarson, "Social Development in 19th-Century Iceland" (in Icelandic), 20–23.

65. Gudmundur Hálfdanarson, "Social Development in 19th-Century Iceland" (in Icelandic), 21.

66. Gísli Gunnarsson, Fertility and Nuptiality in Iceland's Demographic History, 35.

67. Gudmundur Hálfdanarson, "Social Development in 19th-Century Iceland" (in Icelandic), 21–23.

68. National Archives of Iceland, "The Svínavatn District Agricultural Report, 1874" (in Icelandic).

69. Júníus Kristinsson, A Registry of Emigrants to North America, 1870–1914 (in Ice-

landic), 233; National Archives of Iceland, "Census in a Reading Room 1840" (in Icelandic), 226; Páll Kolka, *Father's Fields* (in Icelandic), 152.

70. W. Kristjansson, *The Icelandic People in Manitoba*, 43.

71. W. Kristjansson, *The Icelandic People in Manitoba*, 20, 43–44.

72. W. Kristjansson, *The Icelandic People in Manitoba*, 20.

73. W. Kristjansson, *The Icelandic People in Manitoba*, 43.

74. Albert S. Post, *Olof Krarer*, 23.

75. National Archives of Iceland, "Parish Service Records, 1857–1922" (in Icelandic), 279.

76. National Archives of Iceland, "Parish Service Records, 1857–1922" (in Icelandic); National Archives of Iceland, "Parish Census, 1873–1883" (in Icelandic); Júníus Kristinsson, *A Registry of Emigrants to North America, 1870–1914* (in Icelandic), 235, 236.

77. Júníus Kristinsson, *A Registry of Emigrants to North America, 1870–1914* (in Icelandic), 233–34.

78. Júníus Kristinsson, *A Registry of Emigrants to North America, 1870–1914* (in Icelandic), 233–34.

79. Gudjón Arngrímsson, *New Iceland* (in Icelandic), 93.

80. Pétur Sigurdsson, "Three Farmers in Bólstadarhlíd District in the 19th Century" (in Icelandic), 83.

81. Pétur Sigurdsson, "Three Farmers in Bólstadarhlíd District in the 19th Century" (in Icelandic), 83.

82. Jóhann Schram, "A Diary from 1876–1877" (in Icelandic), 165.

The Promised Land

1. Sigurdur Nordal, *An Epistle on Ólöf Sölvadóttir* (in Icelandic), 10.

2. Gudjón Arngrímsson, *Another Iceland* (in Icelandic), 317–18.

3. Gudjón Arngrímsson, *Another Iceland* (in Icelandic), 316–19.

4. Júníus Kristinsson, *A Registry of Emigrants to North America, 1870–1914* (in Icelandic), 241; Björg Einarsdóttir, *From the Lives and Works of Icelandic Women* (in Icelandic), 1:104–5.

5. Júníus Kristinsson, *A Registry of Emigrants to North America, 1870–1914* (in Icelandic), 299; Vilhjálmur Stefánsson, *Adventures in Error*, 246.

6. Jóhann Schram, "A Diary from 1876–1877" (in Icelandic), 165.

7. Albert S. Post, *Olof Krarer*, 24.

8. Jóhann Schram, "A Diary from 1876–1877" (in Icelandic), 166.

9. Jóhann Schram, "A Diary from 1876–1877" (in Icelandic), 166.

10. Jóhann Schram, "A Diary from 1876–1877" (in Icelandic), 166.

11. Jóhann Schram, "A Diary from 1876–1877" (in Icelandic), 166.

12. W. Kristjansson, *The Icelandic People in Manitoba*, 44.

13. Jóhann Schram, "A Diary from 1876–1877" (in Icelandic), 167.

14. Jóhann Schram, "A Diary from 1876–1877" (in Icelandic), 167.

15. Jóhann Schram, "A Diary from 1876–1877" (in Icelandic), 167.

16. Jóhann Schram, "A Diary from 1876–1877" (in Icelandic), 167.

17. Jóhann Schram, "A Diary from 1876–1877" (in Icelandic), 167.

18. The disease in question is a sort of heat stroke known as "summer complaint." W. Kristjansson, *The Icelandic People in Manitoba*, 45.

19. W. Kristjansson, *The Icelandic People in Manitoba*, 21.

20. W. Kristjansson, *The Icelandic People in Manitoba*, 21–27.

21. W. Kristjansson, *The Icelandic People in Manitoba*, 25.

22. John S. Matthiasson, "Adaptations to an Ethnic Structure," 157–75.

23. John S. Matthiasson, "Adaptations to an Ethnic Structure," 159.

24. John S. Matthiasson, "Adaptations to an Ethnic Structure," 158–60.

25. W. Kristjansson, *The Icelandic People in Manitoba*, 36.

26. W. Kristjansson, *The Icelandic People in Manitoba*, 35.

27. W. Kristjansson, *The Icelandic People in Manitoba*, 35.

28. Nelson Gerrard, March 1, 2001.

29. Nelson Gerrard, March 1, 2001.

30. W. Kristjansson, *The Icelandic People in Manitoba*, 47–48.

31. W. Kristjansson, *The Icelandic People in Manitoba*, 48, 50–51, 52, 55.

32. W. Kristjansson, *The Icelandic People in Manitoba*, 50.

33. W. Kristjansson, *The Icelandic People in Manitoba*, 52.

Westward to the Sea

1. Nelson Gerrard, March 1, 2001.

2. W. Kristjansson, *The Icelandic People in Manitoba*, 153; Fridrik J. Bergmann, "The Colonial History of Icelanders in North America" (in Icelandic), 43.

3. W. Kristjansson, *The Icelandic People in Manitoba*, 153.

4. Tryggvi Oleson, *A History of Icelanders in North America* (in Icelandic), 4:323–24.

5. W. Kristjansson, *The Icelandic People in Manitoba*, 159.

6. W. Kristjansson, *The Icelandic People in Manitoba*, 96.

7. W. Kristjansson, *The Icelandic People in Manitoba*, 96–97.

8. Nelson Gerrard, March 1, 2001; Tryggvi Oleson, *A History of Icelanders in North America* (in Icelandic), 4:324, footnote.

9. 1900 Census, Washington State; Júníus Kristinsson, *A Registry of Emigrants to North America, 1870–1914* (in Icelandic), 355.

10. Carlos Schwanter et al., *Images of a State's Heritage*, 4, 7–8.

11. Carlos Schwanter et al., *Images of a State's Heritage*, 39.

12. Kenneth O. Bjork, *West of the Great Divide*, 427.

13. Carlos Schwanter et al., *Images of a State's Heritage*, 38.

14. Ruth Kirk and Carmela Alexander, *Exploring Washington's Past*, 233.

15. Ruth Kirk and Carmela Alexander, *Exploring Washington's Past*, 296–97; Kay F. Reinartz, "Yankee and Immigrant-Ballardites All," 47.

16. Nordic Heritage Museum, Ballard, Wash.

17. Margaret I. Wandrey, *Four Bridges to Seattle*, 65, 98, 160; Hulda Sigurborg Sigtryggsdóttir, *From Iceland to the New World* (in Icelandic), 238–41.

18. Cheryl Cronander and Thomas Downey, "The Buildings of Old Ballard," 220.

19. Margaret I. Wandrey, *Four Bridges to Seattle*, 94.

20. Carlos Schwanter et al., *Images of a State's Heritage*, 59.

21. 1900 Census, King County, Wash.

22. Key Nelson, "Staying Healthy on Salmon Bay," 190.

23. 1900 Census, King County, Wash.

24. Susan Cook, "A Church for Every Saloon," 121, 117–32; William Moore, "Community Life," 202, 201–16; Hulda Sigurborg Sigtryggsdóttir, *From Iceland to the New World* (in Icelandic), 237, 255.

25. Death Certificate of Sölvi Sölvason, 1903; Seattle Health Department, record 338; King County Health Department, record 11399.

26. Nelson Gerrard, March 1, 2001; Tryggvi Oleson, *A History of Icelanders in North America* (in Icelandic), 4:324.

27. Rhea Hannon, "Rhea Remembers," 1.

28. Rhea Hannon, "Rhea Remembers," 1.

29. *Almanak* of Ólafur S. Thorgeirsson (in Icelandic), 120.

30. This is incorrect. Helga, Thórhildur Sveinsdóttir's grandmother, was not nine years old when her family went to Canada—she was twenty-one. Helga was born in 1855, and her family left the country in 1876. Thórhildur Sveinsdóttir, *Sunset in the Hills* (in Icelandic), 117.

Off Adventuring

1. W. Kristjansson, *The Icelandic People in Manitoba*, 165–66.

2. W. Kristjansson, *The Icelandic People in Manitoba*, 160.

3. W. Kristjansson, *The Icelandic People in Manitoba*, 156–58.

4. W. Kristjansson, *The Icelandic People in Manitoba*, 154, 159.

5. W. Kristjansson, *The Icelandic People in Manitoba*, 149–50.

6. W. Kristjansson, *The Icelandic People in Manitoba*, 150.

7. Fridrik J. Bergmann, "The Colonial History of Icelanders in North America" (in Icelandic), 39; W. Kristjansson, *The Icelandic People in Manitoba*, 149–50.

8. Gudjón Arngrímsson, *New Iceland* (in Icelandic), 280–81.

9. Fridrik J. Bergmann, "The Colonial History of Icelanders in North America" (in Icelandic), 39.

10. Albert S. Post, *Olof Krarer*, 24–25.

11. Betsy Israel, *Bachelor Girl*, 62.

12. Janet M. Davis, *The Circus Age*, 120.

13. See Bluford Adams, *E Pluribus Barnum*. See also Janet M. Davis, *The Circus Age*.

14. Janet M. Davis, *The Circus Age*. See also Matthew F. Jacobson, *Whiteness of a Different Color*.

15. Janet M. Davis, *The Circus Age*, 2–7, 13.

16. Janet M. Davis, *The Circus Age*, 119.

17. Janet M. Davis, *The Circus Age*, 119–20.

18. Janet M. Davis, *The Circus Age*, 67.

19. Matthew Sweet, *Inventing the Victorians*, 136–54.

20. Letter from G. J. Hallson, to B. L. Baldwinson, May 26, 1926, forwarded to Thorstina Jackson.

The Deception Begins

1. Vilhjálmur Stefánsson, *Adventures in Error*, 246.

2. Albert S. Post, *Olof Krarer*, 24–27.

3. Vilhjálmur Stefánsson, *Adventures in Error*, 247. See also Margaret I. Wandrey, *Four Bridges to Seattle*, 138; Helga Ögmundardóttir, "Images, Self-Conceptions, and Power in Icelander-Native American Interactions in North America, 1875–1930" (in Icelandic), 54.

4. Vilhjálmur Stefánsson, *Adventures in Error*, 247.

5. In the opinion of novelist V. S. Naipaul, this is the final fate of all human beings. See V. S. Naipaul, *The Mimic Men*, 25.

6. Hillel Schwartz, *The Culture of the Copy*, 72.

7. Laura Browder, *Slippery Characters*, 2–3. See also Shari M. Huhndorf, *Going Native*.

8. Laura Browder, *Slippery Characters*, 120.

9. Laura Browder, *Slippery Characters*, 212.

10. Donald B. Smith, *From the Land of Shadows*, 41.

11. Donald B. Smith, *From the Land of Shadows*, 189.

12. Laura Browder, *Slippery Characters*, 122; Donald B. Smith, 1982, *Long Lance*, 121.

13. Laura Browder, *Slippery Characters*, 7.

14. Donald B. Smith, *Long Lance*, 125.

15. *The Lyceumite and Talent*, February 1908, 48.

16. Evelin Sullivan, *The Concise Book of Lying*, 88–89.

17. Vilhjálmur Stefánsson, *Adventures in Error*, 248.

18. *Washington Post*, March 16, 1913, 25. See also *Freeborn County Standard*, "Miss Olof Krarer," 7.

Ólöf's Fabricated Biography

1. Albert S. Post, *Olof Krarer*, introduction.
2. Albert S. Post, *Olof Krarer*, introduction.
3. Albert S. Post, *Olof Krarer*, 1. Chapter headings used in this quote are not from Post's original, but were added by the author of this book.
4. Albert S. Post, *Olof Krarer*, 1–2.
5. Albert S. Post, *Olof Krarer*, 2–3.
6. Albert S. Post, *Olof Krarer*, 3.
7. Albert S. Post, *Olof Krarer*, 3–4.
8. Albert S. Post, *Olof Krarer*, 4.
9. Albert S. Post, *Olof Krarer*, 4.
10. Albert S. Post, *Olof Krarer*, 4–5.
11. Albert S. Post, *Olof Krarer*, 5.
12. Albert S. Post, *Olof Krarer*, 6.
13. Albert S. Post, *Olof Krarer*, 6–7.
14. Albert S. Post, *Olof Krarer*, 7.
15. Albert S. Post, *Olof Krarer*, 7.
16. Albert S. Post, *Olof Krarer*, 9–10.
17. Albert S. Post, *Olof Krarer*, 10–11.
18. Albert S. Post, *Olof Krarer*, 12–13.
19. Albert S. Post, *Olof Krarer*, 14–15.
20. Albert S. Post, *Olof Krarer*, 15.
21. Albert S. Post, *Olof Krarer*, 15–16.
22. Albert S. Post, *Olof Krarer*, 16–17.
23. Albert S. Post, *Olof Krarer*, 17–18.
24. Albert S. Post, *Olof Krarer*, 18–19.
25. Albert S. Post, *Olof Krarer*, 19–20.
26. Albert S. Post, *Olof Krarer*, 20–21.
27. Albert S. Post, *Olof Krarer*, 21–22.
28. Albert S. Post, *Olof Krarer*, 23–24.
29. *Washington Post*, March 16, 1913, 25.
30. *Daily Review (Decatur, Ill.)*, July 6, 1899, 8.
31. See photo in *Washington Post*, March 16, 1913, 25.
32. *Freeborn County Standard*, March 27, 1890, 7.
33. *Trenton Times*, November 16, 1889, 3.
34. *Gettysburg Times*, October 8, 1840, 6.
35. Evelin Sullivan, *The Concise Book of Lying*, 89.
36. In recent decades, scholars have theorized that people's bodies and physical stature have no meaning in and of themselves. Instead, our ideas about the body,

about gender, race, and stature, are shaped verbally by cultural forces that are controlled by the ruling classes in society. See, for example, the introduction to Michel Foucault, *Herculine Barbin;* and Judith Butler, *Bodies That Matter.* Ólöf realized the truthfulness of this theory long before it was posited.

37. Albert S. Post, *Olof Krarer,* 18–19.

38. Margaret I. Wandreay, *Four Bridges to Seattle,* 138; Helga Ögmundardóttir, "Images, Self-Conceptions, and Power in Icelander-Native American Interactions in North America, 1875–1930" (in Icelandic), 54.

39. See discussion of this in Erlendur Gudmundsson, *Home and Away* (in Icelandic), as well as Bödvar Gudmundsson, *Letters of the West Icelanders I* (in Icelandic), 186–87, 468–71; Bödvar Gudmundsson, *Letters of the West Icelanders II* (in Icelandic), 11, 15, 24, 78.

40. *West Chester (PA) Republic* in *Miss Olof Krarer,* Slayton Lyceum Bureau Special Publication.

The Race for the North Pole

1. S. Allen Counter, *North Pole Legacy.*

2. Wendell H. Oswalt, *Eskimo Explorers,* 110.

3. Wendell H. Oswalt, *Eskimo Explorers,* 112.

4. Mark Horst Sawin, *Raising Kane.*

5. Mark Horst Sawin, *Raising Kane.*

6. Wendell H. Oswalt, *Eskimo Explorers,* 117–18.

7. Mark Horst Sawin, *Raising Kane,* chap. 13; Wendell H. Oswalt, *Eskimo Explorers,* 117.

8. John Edward Weems, *Peary,* 5–6.

9. John Edward Weems, *Peary,* 5–6.

10. John Edward Weems, *Peary,* 7–8, 52.

11. John Edward Weems, *Peary,* 8.

12. John Edward Weems, *Peary,* 51–67.

13. John Edward Weems, *Peary,* 9, 74.

14. John Edward Weems, *Peary,* 99.

15. John Edward Weems, *Peary,* 271.

16. John Edward Weems, *Peary,* 104.

17. John Edward Weems, *Peary,* 129–30.

18. *Miss Olof Krarer,* Slayton Lyceum Bureau Special Publication.

19. John Edward Weems, *Peary,* 129–30.

20. John Edward Weems, *Peary,* 132.

21. John Edward Weems, *Peary,* 106.

22. John Edward Weems, *Peary,* 136–37.

23. Josephine Peary, *The Snow Baby.*

24. *Miss Olof Krarer,* Slayton Lyceum Bureau Special Publication.

25. See, for example, Alexis Everett Frye, *Geography*, 66, 98–99.

26. Vilhjálmur Stefánsson, *Adventures in Error*, 259.

27. See R. E. Johnson, M. H. Johnson, and H. S. Jeanes, *Schwatka*.

28. M. E. E. Smith, *Eskimo Stories*, 4.

29. M. E. E. Smith, *Eskimo Stories*, 177.

30. Vilhjálmur Stefánsson, *Adventures in Error*, 277.

Chicago

1. Florence Ffrench, *Music and Musicians in Chicago*, 200.

2. Slayton heard Ólöf speak for the first time in Minnesota, most likely in either St. Paul or Minneapolis.

3. *Miss Olof Krarer*, Slayton Lyceum Bureau Special Publication.

4. *Miss Olof Krarer*, Slayton Lyceum Bureau Special Publication.

5. Letter from Wendell Slayton to Vilhjálmur Stefánsson, June 30, 1936.

6. 1900 Census, Cook County, Chicago, Ill.

7. Frances Cheney Bennett, "Henry Lake Slayton," 505.

8. David Ward Wood, *Chicago: Distinguished Citizens*, 132.

9. Frances Cheney Bennett, "Henry Lake Slayton," 505.

10. David Ward Wood, *Chicago: Distinguished Citizens*, 133.

11. Florence Ffrench, *Music and Musicians in Chicago*, 199; David Ward Wood, *Chicago: Distinguished Citizens*, 133; Frances Cheney Bennett, "Henry Lake Slayton," 505–6.

12. Report of Henry Slayton's death, *Chicago Tribune*, June 11, 1910.

13. Frances Cheney Bennett, "Henry Lake Slayton," 507–8.

14. Joseph Kirkland, *The Story of Chicago*, 153, 403.

15. David Ward Wood, *Chicago: Distinguished Citizens*, 133.

16. David Ward Wood, *Chicago: Distinguished Citizens*, 133.

17. Florence Ffrench, *Music and Musicians in Chicago*, 200.

18. Frances Cheney Bennett, "Henry Lake Slayton," 507.

19. *St. Petersburg Times*, September 20, 1932, 2; David Ward Wood, *Chicago: Distinguished Citizens*, 134.

20. A. Augustus Wright, *Who's Who in the Lyceum*, 161; Frances Cheney Bennett, "Henry Lake Slayton," 507.

21. David Ward Wood, *Chicago: Distinguished Citizens*, 134.

22. *Slayton Lyceum Bureau Circular*.

23. Susan E. Hirsch and Robert I. Goler, *A City Comes of Age*, 56.

24. Harold M. Mayer and Richard C. Wade, *Chicago: Growth of a Metropolis*, 35.

25. Florence Ffrench, *Music and Musicians in Chicago*, 200.

26. David Ward Wood, *Chicago: Distinguished Citizens*, 132.

27. David Ward Wood, *Chicago: Distinguished Citizens*, 134.

28. Edgar Lee Masters, *The Tale of Chicago*, 242.

29. The Secretary of State List (the Van Buren address), *Chicago Tribune*, June 11, 1910.

30. Dominic A. Pacyga and Ellen Skerrett, *Chicago: City of Neighborhoods*, 199.

31. 1900 Census, Cook County. Also information received by e-mail from the Chicago Public Library, January 10, 2001.

32. Jóhann Schram, "Diary from 1876–1877" (in Icelandic), 166.

33. A. Augustus Wright, *Who's Who in the Lyceum*, 161.

34. Joseph Kirkland, *The Story of Chicago*, 403; Harold M. Mayer and Richard C. Wade, *Chicago: Growth of a Metropolis*, 150–54.

35. Harold M. Mayer and Richard C. Wade, *Chicago: Growth of a Metropolis*, 256.

36. Charles Simic, "The Thinking Man's Comedy," 13–15.

37. 1900 Census, Cook County, Chicago, Ill.

38. Hördur Ágústsson, *Icelandic Architectural Heritage*, vol. 1, *A Review of Building Construction History, 1750–1940* (in Icelandic), 65.

39. Susan E. Hirsch and Robert I. Goler, *A City Comes of Age*, 55, 128.

40. *Chicago Daily News*, May 12, 1923, 12.

41. Dominic A. Pacyga and Ellen Skerrett, *Chicago: City of Neighborhoods*, 199–200.

42. *Chicago Daily News*, July 8, 1929, 33.

43. *Chicago Daily News*, July 8, 1929, 33.

44. Dominic A. Pacyga and Ellen Skerrett, *Chicago: City of Neighborhoods*, 202.

45. Carl D. Buck, *A Sketch of the Linguistic Conditions of Chicago*, 466.

46. George Thorstein Freeman, "The Viking Hall at Wisconsin's Rock Island State Park," 5.

47. Gudjón Arngrímsson, *Another Iceland* (in Icelandic), 238–43; George Thorstein Freeman, "The Viking Hall at Wisconsin's Rock Island State Park," 5.

Slayton's Business Enterprises

1. Joseph E. Gould, *The Chautauqua Movement*, 3.

2. Joseph E. Gould, *The Chautauqua Movement*, 8.

3. John E. Tapia, *Circuit Chautauqua*, 104–5.

4. Charlotte Canning, "The Most American Thing in America," 104–5.

5. Joseph E. Gould, *The Chautauqua Movement*, 9–10.

6. John E. Tapia, *Circuit Chautauqua*, 104–5; *St. Petersburg Times*, February 25, 1910, 1.

7. A. Augustus Wright, *Who's Who in the Lyceum*, 161.

8. Frances Cheney Bennett, "Henry Lake Slayton," 507.

9. *Slayton Lyceum Bureau Magazine*, 2.

10. *Slayton Lyceum Bureau Magazine*, 40–41.

11. Paul M. Pearson, "A Page about Wagner, " 10; Charles L. Wagner, *Seeing Stars*, 63–64; Edmund Vance Cooke, "Bryan as a Speechmaker," 20–21.

12. A. Augustus Wright, *Who's Who in the Lyceum*, 161.

13. Slayton Lyceum Bureau, 1879–80, 5.

14. Slayton Lyceum Bureau, 1879–80, 5.

15. *Slayton Lyceum Bureau Circular*, 1; See also *Dictionary of American Biography Base Set.*

16. Slayton Lyceum Bureau, 1879–80, 2.

17. Slayton Lyceum Bureau, 1878–79, 2.

18. Slayton Lyceum Bureau, 1878–79, 2.

19. Slayton Lyceum Bureau, 1878–79, 3.

20. Slayton Lyceum Bureau, 1879–80, 4; see also the "Tyler, Moses Coit" entry in *The Columbia Electronic Encyclopedia.*

21. Slayton Lyceum Bureau, 1878–79, 1.

22. Slayton Lyceum Bureau, 1878–79, 1.

23. Slayton Lyceum Bureau, 1878–79, 1.

24. Slayton Lyceum Bureau, 1879–80, 5; *Slayton Lyceum Bureau Magazine*, 52, 54.

25. Charlotte Canning, "The Most American Thing in America," 91.

26. Slayton Lyceum Bureau, 1879–80, 1.

27. S. Russell Bridges, letter to Vilhjálmur Stefánsson, July 31, 1938.

28. *Miss Olof Krarer*, Slayton Lyceum Bureau Special Publication; *Elyria (Ohio) Republican*, "Miss Olof Krarer, Esquimau."

29. *Miss Olof Krarer*, Slayton Lyceum Bureau Special Publication.

30. A. Augustus Wright, *Who's Who in the Lyceum*, 124.

31. *Miss Olof Krarer*, Slayton Lyceum Bureau Special Publication.

32. *Miss Olof Krarer*, Slayton Lyceum Bureau Special Publication.

33. *Daily Review (Decatur, Ill.)*, "Miss Olof Krarer," 8.

34. *Miss Olof Krarer*, Slayton Lyceum Bureau Special Publication.

35. *Miss Olof Krarer*, Slayton Lyceum Bureau Special Publication.

36. *Star and Sentinel*, "An Interesting Lecture," 3.

37. *Miss Olof Krarer*, Slayton Lyceum Bureau Special Publication.

38. *New York Times*, "Greenland by a Native," 2.

39. *Herald and Torch Light (Hagerstown, Md.)*, "A Wonderful Visitor," 4.

40. Mrs. E. A. Carnahan, "Getting a Start in School," 5.

41. Vilhjálmur Stefánsson, *Adventures in Error*, 259.

42. Franz Boas, *The Central Eskimo.*

43. *St. Petersburg Times*, February 8 and 25, 1910.

44. Diane Arbus, *An Aperture Monograph*, 3.

Liar, Liar

1. Evelin Sullivan, *The Concise Book of Lying*, 155.

2. Evelin Sullivan, *The Concise Book of Lying*, 154.

3. Evelin Sullivan, *The Concise Book of Lying*, 152–53.

4. G. J. Hallson, letter to B. L. Baldwinson, May 26, 1926, forwarded to Thorstina Jackson.

5. Evelin Sullivan, *The Concise Book of Lying*, 152–53.

6. See Donald B. Smith, *Long Lance;* Donald B. Smith, *From the Land of Shadows.*

7. Evelin Sullivan, *The Concise Book of Lying,* 88–89.

8. John Schoolcraft, letter to Vilhjálmur Stefánsson, June 19, 1936. In his essay on Ólöf, Vilhjálmur states that John Schoolcraft met Ólöf in Florida (248), but this is incorrect, as they met in Battle Creek, Michigan.

9. John Schoolcraft, "The Story of Olaf Crerar," 2.

10. John Schoolcraft, "The Story of Olaf Crerar," 1–2.

11. Frederick Schwatka, *Children of the Cold,* 181.

12. Josephine Peary, *The Snow Baby,* 41.

13. Josephine Peary, *My Arctic Journal,* 41.

14. Mary E. E. Smith, *Eskimo Stories,* 122–27.

15. *Detroit Free Press* in *Miss Olof Krarer,* Slayton Lyceum Bureau Special Publication.

16. Elisha Kent Kane, *Arctic Explorations,* 361–62.

17. Frederick Schwatka, *Children of the Cold,* 44–65.

18. *Miss Olof Krarer,* Slayton Lyceum Bureau Special Publication.

19. Albert S. Post, *Olof Krarer,* 28.

20. Evelin Sullivan, *The Concise Book of Lying,* 108.

21. Albert S. Post, *Olof Krarer,* 27.

22. Albert S. Post, *Olof Krarer,* 28. Ólöf's own emphasis.

23. William H. Stout, letters to Vilhjálmur Stefánsson, July 13, 1936, and July 21, 1936.

24. *Miss Olof Krarer,* Slayton Lyceum Bureau Special Publication.

25. *Miss Olof Krarer,* Slayton Lyceum Bureau Special Publication.

26. Amy M. Weiskopf, letter to Vilhjálmur Stefánsson, July 23, 1936.

27. John Edward Weems, *Peary,* 132.

28. Dennis Rawlins, *Peary at the North Pole,* 59.

29. John Edward Weems, *Peary,* 129.

30. S. Allen Coutner, *North Pole Legacy,* 27, 34. Vilhjálmur Stefánsson also had a child with an Inuk woman, the son Alex Stefánsson; see Gísli Pálsson, *Travelling Passions.*

31. Josephine Peary, *The Snow Baby,* 30, 38–39.

32. See Lisa Bloom, *Gender on Ice.*

33. Robert E. Peary, *Secrets of Polar Travel,* 186–89.

34. Dennis Rawlins, *Peary at the North Pole,* 59.

35. Dennis Rawlins, *Peary at the North Pole,* 60.

36. Kenn Harper, *Give Me My Father's Body,* 30.

37. Kenn Harper, *Give Me My Father's Body,* 29–30.

38. Kenn Harper, *Give Me My Father's Body,* 29–30.

39. Kenn Harper, *Give Me My Father's Body,* 46.

40. Thorsteinn Th. Thorsteinsson, *Westmen* (in Icelandic). Transcript of a radio broadcast on Icelanders' colonization of North America, 22.

41. John S. Matthiasson, "Adaptation to an Ethnic Structure," 162–65.

42. Bödvar Gudmundsson, interview, March 2004.

43. Jón Ólafsson, *Free Press*, Manitoba, March 8, 1892.

44. Gudjón Arngrímsson, *Another Iceland* (in Icelandic), 196–99.

45. Júníus Kristinsson, *A Registry of Emigrants to North America* (in Icelandic), 305.

46. Gudjón Arngrímsson, *Another Iceland* (in Icelandic), 196–99.

St. Petersburg, Florida

1. A. Augustus Wright, *Who's Who in the Lyceum*, 175; Charles L. Wagner, *Seeing Stars*, 50–51.

2. Paul M. Pearson, "A Page about Wagner," 10.

3. Charles L. Wagner, *Seeing Stars*, 51.

4. Paul M. Pearson, "A Page about Wagner," 10.

5. Frances Cheney Bennett, "Henry Lake Slayton"; *Lyceumite and Talent*, "Henry L. Slayton," 56.

6. Sale agreement, University of Iowa Special Collection.

7. *St. Petersburg Times*, September 20, 1932, 2.

8. *St. Petersburg City Directory*, 1916, 11.

9. *St. Petersburg City Directory*, 1916, 15.

10. *St. Petersburg City Directory*, 1916, 12–13.

11. See Fred J. Alsop III, *Birds of Florida*.

12. David Ward Wood, *Chicago: Distinguished Citizens*, 132.

13. Pinellas County, Fla., MLS, bk. 1, 292.

14. Raymond Arsenault, *St. Petersburg and the Florida Dream*, 144.

15. Raymond Arsenault, *St. Petersburg and the Florida Dream*, 144–45.

16. Raymond Arsenault, *St. Petersburg and the Florida Dream*, 78.

17. *St. Petersburg City Directory*, 1916, 11.

18. *Chicago Tribune*, June 11, 1910.

19. Raymond Arsenault, *St. Petersburg and the Florida Dream*, 120.

20. Raymond Arsenault, *St. Petersburg and the Florida Dream*, 144–45.

21. *St. Petersburg City Directory*, 1922, 31.

22. *St. Petersburg Independent*, July 16, 1964, 3-A.

23. *St. Petersburg City Directory*, 1922, 34.

24. *St. Petersburg City Directory*, 1922, 3.

25. *St. Petersburg City Directory*, 1926, 3.

26. *St. Petersburg Times*, February 25, 1910, 1.

27. *St. Petersburg Times*, February 18, 1916, 1.

28. Scott Taylor Harzell, "Many Carried Mallets and Reveled in Roque's Heyday."

29. *St. Petersburg City Directory*, 1922, 511, 1915; *St. Petersburg City Directory*, 1926, 3.

30. Raymond Arsenault, *St. Petersburg and the Florida Dream*, 123.

31. Vilhjálmur Stefánsson, *Adventures in Error*, 258.

32. *St. Petersburg City Directory*, 1915, 217.

33. *St. Petersburg City Directory*, 1918, 34.

34. *St. Petersburg Independent*, October 8, 1938, 1.

35. Alice Slayton Mundorff, interview, April 1, 2003.

36. S. Russell Bridges, letter to Vilhjálmur Stefánsson, July 1, 1936.

37. Alice Slayton Mundorff, interview, April 1, 2003.

38. *St. Petersburg City Directory*, 1915, 217.

39. *St. Petersburg City Directory*, 1922, 32–34.

40. Raymond Arsenault, *St Petersburg and the Florida Dream*, 136–37.

41. Quad-Cities Memory Project, Marriage Certificates pre 1836 to c1925.

42. *St. Petersburg Independent*, July 16, 1964, 3-A.

43. Alice Slayton Mundorff, interview, April 1, 2003.

44. Clare B. Shank, *St. Petersburg Woman's Club*, 6.

45. Clare B. Shank, *St. Petersburg Woman's Club*, 6.

46. *St. Petersburg Times*, March 8, 1939, 1–2; *St. Petersburg Times*, March 19, 1939, 8; Clare B. Shank, *St. Petersburg Woman's Club*, 4.

47. John Schoolcraft, "The Story of Olaf Crerar," 3.

48. Vilhjálmur Stefánsson, *Adventures in Error*, 259; 1920 Census, Calhoun County, Mich.

49. Fourteenth Census of the United States: 1920 Population.

50. *St. Petersburg Times*, September 20, 1932, 2.

51. John Schoolcraft, "The Story of Olaf Crerar," 3; Vilhjálmur Stefánsson, *Adventures in Error*, 251.

52. John Schoolcraft, letter to Vilhjalmur Stefánsson, June 19, 1936; Vilhjálmur Stefánsson, *Adventures in Error*, 248–49.

53. Alice Slayton Mundorff, interview, April 1, 2003.

54. *St. Petersburg Times*, March 9, 1924.

55. Adrian C. Davis and Barbara Boggess Stephens, *A Historical Scrapbook of Ole St. Pete High*, 93.

56. Raymond Arsenault, *St. Petersburg and the Florida Dream*, 254.

57. Alice Slayton Mundorff, interview, April 1, 2003.

58. Raymond Arsenault, *St. Petersburg and the Florida Dream*, 253–56.

59. Book of Deeds, Pinellas County, Fla., 650:70–74; *St. Petersburg Times*, September 20, 1932, 2.

60. *St. Petersburg Times*, September 20, 1932, 2.

61. *St. Petersburg Times*, September 20, 1932, 2.

62. Alice Slayton Mundorff, interview, April 1, 2003; *St. Petersburg Times*, April 18, 1939, 2.

63. *St. Petersburg Independent*, October 8, 1938, 1; *St. Petersburg Independent*, July 16, 1964, 3-A.

64. Torfi Sveinsson, interview, May 2002.

65. Lorna Lueck, interview, Spring 2004.

66. 1900 Census, Cook County, Chicago, Ill.

67. Charles L. Wagner, *Seeing Stars*, 50.

68. U.S. Department of Labor, Composite Consumer Price Index.

69. W. H. Stout, letter to Vilhjálmur Stefánsson, July 1, 1936; Sale agreement, University of Iowa Special Collection.

70. Frances Finch, letter to Vilhjálmur Stefánsson, November 27, 1932.

71. Documents from St. Petersburg, Pinellas County.

The Death of Miss Krarer

1. W. Stone, letter to Vilhjálmur Stefánsson, June 19, 1936.

2. 1930 Census, Benton Township.

3. W. Stone, letter to Vilhjálmur Stefánsson, June 19, 1936.

4. Alice Slayton Mundorff, interview, April 1, 2003.

5. Wendell Slayton, letter to Vilhjálmur Stefánsson, June 30, 1936.

6. See Death Certificate of Olof Krarer.

7. *Chicago Tribune*, February 1, 1935.

8. E. Edmunds, letter to Vilhjálmur Stefánsson, June 24, 1936; John William Leonard and Albert Nelson Marquis, *Who's Who in Chicago*, 911.

9. Correction of Death Certificate.

10. Thorstina Jackson wrote to Ólöf's relations and old friends in Winnipeg to gather information on behalf of Vilhjálmur Stefánsson, but none of them knew where she was. Ólöf's relatives were willing to provide Thorstina and Vilhjálmur with information in return for Ólöf's location. B. L. Baldwinson, letter to Thorstina Jackson, November 3, 1927.

11. Ólafur S. Thorgeirsson, *Almanac for the Year 1937* (in Icelandic), 111.

12. Torfi Sveinsson, interview, January 19, 2004.

Ólöf Exposed

1. Evelin Sullivan, *The Concise Book of Lying*, 120.

2. Vilhjálmur Stefánsson, *Adventures in Error*, 245–46.

3. Vilhjálmur Stefánsson, *Adventures in Error*, 245–46.

4. Vilhjálmur Stefánsson, *Adventures in Error*, 270.

5. Richard J. Diubaldo, *Stefansson and the Canadian Arctic*, 49–53.

6. Richard J. Diubaldo, *Stefansson and the Canadian Arctic*, 51–54.

7. Richard J. Diubaldo, *Stefansson and the Canadian Arctic*, 51.

8. Vilhjálmur Stefánsson, *Adventures in Error*, 245–46.

9. *Washington Post*, March 16, 1913, 25.

10. Vilhjálmur Stefánsson, *Adventures in Error*, 243.

11. Fred Swanson, letter to Thorstina Jackson, June 5, 1924.

12. Vilhjálmur Stefánsson, *Adventures in Error*, 243–78.

13. Thorstina Jackson, note added on a letter by Baldwinson, November 3, 1927.

14. Vilhjálmur Stefánsson's book was reviewed in the following newspapers in addition to those quoted here: *Book Review Digest*, 912–13; "Popular Delusions," *New York Times*, November 29, 1936, 14; "Truth against Tradition," *New York Herald Tribune*, November 29, 1936, Books section; *Booklist*, December 1936, vol. 33, no. 4, 106.

15. "An Arctic Explorer in Regions of Error," *Boston Evening Transcript*, December 5, 1936.

16. "'Adventures in Error,' Explorer Stefansson Points out Misconceptions," *Springfield Daily Republic*, December 16, 1936.

17. George Sarton, "Vilhjalmur Stefansson. *Adventures in Error*"; Eugene Garfield, "George Sarton," 248–53.

18. Evelyn Stefansson, afterword to *Discovery: The Autobiography of Vilhjalmur Stefansson* by Vilhjálmur Stefánsson, 397–98.

19. George Sarton, "Vilhjalmur Stefansson. *Adventures in Error*," 457–59.

20. George Sarton, "Vilhjalmur Stefansson. *Adventures in Error*," 459.

21. Donald B. Smith, *From the Land of Shadows*.

22. Philip J. Deloria, *Playing Indian*, 2–3.

23. Donald B. Smith, *From the Land of Shadows*, 214.

24. Donald B. Smith, *From the Land of Shadows*, 214.

25. Shari M. Huhndorf, *Going Native*, 85, 100–101.

26. Shari M. Huhndorf, *Going Native*, 85, 100–101.

27. H. Allen Orr, "Darwinian Storytelling. *The Blank Slate*."

28. *Gettysburg Times*, October 8, 1940, 6; *Gettysburg Times*, November 5, 1940, 4.

29. After Sigurdur Nordal gave his radio broadcast, "An Epistle on Ólöf Sölvadóttir," it was published specially in a 450-copy edition. The lecture was also published in the journal *Húnvetningur: The Journal of the Húnavatnssýsla County Society in Reykjavík* 3 (1978): 93–112. The lecture was also published in Sigurdur Nordal, *Descriptions of People III. Expressions* (1986), 73–90.

30. Sigurdur Nordal, *An Epistle on Ólöf Sölvadóttir*, 31. See also Thórhildur Sveinsdóttir on Gísli Ólafsson, "Gísli Ólafsson from Eiríksstadir."

31. Sigurdur Nordal, *An Epistle on Ólöf Sölvadóttir*, 30; Gunnar Árnason, "Gísli Ólafsson from Eiríksstadir."

References

Printed Sources

Ablon, Joan. 1984. *Little People in America: The Social Dimensions of Dwarfism.* New York: Praeger.

Ablon, Joan. 1988. *Living with Difference: Families with Dwarf Children.* New York: Praeger.

Adalsteinn Eiríksson. 1974. *Kvennaskólinn í Reykjavík 1874–1974* [The Women's School in Reykjavík 1874–1974], 89–206. Reykjavík: Almenna bókafélagid.

Adams, Bluford. 1997. *E Pluribus Barnum: The Great Showman and U.S. Popular Culture.* Minneapolis: University of Minnesota Press.

Alsop, Fred J., III. 2002. *Birds of Florida.* New York: DK Publishing.

Arbus, Diane. 1972. *An Aperture Monograph.* New York: Aperture Foundation.

Arsenault, Raymond. 1988. *St. Petersburg and the Florida Dream, 1888–1950.* Norfolk: Donning.

Ártöl og áfangar í sögu íslenskra kvenna [Years and Milestones in the History of Icelandic Women]. 1998. Reykjavík: Kvennasögusafn Íslands.

Bennett, Frances Cheney, ed. 1904. "Henry Lake Slayton." In *History of Music and Art in Illinois,* 505–8. [Societé Universelle Lyrique.] Merrill and Baker.

Bjarni Jónasson. 1977. "Litazt um í Svínavatnshreppi, framhald" [Perspectives on Svínavatn District, continued]. *Húnavaka* 17.

Björg Einarsdóttir. 1984. *Úr ævi og starfi íslenskra kvenna,* I. bindi [From the Lives and Work of Icelandic Women, vol.1]. Reykjavík: Bókrún.

Bjork, Kenneth O. 1958. *West of the Great Divide: Norwegian Migration to the Pacific Coast, 1847–1893.* Northfield, Minn.: Norwegian-American Historical Association.

Björn Bjarnason. 1941. *Brandsstadaannáll* [The Annals of Brandsstadir]. Reykjavík: Sögufélagid Húnvetningur and Húnvetningafélagid í Reykjavík.

Björn Thorsteinsson and Bergsteinn Jónsson. 1991. *Íslandssaga til okkar daga* [A History of Iceland to the Present Day]. Reykjavík: Sögufélag.

Blake, Lille Devereux. 2001. In *Dictionary of American Biography Base Set: American Council of Learned Societies 1928–1936.* Reproduced in Biography Resource Center. Farmington Hills, Mich.: Gale Group.

Bloom, Lisa. 1993. *Gender on Ice: American Ideologies of Polar Expeditions.* Minneapolis: University of Minnesota Press.

Boas, Franz. [1888] 1964. *The Central Eskimo.* Lincoln: University of Nebraska Press.

Bödvar Gudmundsson. 2001. *Bréf Vestur-Íslendinga I* [Letters of the West Icelanders 1]. Reykjavík: Mál og menning.

Bödvar Gudmundsson. 2002. *Bréf Vestur-Íslendinga II* [Letters of the West Icelanders 2]. Reykjavík: Mál og menning.

Bogdan, Robert. 1988. *Freak Show: Presenting Human Oddities for Amusement and Profit.* Chicago: University of Chicago Press.

Browder, Laura. 2000. *Slippery Characters: Ethnic Impersonators and American Identities.* Chapel Hill: University of North Carolina Press.

Bryan, William Jennings. [1896]. 1996. *The Cross of Gold.* Speech Delivered before the National Democratic Convention at Chicago, July 9, 1896. Introduction by Robert W. Cherney. Lincoln: University of Nebraska Press.

Buck, Carl D. 1894. *A Sketch of the Linguistic Conditions of Chicago.* Chicago: University of Chicago Press.

Butler, Judith. 1993. *Bodies That Matter: On the Discursive Limits of "Sex."* New York: Routledge.

Canning, Charlotte. 1999. "The Most American Thing in America: Producing National Identities in Chautauqua, 1904–1932." In Jeffrey D. Mason and J. Ellen Gainor, eds., *Performing America: Cultural Nationalism and American Theater,* 91–105. Ann Arbor: University of Michigan Press.

Carnahan, E. A. 1893. "Getting a Start in School." *Democratic Standard,* December 8.

Cherney, Robert W. 1996. Introduction to William Jennings Bryan, *The Cross of Gold.* Speech Delivered before the National Democratic Convention at Chicago, July 9, 1896. Lincoln: University of Nebraska Press.

Chicago Daily News. 1923. "'Mid-City' Former Home of the Elite." May 12.

Chicago Daily News. 1929. "Union Park." July 8.

Chicago Tribune. 1910. "Lyceum Founder Dead in Chicago." June 11.

Chicago Tribune. 1935. "Miss Krarer, Eskimo, Once a Lecturer, Dies." February 1.

Cook, Susan. 1988. "A Church for Every Saloon." In *Passport to Ballard,* 117–32. Seattle, Wash.: Ballard News Tribune.

Cooke, Edmund Vance. 1908. "Bryan as a Speechmaker: Bryan and the Chautauqua." *Lyceumite and Talent,* July.

Counter, S. Allen. 1991. *North Pole Legacy: Black, White and Eskimo.* Amherst: University of Massachusetts Press.

Cronander, Cheryl, and Thomas Downey. 1988. "The Buildings of Old Ballard." In *Passport to Ballard,* 217–30. Seattle, Wash.: Ballard News Tribune.

Daily Review (Decatur, Illinois). 1899. "Miss Olof Krarer: An Eskimo Dwarf Who Summers in an Improvised Ice Cave Visits an Illinois Town." July 6.

Dasen, Véronique. 1993. *Dwarfs in Ancient Egypt and Greece.* Oxford: Clarendon Press.

Davis, Adrian C., and Barbara Boggess Stephens. 1995. *A Historical Scrapbook of Ole St. Pete High.* St. Petersburg, Fla.

Davis, Janet M. 2002. *The Circus Age: Culture and Society under the Big Top.* Chapel Hill: University of North Carolina Press.

Deloria, Philip J. 1998. *Playing Indian.* New Haven: Yale University Press.

Diubaldo, Richard J. 1978. *Stefansson and the Canadian Arctic.* Montreal: McGill-Queen's University Press.

Elyria (Ohio) Republican. 1903. "Miss Olof Krarer, Esquimau." September 24.

Erlendur Gudmundsson. 2002. *Heima og heiman* [Home and Away]. Reykjavík: Mál og menning.

Ffrench, Florence. [1899] 1979. *Music and Musicians in Chicago: The City's Leading Artists, Organizations and Art Buildings.* Chicago: Florence Ffrench.

Fienup-Riordan, Ann. 1990. *Eskimo Essays.* New Brunswick: Rutgers University Press.

Foucault, Michel. 1980. *Herculine Barbin: Being the Recently Discovered Memoirs of a Nineteenth-Century French Hermaphrodite.* New York: Pantheon Books.

Freeborn County Standard. 1890. "Miss Olof Krarer: A Greenland Lady Tells of the Domestic Life of Her People." March 27.

Freeman, George Thorstein. 2001. "The Viking Hall at Wisconsin's Rock Island State Park." *Lögberg-Heimskringla,* November 16.

French, W. M. 2001. In *Dictionary of American Biography Base Set: American Council of Learned Societies 1928–1936.* Reproduced in Biography Resource Center. Farmington Hills, Mich.: Gale Group.

Fridrik J. Bergmann. 1937. "Safn ad landnámssögu Íslendinga í Vesturheimi" [The Colonial History of Icelanders in North America]. In *Almanak* of Ólafur S. Thorgeirsson, 43:34–76.

Frye, Alexis Everett. 1895. *Geography.* Boston: Ginn.

Garfield, Eugene. 1985. "George Sarton: The Father of the History of Science. Part 2. Sarton Shapes a New Discipline." *Current Comments,* no. 26 (July 1): 248–53. Institute for Scientific Information. www.garfield.library.upenn.edu/essays/v8p248y1985.pdf.

Gettysburg Times. 1940. "Out of the Past." October 8 and November 5.

Gilman, Sander L. 1998. *Creating Beauty to Cure the Soul.* Durham: Duke University Press.

Gísli Gunnarsson. 1980. *Fertility and Nuptiality in Iceland's Demographic History.* Meddelande från Ekonomisk-historiska institutionen 12, University of Lund, Sweden.

Gísli Pálsson. 2003. *Frægd og firnindi: Ævi Vilhjálms Stefánssonar* [Travelling Passions: The Hidden Life of Vilhjalmur Stefansson]. Reykjavík: Mál og menning. English translation by Keneva Kunz published in 2005 by the University of Manitoba Press, Winnipeg.

Gould, Joseph E. 1961. *The Chautauqua Movement: An Episode in the Continuing American Revolution.* State University of New York. New York City: University Publishers.

Gudjón Arngrímsson. 1997. *Nýja Ísland: Örlagasaga vesturfaranna í máli og myndum* [New Iceland: The West Icelanders' Destiny in Words and Pictures]. Reykjavík: Mál og menning.

Gudjón Arngrímsson. 1998. *Annad Ísland: Gullöld Vestur-Íslendinga í máli og myndum* [Another Iceland: The West Icelanders' Golden Age in Words and Pictures]. Reykjavík: Mál og menning.

Gudmundur Hálfdanarson. 1986a. "Börn—höfudstóll fátæklingsins?" [Children—Poor Man's Principal?]. *Saga, Tímarit Sögufélags* 24:121–46.

Gudmundur Hálfdanarson. 1986b. "Takmörkun giftinga eda einstaklingsfrelsi: Íhaldssemi og frjálslyndi á fyrstu árum hins endurreista althingis" [Limitations of Marriage and Personal Freedom]. *Tímarit Máls og menningar* 47, no. 4 (November): 457–68.

Gudmundur Hálfdanarson. 1993. "Íslensk thjódfélagsthróun á 19. öld" [Social Development in 19th-Century Iceland]. In Gudmundur Hálfdánarson and Svanur Kristjánsson, eds., *Íslensk thjódfélagsthróun 1880–1990: Ritgerdir* [Social Development in Iceland 1880–1890: Essays], 9–58. Reykjavík: Félagsvísindastofnun og Sagnfrædistofnun.

Gudmundur Sigurdur Jóhannsson and Magnús Björnsson. 1999. *Ættir Austur-Húnvetninga,* IV. bindi [A Genealogy of East Húnavatnssýsla county, vol. 4]. Reykjavík: Mál og mynd.

Gunnar Árnason. 1974. "Gísli Ólafsson frá Eiríksstödum" [Gísli Ólafsson from Eiríksstadir]. *Húnvetningur* 2:47–63.

Gunnlaugur Haraldsson. 2000. *Læknar á Íslandi* [Physicians in Iceland]. Reykjavík: Thjódsaga.

Hannon, Rhea. 1963. "Rhea Remembers: Early Blakely Days Recalled at Death of 'Mama' Solvason." *Bainbridge Review,* March 20.

Harper, Kenn. 1986. *Give Me My Father's Body: The Life of Minik, The New York Eskimo.* Ontario: Blacklead Books.

Harzell, Scott Taylor. 2002. "Many Carried Mallets and Reveled in Roque's Heyday." *St. Petersburg Times,* June 26.

Helga Ögmundardóttir. 2002. "Ímyndir, sjálfsmyndir og vald í samskiptum Indíána og Íslendinga í Vesturheimi 1875–1930" [Images, Self-Conceptions, and Power Interactions between Icelanders and Native Americans in North America 1875–1930]. Master's thesis, University of Iceland.

Helga Thórarinsdóttir. 1984. *Saga Ljósmædrafélags Íslands 1919–1979* [History of the Icelandic Midwives' Association 1919–1979]. Reykjavík: Ljósmædrafélag Íslands.

The Herald and Torch Light (Hagerstown, Md.). 1890. "A Wonderful Visitor." August 28.

Hirsch, Susan E., and Robert I. Goler 1990. *A City Comes of Age: Chicago in the 1890s.* Chicago: Chicago Historical Society.

Huhndorf, Shari M. 2001. *Going Native: Indians in the American Cultural Imagination.* Ithaca: Cornell University Press.

Hulda Sigurborg Sigtryggsdóttir. 2002. *Frá Íslandi til Vesturheims: Saga Sumarlida Sumarlidasonar gullsmids frá Ædey* [From Iceland to the New World. The Story of Goldsmith Sumarlidi Sumarlidason from Ædey]. Reykjavík: Hid íslenska bókmenntafélag og Sögufélag.

Hördur Ágústsson. 2000. *Íslensk byggingararfleifd,* I. *Ágrip af húsagerdarsögu 1750–1940* [Icelandic Architectural Heritage, vol. 1, A Review of Building Construction History 1750–1940]. Reykjavík: Húsafridunarnefnd ríkisins.

Israel, Betsy. 2002. *Bachelor Girl: The Secret History of Single Women in the Twentieth Century.* New York: William Morrow.

Jacobson, Matthew F. 1998. *Whiteness of a Different Color: European Immigrants and the Alchemy of Race.* Cambridge: Harvard University Press.

Jóhann Schram. 2001. "Dagbók 1876–1877" [Diary 1876–1877]. In Davíd Ólafsson and Sigurdur Gylfi Magnússon, eds., *Burt—og meir en bæjarleid* [Away—And Not Just to Town]. [Diaries and personal writings of emigrants from Iceland to America in the late 19th century.] Reykjavík: Háskólaútgáfan.

Johnson, M. Persis. 1936. "An Arctic Explorer in Regions of Error." *Boston Evening Transcript,* December 5.

Johnson, R. E., M. H. Johnson, and H. S. Jeanes. 1984. *Schwatka: The Life of Frederick Schwatka 1849–1892.* Montpelier, Vt.: Horn of the Moon Enterprises.

Jón Thórdarson. 1950. "Audkúlu-og Svínavatnssóknir, 1857" [Audkúla and Svínavatn Parishes, 1857]. In *Sýslu-og sóknarlýsingar Hins íslenzka bókmenntafélags 1839–1873, I. Húnavatnssýsla* [County and Parish Descriptions of the Icelandic Literary Society 1839–1873]. Akureyri: Bókaútgáfan Nordri.

Jónas B. Bjarnason. 1944. "Saga Búnadarfélags Svínavatnshrepps" [History of the Svínavatn District Agricultural Society]. In *Búnadarfélög Svínavatns-og Bólstadarhlídarhreppa, Aldarminning* [The Agricultural Societies of Svínavatn and Bólstadarhlíd Districts: A Centennial Retrospective]. Akureyri: Sögufélagid Húnvetningur.

Júníus H. Kristinsson. 1983. *Vesturfaraskrá 1870–1914* [A Record of Emigrants to North America 1870–1914]. Reykjavík: Sagnfrædistofnun Háskóla Íslands.

Kane, Elisha Kent. 1996. *Arctic Explorations.* Chicago: R.R. Donnelly and Sons.

Kane, Elisha Kent [1856] 1996. *The U.S. Grinnell Expedition in Search of Sir John Franklin.* Chicago: R.R. Donnelly and Sons.

Kirk, Ruth, and Carmela Alexander. 1990. *Exploring Washington's Past: A Road Guide to History.* Seattle: University of Washington Press.

Kirkland, Joseph. 1892. *The Story of Chicago.* Chicago: Dibble Publishing.

Kristjanson, W. 1965. *The Icelandic People in Manitoba: A Manitoba Saga.* Winnipeg: Wallingford Press.

Lee, Harper [1960] 1982. *To Kill a Mockingbird.* New York: Warner Books.

Leonard, John William, and Albert Nelson Marquis. 1926. *Who's Who in Chicago and*

Illinois: The Book of Chicagoans, a Biographical Dictionary of Leading Living Men and Women of the City of Chicago and Environs. Chicago: A. N. Marquis.

Lyceumite and Talent. 1908. "Henry L. Slayton," May.

Már Jónsson. 1987. "Konur fyrirgefa körlum hór" [Woman Forgive Men's Adultery]. *Ný Saga* 1:70–78, 235–242.

Masters, Edgar Lee. 1933. *The Tale of Chicago.* New York: G. P. Putnam's Sons.

Matthiasson, John S. 1989. "Adaptation to an Ethnic Structure: The Urban Icelandic-Canadians of Winnipeg." In E. P. Durrenberger and Gísli Pálsson, eds., *The Anthropology of Iceland,* 157–75. Iowa City: University of Iowa Press.

Mayer, Harold M., and Richard C. Wade. 1969. *Chicago: Growth of a Metropolis.* Chicago: University of Chicago Press.

Miss Olof Krarer. Slayton Lyceum Bureau Special Publication.

Moore, William. 1988. "Community Life: Tradition in Transition." In *Passport to Ballard,* 201–16. Seattle, Wash.: Ballard News Tribune.

Naipaul, V. S. 1967. *The Mimic Men.* New York: Macmillan.

Nelson, Key. 1988. "Staying Healthy on Salmon Bay." In *Passport to Ballard,* 183–97. Seattle, Wash.: Ballard News Tribune.

New York Times. 1892. "Greenland by a Native." March 23.

Ólafur S. Thorgeirsson. 1904. *Almanak fyrir árid 1903* [Almanac for the Year 1903]. Winnipeg: O. S. Thorgeirsson.

Ólafur S. Thorgeirsson. 1937. *Almanak fyrir árid 1937* [Almanac for the Year 1937]. Winnipeg: O. S. Thorgeirsson.

Oleson, Tryggvi J., ed. 1951. *Saga Íslendinga í Vesturheimi,* IV. bindi [A History of Icelanders in North America, vol. 4]. Reykjavík: Bókaútgáfa Menningarsjóds.

Orr, H. Allen. 2003. "Darwinian Storytelling. *The Blank Slate: The Modern Denial of Human Nature* by Steven Pinker." *New York Review of Books* 50, no. 3 (February 27): 17–20.

Oswalt, Wendell H. 1999. *Eskimo Explorers.* Los Angeles: University of California Press.

Pacyga, Dominic A., and Ellen Skerrett. 1986. *Chicago: City of Neighborhoods.* Chicago: Loyola University Press.

Páll Kolka. 1950. *Föðurtún* [Father's Fields].

Pearson, Paul M. 1908. "A Page about Wagner." *Lyceumite and Talent,* February.

Peary, Josephine [1893] 1975. *My Arctic Journal: A Year among Ice Fields and Eskimos.* New York: AMS.

Peary, Josephine. 1901. *The Snow Baby.* New York: Frederick A. Stokes.

Peary, Josephine. 1903. *The Children of the Arctic.* New York: Frederick A. Stokes.

Peary, Robert E. 1898. *Northward over the "Great Ice": A Narrative of Life and Work along the Shores and upon the Interior Ice-Cap of Northern Greenland in the Years 1886–1897,* vol. 1. New York: Frederick A. Stokes.

Peary, Robert E. 1917. *Secrets of Polar Travel.* New York: Century.

Pétur Sigurdsson. 1987. "Thrír bændur í Bólstadarhlídarhreppi á 19. öld" [Three Farmers in Bólstadarhlíd District in the 19th Century]. *Húnavaka* (1987): 81–83.

Rev. Pjetur Gudmundsson, ed. 1941. *Annáll nítjándu aldar,* III. bindi, *1857–1869* [Annals of the 19th Century, vol. 3, 1857–1869]. Akureyri: Hallgr. Pjetursson and Bókaútgáfan Edda.

Post, Albert S. 1887. *Olof Krarer: The Esquimaux Lady. A Story of Her Native Home.* Ottawa, Ill.: W. Osmon & Sons.

Rawlins, Dennis. 1973. *Peary at the North Pole: Fact or Fiction?* New York: Robert B. Luce.

Reinartz, Kay F. 1988. "Yankee and Immigrant-Ballardites All." In *Passport to Ballard,* 45–55. Seattle, Wash.: Ballard News Tribune.

Sarton, George. 1938. "Vilhjalmur Stefansson. *Adventures in Error."* Isis 29:457–59.

Sawin, Mark Horst. 1997. "Raising Kane: The Making of a Hero, the Marketing of a Celebrity." Master's thesis, University of Texas at Austin. www.ekkane.org/sawin/sawin.htm.

Schwanter, Carlos, Katherine Morrissey, David Nicandri, and Susan Strasser. 1988. *Washington: Images of a State's Heritage.* Spokane, Wash.: Melior Publications.

Schwartz, Hillel. 1996. *The Culture of the Copy: Striking Likenesses, Unreasonable Facsimiles.* New York: Zone Books.

Schwatka, Frederick [1899] 1975. *The Children of the Cold.* Boston: Educational Publishing.

Shank, Clare B. 1982. *St. Petersburg Woman's Club: The Presidents' Book and Brief History.* February 7, 1913—February 1982. St. Petersburg, Fla.

Sigrídur Th. Erlendsdóttir. 1987. "Breytingar á réttarstödu íslenskra kvenna á 20. öld" [Changes in the Legal Standing of Icelandic Women in the 20th Century]. Lecture given before Félag áhugamanna um réttarsögu [The Icelandic Judicial History Society], February 17, 1987. Special publication.

Sigurdur Breidfjörd. 1836. *Frá Grænlandi* [From Greenland]. Copenhagen: Br. Benedictsen.

Sigurdur Breidfjörd. 1937. *Númarímur* [The Rhymes of Númi]. Reykjavík: Snæbjörn Jónsson.

Sigurdur Gudjónsson. 2001. "Afnám vistarskyldunnar og frjálslyndisstefnan: Umrædan um atvinnufrelsi á Íslandi 1888–1893" [Abolition of Labor Bondage and the Liberalism Movement: The Debate about Freedom of Employment in Iceland 1888–1893]. *Morgunbladid,* January 20.

Sigurdur Nordal. 1945. *Tháttur af Ólöfu Sölvadóttur* [An Epistle on Ólöf Sölvadóttir]. Special publication. Reykjavík: Ragnar Jónsson.

Simic, Charles. 2001. "The Thinking Man's Comedy." Review of *Bellow: A Biography* by James Atlas. *New York Review of Books* 48, no. 9 (May 31): 13–15.

Slayton Lyceum Bureau. 1878–79. Chicago, Ill.

Slayton Lyceum Bureau. 1879–80. Chicago, Ill.

Slayton Lyceum Bureau Circular. 1877–78. Chicago, Ill.

Slayton Lyceum Bureau Magazine. 1882–83. Chicago, Ill.

Smith, Donald B. 1982. *Long Lance: The True Story of an Impostor.* Toronto: Macmillan.

Smith, Donald B. 1990. *From the Land of Shadows: The Making of Grey Owl.* Seattle: University of Washington Press.

Smith, Mary Estella E. 1902. *Eskimo Stories.* Chicago: Rand McNally.

Springfield (Mass.) Daily Republic. 1936. "'Adventures in Error,' Explorer Stefansson Points out Misconceptions." December 16.

Star and Sentinel (Gettysburg, Pa.) . 1890. "An Interesting Lecture." November 4.

Stefansson, Evelyn. 1964. "Afterword." In Vilhjalmur Stefansson, *Discovery: The Autobiography of Vilhjalmur Stefansson,* 397–98. New York: McGraw-Hill.

St. Petersburg City Directory. 1915. Florida: R. L. Polk Publishers.

St. Petersburg City Directory. 1916. Florida: R. L. Polk Publishers.

St. Petersburg City Directory. 1918. Florida: R. L. Polk Publishers.

St. Petersburg City Directory. 1922. Florida: R. L. Polk Publishers.

St. Petersburg City Directory. 1926. Florida: R. L. Polk Publishers.

St. Petersburg Independent. 1938. "Local Apartment Houses Are Sold." October 8.

St. Petersburg Independent. 1964. "At a Landmark." July 16.

St. Petersburg Times. 1910. "Eskimo Courtship." February 8.

St. Petersburg Times. 1910. "How Eskimo Women Die." February 25.

St. Petersburg Times. 1916. "Bryan Points to Fallacy of Preparedness." February 18.

St. Petersburg Times. 1924. "Scotchy Thompson Is Winner of Slayton Cup." March 9.

St. Petersburg Times. 1932. "Years of Illness End in Death of Mrs. Slayton." September 20.

St. Petersburg Times. 1939. "Mrs. Slayton Succumbs: Illness Fatal to Social Leader and Clubwoman." April 18.

Sullivan, Evelin. 2001. *The Concise Book of Lying.* New York: Farrar, Strauss and Giroux.

Sweet, Matthew. 2001. *Inventing the Victorians.* London: Faber and Faber.

Tapia, John. 1997. *Circuit Chautauqua: from Rural Education to Popular Entertainment in Early Twentieth Century America.* Jefferson, N.C.: McFarland.

Thórhildur Sveinsdóttir. 1968. *Í gær og í dag* [Yesterday and Today]. Reykjavík.

Thórhildur Sveinsdóttir. 1982. *Sól rann í blíd* [Sunset in the Hills]. Reykjavík: Helgafell.

Thórhildur Sveinsdóttir. 1985. "Gísli Ólafsson frá Eiríksstödum" [Gísli Ólafsson from Eiríksstadir]. *Húnvetningur, Ársrit Húnvetningafélagsins í Reykjavík* 10:71–75.

Thorsteinn Th. Thorsteinsson. 1935. "Vestmenn" [Westmen]. Transcript of a radio broadcast on the Icelandic settlers in North America. Reykjavík: Ísafoldarprentsmidja.

Thorstina S. Jackson. 1926. *Saga Íslendinga í Nordur-Dakota* [A History of Icelanders in North Dakota]. Winnipeg: City Printing and Publishing.

Trenton Times. 1889. November 16.

"Tyler, Moses Coit." 2003. In *The Columbia Electronic Encyclopedia.* Columbia University Press.

U.S. Department of Labor. Bureau of Labor Statistics. Composite Consumer Price Index. www.bls.gov.

Vilhjalmur Stefansson. 1906. "The Icelandic Colony in Greenland." *American Anthropologist*, n.s., 8, no. 2 (April–June): 262–70.

Vilhjalmur Stefansson. 1936. *Adventures in Error.* New York: Robert M. McBride.

Wagner, Charles L. 1939. *Seeing Stars.* New York: G. P. Putnam's Sons.

Wandrey, Margaret I. 1975. *Four Bridges to Seattle: The History of Old Ballard 1853–1907.* Seattle, Wash.: Margaret I. Wandrey.

Washington Post. 1913. "Blond Eskimos Discovered Long before Stefansson Found the Tribe." March 16.

Weems, John Edward. 1967. *Peary: The Explorer and the Man.* Boston: Houghton Mifflin.

Wood, David Ward, ed. 1881. *Chicago: Distinguished Citizens, Progress of Forty Years, Biographical Sketches of Prominent Citizens.* Chicago: M. George.

Wright, A. Augustus. 1906. *Who's Who in the Lyceum.* Philadelphia: Pearson Brothers.

Unpublished Sources

Brandsstadannáll [The Annals of Brandsstadir]. Manuscript National Library of Iceland. 2283, 8vo.

National Archives of Iceland. Skjalasafn Norduramts. Búnadarmálefni B/10. Skýrslur um búnadarástandid 1874. "Búnadarskýrsla Svínavatnshrepps 1874" [Document Registry of he North Region. Agricultural Documents B/10. Reports on Agriculture 1874. "The Svínavatn District Agricultural Report 1874"].

National Archives of Iceland. Skjalasafn sýslumanna og sveitarstjórna. Húnavatnssýsla XVIII, 3. "Afsals-og vedmálabók 1846–1877" [Document Registry of Sheriffs and District Councils. "Húnavatnssýsla County XVIII 3. Property Transactions 1846–1877].

Sale agreement. February 15, 1909. University of Iowa Special Collection.

Schoolcraft, John. 1922. "The Story of Olaf Crerar." Manuscript, Dartmouth College Library.

Church Documents and Censuses

Book of Deeds, Pinellas County, Fla., vol. 650, April 20, 1931, 70–74.

Death Certificate of Olof Krarer. 1935. Cook County, Ill. State of Illinois Department of Public Health—Division of Vital Statistics, record 12.

Death Certificate of Sölvi Sölvason. 1903. Seattle Health Department, record 338.

Fourteenth Census of the United States: 1920 Population. Calhoun County, Mich. Sheet no. 7901.

Grantee Index to all Records, Pinellas County, Fla.

King County (Wash.) Health Department, record 11399.

National Archives of Iceland. Ecclesiastical Collection. Audkúla BA/4. "Prests-thjónustubók 1816–1866" [Parish Service Records 1816–1866].

National Archives of Iceland. Ecclesiastical Collection. Audkúla BA/3. "Prests-thjónustubók Svínavatns 1816–1866" [Parish Service Records for Svínavatn District 1816–1866].

National Archives of Iceland. "Manntal á lestrarsal 1840. Húnavatnssýsla" [Census in a Reading Room 1840. Húnavatnssýsla county], 25.

National Archives of Iceland. Ecclesiastical Collection. Breidabólstadur in West Hóp BA/3. "Preststhjónustubók 1817–1867" [Parish Service Records 1817–1867].

National Archives of Iceland. Ecclesiastical Collection. Audkúla BA/5. "Prests-thjónustubók 1867–1917" [Parish Service Records 1817–1867].

National Archives of Iceland. Ecclesiastical Collection. Audkúla BC/3. "Sóknar-mannatal 1866–1891" [Parish Census 1866–1891].

National Archives of Iceland. Ecclesiastical Collection. Audkúla BA/4. "Prests-thjónustubók 1816–1866" [Parish Service Records 1816–1866].

National Archives of Iceland. Ecclesiastical Collection. Audkúla BA/5. "Prests-thjónustubók 1817–1917" [Parish Service Records 1817–1917].

National Archives of Iceland. Ecclesiastical Collection. Blöndudalshólar in Blön-dudalur BC/1. "Sóknarmannatal 1860–1884" [Parish Census 1860–1884].

National Archives of Iceland. Ecclesiastical Collection. Bergsstadir in Svartárdalur BA/6. "Preststhjónustubók 1857–1922" [Parish Service Records 1857–1922].

National Archives of Iceland. Ecclesiastical Collection. Bergsstadir in Svartárdalur BC/3. "Sóknarmannatal 1873–1883" [Parish Census 1873–1883].

1900 Census, Cook County, Chicago, Ill.

1900 Census, King County, Wash. Microfilm 1743. Census dated June 19, 1900.

1920 Census, Battle Creek, Calhoun County, Mich.

1930 Census, Benton Township, Benton Harbor, Berrien County, Mich.

1920 Census, St. Petersburg, Pinellas County, Fla.

Pinellas County, Fla., MLS, book 1, 292.

Quad-Cities Memory Project. Marriage Certificates pre 1836 to c1925. Richardson-Sloane Special Collections Center, Davenport Public Library, Davenport, Iowa. www.qcmemory.org.

Interviews

Bödvar Gudmundsson, March 2004.

Nelson Gerrard, March 2001.

Lorna Lueck, Spring 2004.

Alice (Slayton) Mundorff, April 2003.

Nordic Heritage Museum, Ballard, Seattle, Wash.

Torfi Sveinsson of Saudárkrókur, May 2002 and January 2004.

Letters

B. L. Baldwinson to Thorstina Jackson. Written in Winnipeg, Manitoba, November 3, 1927. Dartmouth College Library.

S. Russell Bridges to Vilhjálmur Stefánsson. Written in Atlanta, Ga., July 31, 1936. Dartmouth College Library.

E. C. Edmunds to Vilhjálmur Stefánsson. Written in Benton Harbor, Mich., June 24, 1936. Dartmouth College Library.

Frances A. Finch to Vilhjálmur Stefánsson. Written in Skaneateles, N.Y., November 27, 1932. Dartmouth College Library.

G. J. Hallson to B. L. Baldwinson, forwarded to Thorstina Jackson. Written in Hallson, N.Dak., May 26, 1926. Dartmouth College Library.

G. J. Hallson to Thorstina Jackson. Written in Hallson, N.Dak., May 26, 1926. Dartmouth College Library.

John Schoolcraft to Vilhjálmur Stefánsson. Written in Providence, R.I., June 19, 1936. Dartmouth College Library.

Wendell P. Slayton to Vilhjálmur Stefánsson. Written in Chicago, Ill., June 30, 1936. Dartmouth College Library.

Irving K. Stone to Vilhjálmur Stefánsson. Written in Battle Creek, Mich., June 19, 1936. Dartmouth College Library.

Williams H. Stout to Vilhjálmur Stefánsson. Written in Greenwood, Ind., July 1, 1936; July 13, 1936; and July 21, 1936. Dartmouth College Library.

Fred Swanson to Thorstina Jackson. Written in Winnipeg, June 5, 1924. Dartmouth College Library.

Amy M. Weiskopf to Vilhjálmur Stefánsson. Written in Dallas, Tex., July 23, 1936. Dartmouth College Library.

Credits

P. xii. Olof the Aristocrat. Photographer unknown. From a Slayton Lyceum Bureau publication. Dartmouth College.

P. 4. William Jennings Bryan. Photographer unknown.

P. 6. Sölvi Sölvason, Ólöf's father. Photographer unknown. From *Father's Fields* (in Icelandic) by P. V. G. Kolka. Reykjavík, 1950. P. 141.

P. 12. Hólshús in Eyjafjördur, about 1900. The photographer is probably Anna Schiöth. Photo courtesy of Örlygur Hálfdánarson.

P. 15. Women carding wool in a *badstofa*. Photographer Daniel Bruun. Photo courtesy of Örlygur Hálfdánarson.

P. 23. Saudárkrókur in the late nineteenth century. This is the first photograph ever taken in Saudárkrókur, and it dates to sometime in 1887–88. Photographer unknown. Skagafjördur Regional Library, Saudárkrókur.

P. 26. Emigrants on board *Camoens* on their way to Granton, Scotland, in 1883 or 1884. Photographer Sigfús Eymundsson. National Museum of Iceland.

P. 31. Landing at Willow Point in Winnipeg, 1875. Painting by Árni Sigurdsson, 1930.

P. 33. Log cabin of Icelandic settlers at Spanish Fork, Utah, erected in 1875. Photographer unknown. National Museum of Iceland.

P. 35. Shanty Town in Winnipeg, ca. 1880. Photographer unknown. Manitoba Provincial Archives.

P. 38. A map of New Iceland. From *The Icelandic People in Manitoba*, by Wilhelm Kristjanson.

P. 39. Icelandic women in Ballard at a party in honor of midwife Ormsson's birthday in 1921. Photographer J. H. Mendenhall. Ballard Historical Society.

P. 47. Advertisement for a curiosity show in the United States. From *Pictorial History of the American Circus*, by John and Alice Durant. New York: A. S. Barnes and Company 1957.

P. 48. Ólöf and her supposed husband. Photographer unknown. Dartmouth College.

P. 50. Human curiosity show in the United States, 1932. From *Pictorial History of the American Circus*, by John and Alice Durant. New York: A. S. Barnes and Company, 1957. Pp. 128–29.

P. 55. Ólöf in Eskimo garb. Photographer unknown. Dartmouth College.

P. 59. Grey Owl. Photographer unknown. From *Wilderness Man* by Lovat Dickson. Toronto, 1973. Unnumbered page.

P. 60. Long Lance. Photographer unknown. *American Indian Intellectuals.* Ed. Margot Liberty. St. Paul: West Publishing, 1978. P. 196.

P. 84. Elisha Kent Kane. Photographer unknown.

P. 86. Robert E. Peary. Photographer unknown. From *Gender on Ice* by Lisa Bloom. Minneapolis: University of Minneapolis Press, 1993. P. 16.

P. 88. Setting out on a long dogsled journey. Artist unknown.

P. 89. A bear defeated. From *The North Pole* by Robert E. Peary. Photographer unknown. New York: Frederick A. Stokes Company, 1910. P. 157.

P. 90. Josephine Peary with native women in north Greenland. From *My Arctic Journal: A Year among Ice Fields and Eskimos* by Josephine Peary (1893). Contemporary Reprint. New York: AMS, 1975. Photographer unknown. Unnumbered page.

P. 91. Marie Peary (Snow Baby), born in Greenland. From *The Snow Baby*, by Josephine Peary. New York, 1901.

P. 92. Marie Peary with native friends. From *The Snow Baby*, by Josephine Peary. New York, 1901. P. 53.

P. 96. Henry Slayton, Ólöf's employer and protector. Photographer unknown. History of Music and Art in Illinois, 1904. P. 504.

P. 101. Mina Slayton. Photographer unknown. Photo courtesy of Alice Slayton Mundorff.

P. 102. Advertisement from the Slayton Lyceum Bureau. "The Colored Ideals." *Slayton's Lyceum Magazine* 1876–77, p. 133.

P. 104. The Slayton Lyceum Bureau was housed in this building in downtown Chicago. Photographer unknown. Chicago Historical Society.

P. 108. Advertisement for one of Ólöf's lectures for the Slayton Lyceum Bureau. *The Lyceumite and Talent* 1908.

P. 117. A Greenlandic love poem that Ólöf often sang. Reproduced after an image in the *Washington Post*, March 16, 1913, p. 25.

P. 120. Olof Krarer, a nobly born aristocrat. Photographer unknown. From a Slayton Lyceum Bureau publication. Dartmouth College.

P. 127. Four Inuit women with their children. Photographer unknown. From *Nearest the Pole* by Robert E. Peary. London, 1907. Unnumbered page.

P. 129. An Inuit family by a summer tent. From *The Secrets of Polar Travel* by Robert E. Peary. Photographer unknown. New York: The Century Company, 1917. P. 181.

P. 132. Inuit in summer garb. From *The Secrets of Polar Travel* by Robert E. Peary. Photographer unknown. New York: The Century Company, 1917. P. 194.

P. 137. Ahlikasingwah, Robert E. Peary's lover and the mother of two of his children. From *Northward over the "Great Ice"* by Robert E. Peary. Photographer unknown. New York: Frederick A. Stokes Company, 1898. P. 500.

P. 139. The Inuk girl Aviaq and boy Minik. From *Give Me My Father's Body: The Life of Minik, the New York Eskimo* by Kenn Harper. Ontario, 1986. Unnumbered page.

P. 149. Seven Gables. Photographer unknown. St. Petersburg Historical Society.

P. 152. Ólöf in St. Petersburg with a young friend. Photographer unknown. Dartmouth College.

P. 153. Ólöf in front of Seven Gables. Photographer unknown. From *An Epistle on Ólöf Sölvadóttir* by Sigurdur Nordal. Reykjavík, 1945.

P. 163. The Baptist Retirement Home in Maywood, Illinois, where Ólöf spent the last years of her life. It was then called Baptist Old People's Home. Photographer Inga Dóra Björnsdóttir.

P. 165. Here lies Ólöf Sölvadóttir from Outer Langamýri as the Esquimaux Lady, Olof Krarer. Photographer Inga Dóra Björnsdóttir.

P. 166. Ólöf's death certificate and correction. Department of Public Health—Division of Vital Statistics. State of Illinois.

P. 170. Vilhjálmur Stefánsson, ca. 1936. Photographer unknown. Dartmouth College.

P. 172. Copper Inuit. From *My Life with the Eskimo* by Vilhjálmur Stefánsson. Photographer unknown. New York: The MacMillan Company, 1924. Unnumbered page.

P. 174. Thorstina Jackson. Photographer unknown. From *A History of Icelanders in North Dakota* by Thorstina S. Jackson. Winnipeg, 1926.

P. 180. Sigurdur Nordal, Ólöf's admirer. Photographer unknown. Photo courtesy of Jóhannes Nordal.

Index

Icelandic personal names are alphabetized by the first name, according to Icelandic custom.